Alive at 5
Victory in Retrospect
Volume 1

By: L. David Harris

To: Clif

You've been a great son to your
parents. You are an example
to us all. Only trust JESUS.

L. David

XULON PRESS

For information regarding other books and publications by
L. David Harris visit:
www.TheWritingsOfDavidHarris.com

Alive at 5—Victory in Retrospect, Volume 1
by L. David Harris

Printed in the United States of America

ISBN 1-594678-38-3

Unless otherwise indicated, Bible quotations are taken from the King James Version (KJV) of the Bible.

www.TheWritingsOfDavidHarris.com

www.xulonpress.com

CONTENTS

SPECIAL THANKS

━┿═┿━

As you might imagine, writing any book of substance requires persistent and deliberate effort. It is very easy to get sidetracked. The goal I set for myself for writing these two volumes simultaneously was almost ridiculous. The blessing is that the Lord was able to accomplish it through me, in spite of the truly incredible odds.

I am constrained to first thank the Lord. He has been wonderful to me. Everything I have ever written concerning Him was done *only* by His grace. He has been patient with me as I tried desperately to hear His voice, while struggling with my *humanness*, at the same time. I am certain that I have not always followed His will perfectly, which is why I praise Him. He could have chosen to foreclose on my breath, but He didn't. He could have allowed the enemy to take complete advantage of me, but He didn't. He could have arrested my progress as I pressed forward writing these books, but He didn't. For this and much more, I am eternally grateful. Above all, I praise Him for giving me the gift of salvation, free of charge. Jesus paid it all!

There are many people that have been a blessing to me as I wrote these volumes. I kept a faithful record of the names, but it is possible that I omitted some. If *you* know that you prayed for me, or otherwise supported me, and I neglected to mention you by name, please choose to think the best and not the worst. I did not intend to forget you. The Lord in heaven has the faithful record and your contribution to the blessing of perhaps millions of souls through this work, will not go unrewarded.

My wife Simone is the best woman I could possibly have married. She has been loving, kind, and supportive. Although it was not an easy process, she gave me the freedom to rearrange the daily schedule of our family worship and quiet times to accommodate my writing schedule. She never complained about the times that I spent eight or more hours sometimes in my *office* working to get this project completed. I could say more, but let me simply say this; I love you Simone!

My mom has been more supportive of all of my ministries than any person can imagine. I am certain, based on the ways she expresses herself, even nonverbally, that I do not even know the half. She has been the most responsible, *practically* speaking, for me becoming a published writer/author. Her ministry of prayer and love has been a blessing. For this, I am thankful.

My sister Lisa has been a great, upbeat friend. She has encouraged me in the way of getting the word out about the Lord and these volumes. I know that I could not possibly afford a better morale booster, publicist, cheerleader, or marketing person than her. She's the best!

My brother-in-law, Nigel has been the absolute most influential person when it comes to my writing. Nobody has been more steadfast and determined to see me use this special gift. He has counseled me for years to stop chasing all of the other ideas I have had to produce a better lifestyle for myself, and now my family. Gently and patiently, he has stayed in my corner, just waiting for the day that I would finally see what he saw for many years. When I finally realized that I *must* begin writing books, he was the first person I called. Accordingly, I dedicate this book first to Christ, but secondly, to Nigel S. Quailey. Thanks for not giving up on me like so many others have. Thank you for being the most consistent male in my life besides my late uncle, Chester G. Sparks. I love you bro.

Here is a list of the others that have been a great blessing to me: Ron and Deria Gadsden, Anthony and Lisa Reeves, Rosalee Van Putten Daryl and Nevea Davis, Harold and Debbie Sanford, Randy Preston, Jermaine and LaJoya Assent, Ed and JoAnn Crosby, Carolyn Harraway, Al and Jeanette Joyner, Gary Nelson and Loretta LaMar-Nelson, Sylvia Williams, Harry Walker, Pam Smith, Terry-Ann Walters, Dieter and Tia Montgomery, Ralph and Delores Rhyne, Bro. and Sis. Steele, James and Judy Lovick, Margo Haskins, Frank and Michell Baker, Bro. and Sis. Belmo, Kieth and Jennifer Bramble, Carol Wright, Wesley Sadler, Carlsen Griffith, Eric and Judith Desarme, Noralyn Wilson, Aeisha Thomas, Karen Hart, Jewell Elliott, Chris Sealey, Jimmy and Maribel Sanders, and Joan Hutcheson. May the Lord bless you all!

PREFACE

he gospel of Jesus Christ is the most influential
story ever told. It is an eternal, panoramic movie
projected on a universe-sized monitor for all generations to
see. God loved us so much that He could not stand the
prospect of living without us. Since sin drove a seemingly
impregnable wall between us and God, He had to imple-
ment His plan of salvation.

Jesus was the gift God chose to give us in order to
release us from the bondage of sin that would certainly end
in eternal separation from God. He could not endure the
prospect of losing His prized creation to the cold hands of
eternal ruin. Jesus assumed human flesh and lived in absolute submission to the will of His Father. He brought to
view, in living color, the many facets of redemption. In
order to begin understanding God's love for us, we need to
look no further than Jesus Christ. His perfect life, sacrifice,
resurrection, and heavenly ministry have transformed the
impossibility of our survival into an oasis of prosperity. He
has transformed the dismal prospect of damnation into a
utopia of relationship with the Creator of the universe.

Alive at 5 – Victory in Retrospect - Volume 1 is an eclec-
tic compilation of Old Testament daily devotional entries
covering six months that highlight many facets of God's
grace. Within its pages, one may find entries varying in
length, focused on the great news of Jesus Christ. It may not
be apparent at first, since it is predominantly based on the
Old Testament, but a closer examination of the topics should
only lead to one place–Jesus Christ.

The inspiration behind the title is based on our need to live victorious lives. In the United States, the traditional working day is eight hours, beginning at nine in the morning and ending by five in the evening. Most people with jobs work many more that eight hours per day, but people understand what is meant by the phrase, "nine to five." Also, in the American culture, many television news programs are aired at five in the evening. Wouldn't it be wonderful if the latest breaking news for your life everyday was how you lived triumphantly over self, sin, and the devil? Wouldn't it be wonderful if the telecast highlighted the method you used daily to enjoy this success?

This devotional is intended to be used as a *catalyst* for victorious living; one day at a time. It is not a how-to-book per se. It does not have a certain set formula for people to follow, but there is an underlying spiritual principle subtly inferred. When we begin our days with deep spiritual emphasis, meditation, and prayer, we are planted on a firm foundation to meet the struggles that we will invariably face. When the day ends, we should be able to reflect on our experiences and know that our victory was jumpstarted by an early morning encounter with God, which ignited a zeal to live like Jesus all day long.

You will find the subject matter in many cases quite filling, yet digestible. It is a blessing to have devotional readings that inspire diligent Bible study. Written on the pages of this book, you will find truths gently incorporated into a readable format, with astounding last-day implications. The intent of this devotional *is* to give a slightly meatier focus on Christ and the Bible, but not to be a quick substitute for individual study. This point must be clear. The Lord often blesses us with good spiritual aids that we sometimes use to replace personal quiet time with Him, and our own reasoning abilities become weakened. Our experience is limited by that of another. Please use this devotional resource as a *catalyst* for change, evangelistic tool, springboard for spiritual growth, inspiration to find Jesus, but never as a shortcut, quick fix, or replacement for intimate encounters with God. The Lord has revealed too much in His word for us to settle for few hundred word thoughts from someone else's point of view.

I pray that you will find peace, joy, and better understanding of God by reading this devotional. I pray that God's prosperity, love, and eternal rewards will begin to overtake you. I pray most of all, that reading this book will lead you to a refreshing, effervescent, and contagious relationship with God. It is by presently and continually experiencing God for ourselves that we can be His witnesses and make disciple makers for Christ. "How beautiful are the feet of them that preach the gospel of peace, and bring glad tidings of good things!" Romans 10:15b.

Let the reading begin...

GOD'S IMAGE

Genesis 1:26, 27
"And God said, Let us make man in our image, after our likeness: and let them have dominion over the fish of the sea, and over the fowl of the air, and over the cattle, and over all the earth, and over every creeping thing that creepeth upon the earth. So God created man in his own image, in the image of God created he him; male and female created he them."

God created most everything by His word. He spoke and things began to happen. The crowning work of His creation was when He created humankind from the dust of the earth. The Bible says that He created man from the dust of the earth and breathed His own breath into their nostrils, and then man became a living soul. It is this unity of God's breath and dust (our bodies) that composes our being. Without this unity, life for us never would have existed.

The thought of God creating us in His image is staggering. How could God love us so much that He would make us an extension of Himself? The Psalmist David was astonished by this great honor when he wrote: "What is man, that thou art mindful of him? And the son of man, that thou visitest him? For thou hast made him a little lower than the angels, and hast crowned him with glory and honour. Thou madest him to have dominion over the works of thy hands; thou hast put all things under his feet: All sheep and oxen, yea, and the beasts of the field; The fowl of the air, and the fish of the sea, and whatsoever passeth through the paths of the seas. O LORD our Lord, how excellent is thy name in all the earth!" Psalm 8:4-9.

At some point after God created Adam and Eve, they chose to ignore the special guidelines that protected them from ruin. They decided to betray their origins by sinning against God. As a result, a peculiar shift in language occurs in the scriptures. "And Adam lived a hundred and thirty years, and begat a son in his own likeness, after his image; and called his name Seth:" Genesis 5:3. I do not want to make too much of this because it may just mean that Adam's son came from his own loins and reflected that. Whatever the meaning, it makes me think that our natural birth after sin maintained the separation from God that occurred in Eden. "That which is born of the flesh is flesh; and that which is born of the Spirit is spirit. Marvel not that I said unto thee, Ye must be born again." John 3:6, 7.

One of the blessings of the image of God being placed in us is that it has the power of choice. The way Adam and Eve chose to ruin their lives is how we can choose everlasting life (Deuteronomy 30:19). Once we make the decision to follow the God all the way, His perfect image begins being restored in us. We look forward to the day when His image will never be effaced from His people.

As we go out into the world everyday, let us work, study, and play as those being elevated to the image of God Himself.

FOR MAN

Genesis 2:1-3
"Thus the heavens and the earth were finished, and all the host of them. And on the seventh day God ended his work which he had made; and he rested on the seventh day from all his work which he had made. And God blessed the seventh day, and sanctified it: because that in it he had rested from all his work which God created and made."

The creation of God was perfect in every way. He moved out into the darkness and commanded light to appear, and it was so. His essence breached the darkness since the heavenly bodies had not yet been created. The next six days would prove to be nothing short of astounding. From His emanating light would erupt creative power. All that we see now and more would be called into existence. Vegetation, dry land, water, every species of creature, and all of the heavenly bodies would obey His command and assume their positions.

Once all of this was complete, God crowned His work as Creator and molded humankind. The man Adam was created from the dust of the ground, and God shared His own breath with him making him a living being. After Adam agreed with the names God had in mind for all of the creatures, God caused him to fall into a deep sleep. He took a rib from Adam and made a woman, the mother of all living, and brought her to him (Genesis 2:21, 22). Adam called her woman, because she was taken from man. She was indeed created for man.

Finally, the holy couple was ready. They had all of the things they needed in order to live blissful lives, except one. The Bible says that God rested on the seventh day, setting it aside as holy. He prepared a special time for His children to come aside from their everyday activities for something special. Truly, God set this time aside for the benefit of man, that is, humankind. "And he said unto them, The sabbath was made for man, and not man for the sabbath:" Mark 2:27. Four thousand years later, when humankind forgot the purpose of Sabbath time, Jesus reminded them. I digress.

Can you imagine what the first Sabbath must have been like? I imagine the Creator coming to His new children and opening many of the mysteries of the universe to their prefect minds. I can see them in awe of the One who loved them so much that He provided everything they needed, and then set them in the midst to enjoy it all. The songs that they sang together must have been glorious. How does a voice untouched by sin sound? Their gratitude must have been pure and sincere. They had no need of a pastor. God Himself was with them face to face.

If the perfect pair needed the blessings of the Sabbath, how much more do we, during this time in earth's history? Sabbath is special time for us to be re-energized by God. As we worship Him daily, we look forward to the seventh day, which He made holy, to worship Him on a higher level. We are able to worship without the burden of ordinary, everyday thoughts. We truly come aside and rest. I praise the Lord for that rest. How about you?

WHAT'S THE BIG DEAL

Genesis 2:16, 17
"And the LORD God commanded the man, saying, Of every tree of the garden thou mayest freely eat: But of the tree of the knowledge of good and evil, thou shalt not eat of it: for in the day that thou eatest thereof thou shalt surely die."

Adam was created in the image of God and given every human luxury imaginable. He had pure air and water. The temperature in Eden was always perfect; never too cold or hot. He was able to interact with other species without the fear of hurting or being hurt. God provided a companion for him named Eve to help complete him. There was no intrinsic inclination within either of them to sin against God.

As time progressed, the devil came into Eden to tempt Adam and Eve. He found occasion to engage Eve in conversation at the tree of the knowledge of good and evil. She entertained the enemy at a tree that the Lord forbade, and fell powerless to Satan's temptation. Eve ate the forbidden fruit. Though not deceived, Adam did eat as well.

What was their great sin? Did they kill or steal? Did they lie or covet? The sin they committed was that they ate a piece of fruit. The Lord said that they should not eat of the fruit from that tree, yet they disobeyed. As a result, Satan gained access to the human race. With the exception of Jesus, Satan was then able to plant seeds of rebellion in everyone that was ever born.

This ordeal is instructive to those who think that sin is trivial. While there are varying degrees of sin, no sin is insignificant in God's sight. "If there be a controversy between men, and they come unto judgment, that the judges may judge them; then they shall justify the righteous, and condemn the wicked. And it shall be, if the wicked man be worthy to be beaten, that the judge shall cause him to lie down, and to be beaten before his face, <u>according to his fault</u>, by a certain number. Forty stripes he may give him, and not exceed: lest, if he should exceed, and beat him above these with many stripes, then thy brother should seem vile unto thee." Deuteronomy 25:1-3. "Behold, all souls are mine; as the soul of the father, so also the soul of the son is mine: the soul that sinneth, it shall die." Ezekiel 18:4.

There are those who wonder, with regard to holy deportment, what the big deal is. I mean, there are those who think God is not interested in the foods we eat, whether or not we drink alcohol, use drugs, hold a grudge against someone who has wronged us, or tell little lies once in a while to save our reputations. This could not be further from the truth. He has given us truths to model our lives after, and He *is* concerned with the details. We do not follow the Lord's plan in order to be saved, but because we are saved, we are empowered and honored to do so.

If you are tempted to think that a certain issue of sanctification is trivial, ask your self a question. What could be smaller than eating a piece of fruit? Adam and Eve ate some fruit and it brought woe and degradation upon every human born after them. When God instructs us to live in certain ways, it is no small matter. It is of the utmost importance. It is a big deal to disobey God. When we surrender to Him, we begin to sense the exceeding sinfulness of sin, and do all that we can to avoid it.

HELP MEET

Genesis 2:18
"And the LORD God said, It is not good that the man should be alone; I will make him an help meet for him."

Every detail of our lives is planned and organized by God. When we are happy, it is because He is the happiness of the entire universe. When we are sad, He is experiencing our pain. When we are lonely, not only does He want to comfort us, but He often extends His hands through the endless corridor of countless galaxies and hugs us through the arms of another.

Adam had been given every imaginable luxury and blessing. He had just the right atmosphere in which to exist and breathe. He was able to imbibe the sweet aromas of beautiful flowers, and behold the colors in their rich profusion. His companions were four footed beasts, creeping things, graceful birds of the air, and mammals of the sea. The majestic trees and free flowing waters seemed to sing together in harmony that their Lord created all of this just for Adam. An internal soul silence deafened him because all of these blessings were incredible and tailor-made for his enjoyment, yet there was still something missing.

Then it happened! The Lord caused a deep sleep to come over the man whom he had perfectly formed, and God satisfied Adam's need for custom fitted companionship. God gave Adam a woman from his own rib. He formed her from the man's own flesh and saw that it was very good.

This same attentive God is interested in us today. Whenever we need the gentle touch of a caring hand, He is there to abundantly satisfy. He created us with a need for love and He continues to fulfill that need. Reach out for His love. I promise you will not be disappointed.

IT WAS GOD'S IDEA

Genesis 2:21, 22
"And the LORD God caused a deep sleep to fall upon Adam and he slept: and he took one of his ribs, and closed up the flesh instead thereof; And the rib, which the LORD God had taken from man, made he a woman, and brought her unto the man."

God had completed His work creating the heavenly bodies, land, waters, animals, and the first man. All of His work was perfect. The man whom God created realized, having completed the work of actively agreeing with the names God had in mind for each of the animals, that they all had other selves. That is to say, each had a companion. His God-given super intelligence noticed the fact that He should also have a companion, someone with whom He could enjoy all of the blessings of God's creation.

The Lord caused Adam to fall into a deep sleep; He then performed the first surgery, and formed from his rib, a woman. This woman would complete Adam. If God had created two men, they both would have been incomplete. If He had created two women, they would also have been incomplete. This is why He created Eve for Adam and Adam for Eve. These two together would complete the image of God in the earth. Adam would posses the sterner, stronger characteristics of God. Eve would posses the more tender, nurturing, compassionate attributes.

It is clear, even from a surface view of this event, that the Lord originated marriage. I hope that did not slip by you. The fact that God created Eve from Adam's rib and then presented her to him in order to complete him is evidence of the first marriage. Marriage was and is God's idea. Together the holy pair and all that would follow until the end of time, were to stand as a composite sketch, representing the character of

God. The earth was to be populated through the gift of procreation that the Lord specifically gave to men and women joined in holy matrimony.

When considering marriage, examine the first marriage that took place in Eden for guidance, it is always safer to do so. We do not need to be confused about what God intended. As we stay close to the model of Edenic marriage, we remain close to the revealed will of God on this subject. Since marriage was God's idea. Why not ask *Him* to teach us about it?

VULNERABLE

Genesis 2:25
*"And they were both naked, the man and his wife, and
were not ashamed."*

The creation account is the perfect place to gather insight into how wonderful God intended things to be. The environment surrounding Adam and Eve was incredible. All creatures lived in harmony. There was no miasma of rotting flesh to disturb the water flow. The ground was unencumbered by predators making sure of their prey. Nothing was out of alignment with God's perfect will. I am certain that the beginning of each morning was the most beautiful spectacle that any human could possibly imagine. All of the birds sang praises to the Creator, while the holy pair anticipated His daily meeting with them. I suppose the word perfect still limits the splendor of their first home and all that surrounded it.

One very beautiful aspect of the Edenic experience was the relationship of Adam and Eve. Not only were they created especially for one another, but they were also vulnerable. This word probably did not mean the same thing to them as it does to us today, since they had no weaknesses to speak of. The Bible does say, however, that they were naked, yet unashamed. Certainly, the principle thought surrounding this has to do with their relationship to God. They were clothed with the righteous covering of light; therefore, they could be exposed in every way without apprehension or guilt. Along with this, they were able to share a level of intimacy that we cannot even imagine. I wonder what their conversations must have been like. I wonder how Eve expressed her feelings concerning the family they would soon start. What were Adam's thoughts about how they would relate to Jesus, as the children became old enough to recognize Him? They must have had the best time worshipping together without the need to seek forgiveness. When they shared their innermost thoughts, they were uninhibited because they did not need to worry about being misunderstood.

Although things have changed because of the existence of sin, we can learn a lesson in vulnerability today. If Adam and Eve were able to be free and open with one another, largely because of their relationship with God, how much more can we? If God's presence could enhance their experience even though they were perfect, do you think He can improve ours? As we come together to share ourselves, let the Lord be at the head. He is the holy Moderator. As long as He is in control, we can be as free and vulnerable as we need to be. With Jesus in control, we can expect great things from our relationships. It is good to be completely open with someone who loves the Lord because He will always show them how to relate in the most caring and gentle manner. With Christ at the center of our relationships, it is a blessing to be uncovered and unashamed. With Christ in control, it is a blessing to be vulnerable.

CRAFTY

Genesis 3:1
"Now the serpent was more subtil than any beast of the field which the LORD God had made. And he said unto the woman, Yea, hath God said, Ye shall not eat of every tree of the garden?"

The enemy of our souls has thousands of years of experience in the diabolical practice of deception. He first deceived himself into thinking that he was worthy of worship. He allowed himself to believe that he was a match for the Son of God, the Captain of the heavenly hosts. He continued his deception by convincing a large number of the angels that they should revolt against God, and that it was a better option than strict obedience. This caused the devil and his allies to be eternally banned from heaven (Revelation 12:9). Their persistent resistance to the appeals of God for repentance was not accepted, and Satan and his angels will reap what they had sown.

The devil, along with his angels, brought their craft down to this earth, where they hoped to recruit the apple of God's eye; those created in His image. In the Garden of Eden, he unleashed his greatest weapon of deception. It was with subtlety that he approached Eve. If he had openly and directly refuted the Lord's words or called Him a liar, the deception would have lost some of its effectiveness. If Satan had told Eve that he was the enemy of God, and that his mission was to recruit as many humans to his cause as possible to one day fight against heaven, she certainly would have fled the scene. He knew that his approach needed to be cunning like a feline predator. He knew that his only chance was to confuse the issue and cloak himself in the garb of innocence.

The story of sin on earth is an intricate one. What we

need to understand, just on the surface of it all, is that we must not entertain any deviation from righteousness. Which deception is more effective, attempting to sell a car with shiny paint, a clean interior and a defective engine, or a car with a rusted body, torn seats, and a bad transmission? Certainly, the car that looks great on the surface but has a defective engine is a more effective deception.

Our best work is to stay close to the side of Jesus. He is our *only* hope. His Word is light to those who take heed. The devil cannot overcome those who experience God through the Scriptures. In our own strength, we are no match for such a crafty foe, but Jesus said that he is utterly defeated by the blood of the Lamb (Revelation 12:11). "Submit yourselves therefore to God. Resist the devil, and he will flee from you." James 4:7, 8.

YE SHALL NOT SURELY DIE

Genesis 3:4
"And the serpent said unto the woman,
Ye shall not surely die:"

Death is one of the most difficult realities to cope with. Almost from the beginning of time, human beings have been stalked by the certainty of death. We have known that it was just a matter of time before we or someone we love would no longer be around. There is an obsession with death on television and on video games. So many movies are centered on guns and violence. Many video games desensitize our youth to the morbidity of malicious violence by engaging them to participate. Soon their reality and the fiction of the games become one. Unfortunately, it is no longer a big deal to hear of someone being massacred, because we are so inundated with death.

Many are distressed because they are uncertain where they or their loved ones will go after death. Will they go to heaven or hell? Will they be held in limbo or purgatory awaiting sufficient payment, prayers, or vicarious baptisms in order to be allowed into heaven? Will they become guardian angels? There are so many questions.

When Satan accosted Eve at the tree of the knowledge of good and evil, he obscured the truth concerning the vital questions about death. He implied that she would not surely die if she disobeyed God. He promised that she would be just like God, through disobedience. Today, the devil still tries to calm our fears about death by leading people to believe that their loved ones are in heaven. He tries to intensify the hopelessness of others by suggesting that they go straight to hell or are held in limbo. He still teaches people that the dead are not really dead. He tries to teach us that we are immortal just like God, however, the Bible teaches that, if we are found faithful, we receive immortality at the second coming of Christ; no sooner (I Corinthians 15:51-58).

The Lord has given us truth that provides real comfort and peace to the faithful. "For the living know that they shall die: but the dead know not any thing, neither have they any more a reward; for the memory of them is forgotten. Also their love, and their hatred, and their envy, is now perished; neither have they any more a portion for ever in any thing that is done under the sun." Ecclesiastes 9:5, 6. This reality is a blessing because we no longer need to be uncertain. Imagine if your deceased loved one had to watch from heaven as you struggle through life? Would heaven be a pleasant place to be? How about hell? Could God send people directly to hell, not having been judged? Would that be fair?

Find peace in the fact that, as Jesus rested in the tomb, not having ascended to the Father, we too will rest in the grave if death should occur. (John 20:17). We do not need to be uncertain concerning death. We need only to be faithful, and one day we will see Jesus coming with clouds to take His people home (Revelation 2:10).

UNRESTRICTED ACCESS

Genesis 3:24
"So he drove out the man; and he placed at the east of the garden of Eden Cherubims, and a flaming sword which turned every way, to keep the way of the tree of life."

Adam and Eve recovered from the spiritual hangover of sin. They finally came to the realization of the implications of their actions. They faced the Lord, and with fear and trepidation attempted to explain themselves. Because of God's love for them, He had to make drastic decisions, which, at first, they may not have understood.

The Tree of Life had life-sustaining properties for those who ate of it. Before sin, the holy couple had free access to it. What would have happened if they had eaten the fruit after they sinned? "And the LORD God said, Behold, the man is become as one of us, to know good and evil: and now, lest he put forth his hand, and take also of the tree of life, and eat, and live for ever:" Genesis 3:22. If they had eaten from the tree of life, they would have been on a never-ending roller coaster of sin. By their eating from the tree, their lives would have been sustained in a sinful state. What a miserable existence that would have been. With the compassion of a tender, loving parent, and the foresight of a good manager, the Lord made certain that they did not have that opportunity. He understood what they could not understand, and barred access to the tree.

One of the things that we may not be anticipating as much as we should, is the end of sin. In some ways, many of us are probably tired of the ill effects of it, but we should loathe it. We should even loathe what we now consider pleasurable. The blessing is that God understands our deficiencies. He knows that we need Him to intervene so we do not become attached to sin. He instills the power of the Holy

Ghost within us to awaken our consciences to begin seeing sin for what it really is. It is a long protracted process, but as we grow in the Lord, we begin to separate from our evil habits and are brought into conformity to His will.

One day soon, we will be able to reach forth our hands to the tree of life. We will live forever in a state of holiness and sin will be no more. We will have unrestrained access to the Tree of Life.

SIN AT THE DOOR

Genesis 4:8
"And Cain talked with Abel his brother: and it came to pass, when they were in the field, that Cain rose up against Abel his brother, and slew him."

Adam and Eve were readily able to see sin's ill effects immediately after they committed their first sin. Undoubtedly, nature began to change right before their eyes. Majestic beasts that were vegetarians before sin became predators stalking weaker species. Flowers that were always beautiful and in full bloom, now wilted under the scorching heat of the sun. The temperature that was always pleasant now fluctuated unpredictably creating the need for shelter from both heat and cold. Perhaps the saddest effect of sin on the human family, besides being separated from God, was the violence that ensued.

God spoke to Cain and Abel and commanded them to offer a sacrifice to Him. Judging from the fact that following their disobedience, God covered Adam and Eve with coats of skins from a slain animal, there can be no doubt that God immediately revealed the role that the sacrificial system played in the plan of salvation. Cain and Abel were well aware of God's requirements for an acceptable sacrifice. He chose animal sacrifices to represent the future sacrifice of Jesus in behalf of humankind. "And in process of time it came to pass, that Cain brought of the fruit of the ground an offering unto the LORD. And Abel, he also brought of the firstlings of his flock and of the fat thereof. And the LORD had respect unto Abel and to his offering: But unto Cain and to his offering he had not respect. And Cain was very wroth, and his countenance fell. And the LORD said unto Cain, Why art thou wroth? and why is thy countenance fallen? If thou doest well, shalt thou not be accepted? and if thou doest not well, sin lieth at the door. And unto thee shall be his desire, and thou shalt rule over him." Genesis 4:3-7.

Why was Cain so angry when all he needed to do was to obey God by giving Him a worthy sacrifice? Because of Cain's unyielding animosity against both his own brother and God, he committed the first murder. He could not stand in the light of Abel's righteous offering because it revealed the inadequacy of his own.

There are many, even today, who look at the people of God and become angry. In the presence of God's people, their own evil deeds become more apparent. The unwillingness to change of some of those who hate the Lord will cause them to persecute His friends. Whether it is on the job, in the home, or even in church, when we choose faithfulness, we will be hated and despised. What we must remember is that Jesus said, "If the world hate you, ye know that it hated me before it hated you." John 15:18. Do not allow the enemy to cause you to feel that living right before God is not worth the trouble. Jesus endured all that the devil had in his arsenal in order to make us holy. Let us give Jesus the satisfaction of seeing that His work for us was not in vain.

WHOSE IMAGE

Genesis 5:3
*"And Adam lived an hundred and thirty years, and begat
a son in his own likeness, after his image;
and called his name Seth:"*

When the Lord put the icing on His creative cake by creating humankind, He did a wonderful thing. He created them, male and female, representing both His stern and tender characteristics. They stood as a composite sketch of God. They were created in His image. "So God created man in his own image, in the image of God created he him; male and female created he them." Genesis 1:27. He gave humankind dominion over all living creatures, the ability to procreate, super intelligence with the capacity to discern God, and the blessing of loving companionship. Mentioned here are just a few of the ways that we were created in His image.

This God-given image was tainted by sin. Those that were originally created in God's holy image were degraded to the image of a fallen human being. We were created to experience life forever without ever tasting death, yet we now suffer the deadly effects of sin. We are all subject to death in this life, and those who choose not to follow the Lord implicitly, will also suffer eternal death.

I realize that our text for today is simply stating that Adam and Eve had a child just like themselves. The child was after their kind, even as every species of animal produces offspring after their kind. Apes do not conceive people and cats do not conceive alligators. There is divine order in creation. That being said, look at the spiritual view of the verse. Jesus said, "That which is born of the flesh is flesh; and that which is born of the Spirit is spirit. Marvel not that I said unto thee, Ye must be born again." John 3:6, 7. After Adam sinned, the human race had to be redeemed from sin and restored to God's original plan. God in Christ, needed to reconcile willing souls to Himself (II Corinthians 5:19-21). Through the gospel of Jesus Christ, we receive power to become the children of God (John 1:12). The question that I must ask myself daily is, "whose image am I in?" Am I allowing the Lord to re-create me in His image, or do I represent the image of fallen, condemned humanity? It is our privilege today to accept the gift of salvation that God gives and to be restored into His image.

DIVINE INFOMERCIAL

Genesis 5:24
*"And Enoch walked with God: and he was not;
for God took him."*

Almost every time I watch an infomercial on television, no matter what it is about, I can feel my pulse quicken. My interest is sparked through the effective advertising and marketing of those who produce the infomercials. I believe that the element that makes their campaigns so effective is their use of testimonials. They showcase *ordinary* people who are willing to say that the product or service absolutely changed their lives, and can change yours too. They say that if they have benefited so tremendously, so can you. I have caught myself imagining that I was actually experiencing the results they claimed that I would. From the perfect knives, vacuum cleaners, massagers, and food processors, to the best real estate investment, currency trading, and internet business programs, all are compelling. The reason had everything to do with the testimonials. If God were to produce an infomercial advertising the power of relationship with Him, who might He get to give testimonials?

The Bible says that Enoch walked with God. His experience with God was so rich that God translated him to heaven without seeing death. God must have been included as the center of all that Enoch's everyday life entailed. He must have been so interwoven into Enoch's life that they were close friends. Enoch probably consulted the Lord before making any decision, because He valued God's input so much. Enoch and the Lord became so close that God could not bear to wait thousands of years for Jesus to come in the clouds, to have him in heaven. God took him into heaven early, so he could have that much more time with him, and demonstrate to us how wonderful a relationship with God is.

I am sure that God would use the testimonials of people like, Rahab, David, Joseph, Mary Magdalene, and Abraham as well. If I were watching their testimonies, my pulse would quicken knowing that if these ordinary people could live victorious lives, I can too. God's infomercial would leave us with no need for doubt or apprehension. We could fully believe the claims of the producer and totally invest ourselves to receive the benefits shown. I am so glad that God has shown through so many people just like me, that we can have a successful life in Christ. This gives me hope.

WALK WITH GOD

Genesis 5:24
"And Enoch walked with God: and he was not;
for God took him."

Is it possible to walk together with someone if you and that person are traveling in opposite directions? Can you walk together if you do not agree? Enoch was a man of God living in one of the worst eras of human history. He lived during the years just before the flood. God looked down and saw that the wickedness upon the earth had risen to critical levels. He saw that it had grown to epidemic proportions and if He did not do something drastic, things would spiral completely out of control. In the midst of this, Enoch still chose to walk with the Lord. Enoch did not allow the influences of wickedness to impact him and then blame his surroundings for his unfaithfulness. Instead, he chose to be God's friend. As a result of this close friendship, God could not resist having him right by His side with nothing separating. The Bible says that God took him.

This model of human relationship with God was just before the time of the worldwide flood. If things in the last days are as they were during the time of Noah, we do not have to guess what was going on. There must have been crime on every hand, people dreaming of more evil to commit, sexual indiscretion, and riotous living. If our time is any indication, children must have been disobedient to parents, men loved themselves more than God, and were unholy. We have mad scientists amalgamating men with beasts in secret and cloning other species openly, so this must have been the case then. In spite of all of this, Enoch walked with God.

Are you walking with God daily? Is He your very best friend? Do you consult Him before making every decision?

When I am with my friends, I like to know what they are thinking. I like to know what makes them happy and what makes them sad. Why don't we follow the example of Mr. Enoch who chose to live a holy life against all odds? Walk with the King. He will never lead you astray.

PROBATION

Genesis 6:17, 18
"And, behold, I, even I, do bring a flood of waters upon the earth, to destroy all flesh, wherein is the breath of life, from under heaven; and every thing that is in the earth shall die. But with thee will I establish my covenant; and thou shalt come into the ark, thou, and thy sons, and thy wife, and thy sons' wives with thee."

Sin covered the face of the earth with a dark shadow. Humankind overwhelmingly employed its super intelligence to defile themselves and defy their God. "And GOD saw that the wickedness of man was great in the earth, and that every imagination of the thoughts of his heart was only evil continually." Genesis 6:5. This was not what God intended. His plan was that all creation should live in harmony with His will and that peace would always prevail. The devil gained a foothold so deep that it seemed that all was out of control. "And it repented the LORD that he had made man on the earth, and it grieved him at his heart. And the LORD said, I will destroy man whom I have created from the face of the earth; both man, and beast, and the creeping thing, and the fowls of the air; for it repenteth me that I have made them." Genesis 6:6, 7.

God selected Noah, a man who demonstrated fidelity toward God, to carry His message of warning to the world. For a probationary period of 120 years, Noah was to preach the same message; the flood is coming. Turn toward God and repent. For all of the wickedness you have imagined, repent. For misusing the broad and intelligent mind that God has given each of you, repent. For not worshipping the Lord with your entire being, repent. The end of all flesh is at hand.

The burden of salvation for the entire world rested upon Noah's shoulders. In the time of this crisis, you would think that many people would heed the warnings, but such was not the case. As every year passed without a drop of rain, the hearts of the wicked hardened. Perhaps there were those who repented and died prior to the flood. Certainly there were righteous ones, whom God laid to rest before the flood came, but those who lived up until the flood wasted their time and all were lost. Only Noah and His family were spared.

The Lord has appointed a probationary time for *us* to be prepared for the end of all things. "But of that day and hour knoweth no man, no, not the angels of heaven, but my Father only. But as the days of Noe were, so shall also the coming of the Son of man be. For as in the days that were before the flood they were eating and drinking, marrying and giving in marriage, until the day that Noe entered into the ark, And knew not until the flood came, and took them all away; so shall also the coming of the Son of man be." Matthew 24:36-39. Although the Lord has not shared with us how long our probation will be, we know that His coming is near. The signs around us all point to a soon-coming King. Will we be ready like Noah and his family, or will we be swept away like the others? God has prepared a way through Jesus Christ for us to be saved from condemnation. *He* is the ark of safety. If we choose to listen to God and go into the ark, we will be saved.

The message today is simple. The end of time is at hand. God has given time today to turn from our sinful lives and begin to experience Him in good relationship. Let us dedicate our lives to Him, and one day soon, He will come to take us home to live forever with Him.

I WILL REMEMBER

Genesis 9:15
*"And I will remember my covenant, which is between me
and you and every living creature of all flesh; and the
waters shall no more become a flood to destroy all flesh."*

Have you ever looked up to the sky and seen a rainbow rich
with the colors of the spectrum? The first time I recall
seeing a rainbow, I was driving and almost had an accident,
because it was so beautiful. It stretched across the expanse
of sky that I imagine measured hundreds of miles.

A friend of mine once told me that he loves to see the
rainbow because it reminds him of the covenant God made
with us. God promised that He would never destroy this
earth by water again. When there are torrential downpours,
it is easy to forget the Lord's promise. When floods come
and homes are destroyed, remember what the Lord said.
Likewise, when the rains of life's trials threaten to destroy
us, and we are tempted to give up hope, we must recount
these words: "But now thus saith the LORD that created
thee, O Jacob, and he that formed thee, O Israel, Fear not:
for I have redeemed thee, I have called thee by thy name;
thou art mine. When thou passest through the waters, I will
be with thee; and through the rivers, they shall not overflow
thee: when thou walkest through the fire, thou shalt not be
burned; neither shall the flame kindle upon thee." Isaiah
43:1, 2.

This promise is even more beautiful than the impressive
rainbow. More than that, God has made provision for everyone who ever lived on this earth to live in a sin-free world
beyond the sky. Jesus is coming in the clouds, and if we are
faithful, we will see Him in peace. We who have accepted
Jesus Christ will receive the inheritance of Abraham in that
day. The beauty of salvation and the covenant signified by

48

the rainbow is, that the Lord always keeps His promises. He said that He would look into the sky, see the rainbow, and remember His promise. Since we can see that He is still making good on this promise, we can believe His promise to come again and take us home to live with Him forever in the absolute absence of sin. "Let not your heart be troubled: ye believe in God, believe also in me. In my Father's house are many mansions: if it were not so, I would have told you. I go to prepare a place for you. And if I go and prepare a place for you, I will come again, and receive you unto myself; that where I am, there ye may be also." John 14:1-3.

CONFUSION

Genesis 11:4
"And they said, Go to, let us build us a city and a tower,
whose top may reach unto heaven; and let us make us a
name, lest we be scattered abroad upon the face
of the whole earth."

Not long after the worldwide flood that covered the earth to purify it from sin, many of the ultra-intelligent inhabitants of earth, to represent their pride, united to build a tower that would reach heaven. Perhaps they thought there was safety in numbers since they said that they were building in order to avoid being scattered over all the earth. I imagine that they sought refuge from the fury of another flood, although God had promised with the rainbow, that He would not destroy the earth with water again. Certainly, they wanted to proudly demonstrate their greatness. If God had not intervened, nothing would have hindered their plans, since they were intelligent, and had one common language.

The Lord saw the tower builders' pride and thwarted their plans by confusing their language. The very thing they wanted to avoid by building the tower would occur anyway because of their pride. God ultimately scattered them all around the then known world and destroyed their tower.

Oftentimes we build for ourselves, towers of pride, hoping to make ourselves great. Sometimes we earn degrees, buy large homes, and develop associations with influential people so that we can be noticed and complimented. As in the days of the confusion of Babel, God is willing to demonstrate His jealousy over His people. He would not hesitate to remove anything that competed for His place in our lives. Isn't it better to simply surrender those things that threaten to take God's place? God is willing to reveal what they are to us and give us the ability to live victoriously. "For the grace of God that bringeth salvation hath appeared to all men, Teaching us that, denying ungodliness and worldly lusts, we should live soberly, righteously, and godly, in this present world; Looking for that blessed hope, and the glorious appearing of the great God and our Saviour Jesus Christ; Who gave himself for us, that he might redeem us from all iniquity, and purify unto himself a peculiar people, zealous of good works." Titus 2:11-14.

TRUST THE LORD'S PLAN

Genesis 16:2
"And Sarai said unto Abram, Behold now, the LORD hath restrained me from bearing: I pray thee, go in unto my maid; it may be that I may obtain children by her. And Abram hearkened to the voice of Sarai."

The Lord went to Abram and Sarai to share a wonderful plan with them. He promised that they, together, would have a son. Eventually they would understand that the Messiah would come through this son. Abram and Sarai both were well stricken in years and thought surely the Lord must not be referring to natural means. Abram even suggested that perhaps his servant's son would be considered the promised seed since technically he would be from Abram's household.

Sarai went to her husband and suggested that he go in to her handmaid and make a baby. If they were successful, the Lord's purposes would be accomplished. Abram did what his wife suggested and they had a son whom they named Ishmael.

To make a long story short, there were a number of problems that arose as a result of the couple interfering with God's plan for them. In fact, the Lord had to test Abraham severely because of this. If they had simply believed the Lord's promise as He communicated it, they could have spared themselves and the world many problems.

There are valuable lessons we can learn form this situation. When the Lord makes a promise, we can rest assured that He will bring it to pass. If we choose not to believe the Lord and begin contriving ways to make sure that His promises are kept, we unnecessarily interfere with the desired results. Breaking the law of God, as Abram did by having sexual relations with Hagar was not a good way to receive His promise.

We do know that in the end, the Lord's will was done and they did have a son named Isaac, just as the Lord said. To this day, the peoples of the Middle East are still experiencing the ill effects of Abram's temporary lack of trust.

I pray that I will learn how to trust God's word implicitly. It is always better to cooperate with the Lord since He is sovereign. May the Lord help us all to conform to His will.

YE ARE THE SALT OF THE EARTH

Genesis 18:23, 32, 33
"And Abraham drew near, and said, Wilt thou also destroy the righteous with the wicked? And he said, Oh let not the Lord be angry, and I will speak yet but this once: Peradventure ten shall be found there. And he said, I will not destroy it for ten's sake. And the LORD went his way, as soon as he had left communing with Abraham: and Abraham returned unto his place."

It was solemn scene. Jesus and two angels came to earth to meet with Abraham and Lot. The wickedness of Sodom and Gomorrah had reached its limit. The Lord's mercy was stretched almost to the point of popping. As the Lord told His friend Abraham of His plan to destroy those wicked cities, Abraham stood before Him reverently. He asked the Lord to spare the cities. He asked if there were still a certain number of righteous people living there, whether the Lord would spare the city. Step by step Abraham reduced the number of righteous people he hoped would be left in the cities, and when the number went down to ten, the Bible says that the Lord went away and ended communing with Abraham. This was indicative of the sadness, which the Lord must have felt having to judge those cities to the point of destroying them. With His sadness was mingled righteous wrath that could no longer tolerate their blatant disregard for His truth. They had become so depraved that the men of the town almost beat down the doors of Lot's home in order to have sex with the two angels whom they thought were just ordinary men. "But before they lay down, the men of the city, even the men of Sodom, compassed the house round, both old and young, all the people from every quarter: And they called unto Lot, and said unto him, Where are the men which came in to thee this night? bring them out unto us, that we may know them. And Lot went out at the door unto them, and shut the door after him, And said, I pray you, brethren, do not so wickedly." Genesis 19:4-7. The cup of God's indignation was full, there were not even ten righteous in the cities, that would cause the Lord to stay His wrath.

What was the significance of Abraham asking the Lord not to destroy the cities if there were a certain number of righteous folk there? Notice what the Bible says: "Ye are the salt of the earth: but if the salt have lost his savour, wherewith shall it be salted? it is thenceforth good for nothing, but to be cast out, and to be trodden under foot of men." Matthew 5:13. Salt has a number of uses. One use, in particular, was important in ancient Israel in the absence of refrigeration. Salt has preservative properties. The people of the day kept certain foods from spoiling by salting them. This is why we see salted fish in kosher markets until this day. If we are to be salt, that means we are to preserve the places in which we dwell from the judgments of God. As we continue living there, our purpose is to save as many as we can from the impending doom that is coming upon the unrepentant. Patiently and lovingly we are to teach them whatsoever the Lord has commanded, knowing that He is with us always.

The problem is, many of us are just like those living in Sodom and Gomorrah. We have lost our saltiness and are not doing what the Lord has called us to do. If you and nine of your friends lived in those cities during that time, would they have been destroyed? We all must ask this question of ourselves as we prepare for the coming of the Lord. How can we be salt and light? The Bible says, "But as many as received him, to them gave he power to become the sons of God, even to them that believe on his name:" John 1:12. As we continually receive the Lord into our lives, enabling us to live according to His word, we are the salt and light He ordained us to be. My prayer is that we will not lose our saltiness, but remain faithful so we can lead others to Jesus. The end of time is at hand.

THE LORD WILL PROVIDE

Genesis 22:8
"And Abraham said, My son, God will provide himself a
lamb for a burnt offering: so they went both
of them together."

Abraham was accustomed to hearing the voice of God. It was this familiar voice that made the promise of the son though nature seemed to say otherwise. Although Abraham and Sarah had a temporary lapse of faith, God kept His word. When the son of promise was a young lad, the Lord brought upon Abraham the most severe test imaginable. God commanded Abraham to sacrifice His promised son, the one through whom Messiah would come. Surely God must be mistaken, right? Abraham, fully armed with faith did not flinch at the command, though the road was a difficult one. Abraham demonstrated that he believed that by some miracle God would bring Isaac back to life. "And Abraham said unto his young men, Abide ye here with the ass; and I and the lad will go yonder and worship, and come again to you," Genesis 22:5. The last phrase is instructive, although he fully intended to sacrifice his son, he told his servants that they both would worship and return. This is a model of great faith.

At a critical point in their journey, the strong young man realized that all that was necessary for the sacrifice was present besides except sacrifice itself. A double meaning burst into my thoughts when Abraham responded by saying, "The Lord will provide himself a ram." On one hand God Himself (the Father) would provide the ram. On the other hand, God (the Son) would provide himself as the ram. The first interpretation is preferable, although the second is also glorious. Whatever the case, when the moment came for Abraham to lower the knife, God revealed the ram of provision (Genesis 22:13).

Isn't it curious that the story of the sacrifice is about a loving father and a strong, yet submissive son? Isn't it interesting that the ram was caught in a thicket? Isn't it also interesting that the ram was sacrificed instead of the boy?

Our heavenly Father loved us so much that he provided Jesus, the only Lamb, which takes away the sins of the world. God the Son, who could have decided not to be sacrificed just as Isaac could have refused, decided to submit to the will of His father. Jesus wore a crown of thorns, just as the ram had its horns caught in a thicket. The Lord stopped the sacrifice of a mere human, signifying the insufficiency of such a sacrifice. God provided, in Jesus Christ, the perfect sacrifice for our sins. The Lord will provide!

JACOB'S LADDER

Genesis 28:10-12
"And Jacob went out from Beer-sheba, and went toward Haran. And he lighted upon a certain place, and tarried there all night, because the sun was set; and he took of the stones of that place, and put them for his pillows, and lay down in that place to sleep. And he dreamed, and behold a ladder set up on the earth, and the top of it reached to heaven: and behold the angels of God ascending and descending on it."

The Lord was slowly revealing Himself to Jacob. He knew that as He continued to lead Jacob, he would soon become the faithful man that God intended him to be. After Jacob was blessed by his father and sent on his way, he traveled toward Haran. As the sun set, he found a place to sleep for the night. The Lord gave him a dream of a ladder reaching into heaven. He saw a vision of angels ascending and descending upon it, with the Lord at the top. The Lord proclaimed His name and promised Jacob that He would make of him a great nation and would give him the land where he slept as an inheritance. This was the hope Jacob had. God said, "And, behold, I am with thee, and will keep thee in all places whither thou goest, and will bring thee again into this land; for I will not leave thee, until I have done that which I have spoken to thee of. And Jacob awaked out of his sleep, and he said, Surely the LORD is in this place; and I knew it not. And he was afraid, and said, How dreadful is this place! this is none other but the house of God, and this is the gate of heaven." Genesis 28:15-17.

Did you know that Jesus expounded on this dream in the New Testament? "Nathanael answered and saith unto him, Rabbi, thou art the Son of God; thou art the King of Israel. Jesus answered and said unto him, Because I said unto thee,

I saw thee under the fig tree, believest thou? thou shalt see greater things than these. And he saith unto him, Verily, verily, I say unto you, Hereafter ye shall see heaven open, and the angels of God ascending and descending upon the Son of man." John 1:49-51. Jesus is our connection with heaven. With His humanity, Jesus lays hold on us; with His divinity, He lays hold upon God. In truth, He is our mediator. There is no other way that we can have access to the throne of God. As with Jacob, He promises that those who are faithful will inherit the place whereon we stand.

One thousand years following the return of Christ, we will inherit the earth made new (Revelation 20, 21). The New Jerusalem will descend to the earth and we will see the prophecies of Isaiah 65 fulfilled. All of this will be possible, not because of any good that we have done, but because of the Ladder, Jesus Christ. Through Christ is communicated the power that we need in order for us to submit to God and be renewed by His Spirit.

We are blessed to have such a good friend in Jesus. Thank the Lord for being willing to give us all of heaven in one gift, the person of Christ.

PENIEL

Genesis 32:30

"And Jacob called the name of the place Peniel: for I have seen God face to face, and my life is preserved."

It was a turbulent night. Jacob was stressed because of an ongoing altercation he was having with his brother Esau who sought to do him harm. "And Jacob was left alone; and there wrestled a man with him until the breaking of the day. And when he saw that he prevailed not against him, he touched the hollow of his thigh; and the hollow of Jacob's thigh was out of joint, as he wrestled with him. And he said, Let me go, for the day breaketh. And he said, I will not let thee go, except thou bless me. And he said unto him, What is thy name? And he said, Jacob. And he said, Thy name shall be called no more Jacob, but Israel: for as a prince hast thou power with God and with men, and hast prevailed. And Jacob asked him, and said, Tell me, I pray thee, thy name. And he said, Wherefore is it that thou dost ask after my name? And he blessed him there. And Jacob called the name of the place Peniel: for I have seen God face to face, and my life is preserved." Genesis 32:24-30.

The experience Jacob had with God is very important for us in this day. Everyday that passes draws us closer to the end of time. If we are truly God's children, we will begin facing trials that are greater than any we have ever encountered. The Lord's message to us is that we must prevail in prayer. We must lay hold upon God with the hand of faith and never let go. No matter how the heavens seem shut up unto us, we must not cease praying. There is coming a time of trouble never before seen on the earth and the Lord expects His people to have learned to prevail in prayer in order to make it through that time. "And at that time shall Michael stand up, the great prince which standeth for the children of thy people: and there shall be a time of trouble, such as never was since there was a nation even to that same time: and at that time thy people shall be delivered, every one that shall be found written in the book." Daniel 12:1. "Because thou hast kept the word of my patience, I also will keep thee from the hour of temptation, which shall come upon all the world, to try them that dwell upon the earth. Behold, I come quickly: hold that fast which thou hast, that no man take thy crown. Him that overcometh will I make a pillar in the temple of my God, and he shall go no more out: and I will write upon him the name of my God, and the name of the city of my God, which is new Jerusalem, which cometh down out of heaven from my God: and I will write upon him my new name." Revelation 3:10-12.

As we learn to prevail in prayer and persevere during hard trials, we, like Jacob, will have a revelation of God and be in awe. Soon, time will be no more and the struggles of this life will cease. Jesus will part the sky and will be ushered in to take His people home. Will you be in that number? If not, why not? No matter your answer, pray that the Lord will make you more faithful today and commit yourself to Him. He will never disappoint, but will keep what you have committed to Him until that day.

SUPREME ELEVATION

Genesis 50:19-21
"And Joseph said unto them, Fear not: for am I in the place of God? But as for you, ye thought evil against me; but God meant it unto good, to bring to pass, as it is this day, to save much people alive. Now therefore fear ye not: I will nourish you, and your little ones. And he comforted them, and spake kindly unto them."

The story of Joseph is amazing. He was one of the twelve sons of Jacob. He had one brother that was younger than him, named Benjamin. When Joseph was young, Jacob showed partiality toward him. Eventually, a seed of envy was planted in his elder brothers to the point of nearly killing him, but instead, they sold him into slavery for thirty pieces of silver.

As the story continues, while in jail, Joseph grows in favor with prominent people, and in a strange turn of events, one such leader's wife tried to seduce him into fornication. "But he refused, and said unto his master's wife, Behold, my master wotteth not what is with me in the house, and he hath committed all that he hath to my hand; There is none greater in this house than I; neither hath he kept back any thing from me but thee, because thou art his wife: how then can I do this great wickedness, and sin against God?" Genesis 39:8, 9. Instead of Joseph being delivered from jail, as he deserved, he stayed longer. Eventually, by divine intervention, he was released to govern the seven-year process of storing grain in all of the land; a seven-year famine loomed on the horizon. As a result of his godly resolve and spiritual witness, he was elevated before the people.

When the years of famine came, Joseph's long-lost betrayers resurfaced not knowing who the powerful governor was at first. Through a series of tests, Joseph revealed himself. The brothers were repentant. "And Joseph said unto them, Fear not: for am I in the place of God? But as for you, ye thought evil against me; but God meant it unto good, to bring to pass, as it is this day, to save much people alive. Now therefore fear ye not: I will nourish you, and your little ones. And he comforted them, and spake kindly unto them." Genesis 50:19-21.

Did you know that Jesus bound Himself in the prison of earth? The divine Son of God did not deserve to be here to suffer the punishment that we deserve. The devil, in leading human beings to transgress God's law, intended it for evil against us, but God meant it for good. He intended that we be eternally separated from God and be condemned to eternal death. He used Judas, one who claimed to be close to Jesus, to betray Him into the hands of His enemies. Jesus, having taken all of this into account still became the Savior of the world by dying on the cross and being raised on the third day.

You may wonder how anything good could come out of the human predicament. The answer is simple, yet glorious. While God never intended that humankind sin, He saw an opportunity through sin to elevate us. Jesus adopted the humanity of Abraham in order to live as our example, vanquish the enemy, vindicate God's character, and effect our salvation (Hebrews 2:14-18). Through the process of God, that is, Jesus Christ, becoming human, He elevated us. The fact that Jesus clothed His divinity with our humanity brings those that have faith in Him to a supreme level. It is an honor to have Jesus as our representative in the heavens, having suffered the second death and overcoming it for us.

It is true that God's ideal was that we had never sinned, but since we did, He can be glorified. He now can demonstrate His love and power on a level that we cannot imagine. With divinity and humanity united, we experience a supreme elevation. It is a blessing to know that God loved us so much that He became a man (I Timothy 3:16). Having done so, He united us with the divine by an unbreakable cord of love. What Satan meant for evil, God turned around and made it for good.

NULLIFIED INFLUENCE

Exodus 2:14
"And he said, Who made thee a prince and a judge over us? intendest thou to kill me, as thou killedst the Egyptian? And Moses feared, and said, Surely this thing is known."

Moses was a Hebrew; therefore, he was called to the faithfulness of Abraham. He and his people, even before the writing of the law in stone, were called to holiness. God had revealed His ability to set aside God-fearing people through the patriarchs who had lived before Moses.

One day Moses saw an Egyptian beating a Hebrew as he worked. With indignation, he descended on the Egyptian, killed him, and buried him in the sand. All of this he did after looking around to make sure nobody was watching. "And when he went out the second day, behold, two men of the Hebrews strove together: and he said to him that did the wrong, Wherefore smitest thou thy fellow? And he said, Who made thee a prince and a judge over us? intendest thou to kill me, as thou killedst the Egyptian? And Moses feared, and said, Surely this thing is known." Exodus 2:13, 14.

In this one thoughtless act on the part of Moses, the devil sought to nullify his influence forever. He knew that if he could cause Moses to fall, his iniquity would separate him from God (Isaiah 59:2). He knew that whatever God was planning to do through Moses could be hampered if Moses lost his spiritual composure.

Pharaoh heard about what Moses had done and wanted to kill him. Moses, fearing his life, fled into Midian where He kept the sheep of his father-in-law Jethro. Eventually the Lord appeared to Moses in a burning bush. "And Moses said, I will now turn aside, and see this great sight, why the bush is not burnt. And when the LORD saw that he turned aside to see, God called unto him out of the midst of the bush, and said, Moses, Moses. And he said, Here am I. And he said, Draw not nigh hither: put off thy shoes from off thy feet, for the place whereon thou standest is holy ground. Moreover he said, I am the God of thy father, the God of Abraham, the God of Isaac, and the God of Jacob. And Moses hid his face; for he was afraid to look upon God." Exodus 3:3-6. During this encounter, God gave Moses his commission to act as a deliverer of His people from Egyptian slavery.

The devil intended that Moses' influence for good be eternally nullified, but God had another plan. He taught Moses humility and patience through his experience in Midian. God called Moses to his mission when the time was right.

On some level, this is the case with all of us. When we could have a godly influence on people and lead them to relationship with Christ, sometimes we fail. Sometimes we allow self to get in the way of God's mission for our lives. All is not lost. God, in His faithfulness, teaches us through our own Midian experiences what it means to patiently trust Him and become meek. As He develops our character, He entrusts us with more and more responsibilities to do His service. Will we accept the charge or remain nullified? Moses tried to resist his call, but the Lord persisted and Moses obeyed. What is God calling you to do? Do not allow your past to intimidate you. Trust the Lord to nurture and guide you into your mission for Him. Do not allow your influence for good to be nullified.

EVEN THE GROUND IS HOLY

Exodus 3:4, 5
"And when the LORD saw that he turned aside to see,
God called unto him out of the midst of the bush, and
said, Moses, Moses. And he said, Here am I. And he said,
Draw not nigh hither: put off thy shoes from off thy feet,
for the place whereon thou standest is holy ground."

Much can be said about the holiness of God. At the sound His name demons flee, diseases lose their grip, and broken hearts are bound up. God's presence inspires unholy men to become worldwide evangelists, prostitutes to become His witnesses, and the dumb cannot help but to speak eloquently.

Moses had a close encounter with this God, the One whom angels adore and humankind worships. During the beginning stages of Moses' ministry, God spoke to him through a bush that, though on fire, was not consumed. As Moses sought to understand the nature of this grand display, the Lord spoke to him. The first thing He told Moses was to take off his shoes, because the very ground beneath him was holy. This is not the only time this occurred in Bible history. "And it came to pass, when Joshua was by Jericho, that he lifted up his eyes and looked, and, behold, there stood a man over against him with his sword drawn in his hand: and Joshua went unto him, and said unto him, Art thou for us, or for our adversaries? And he said, Nay; but as captain of the host of the LORD am I now come. And Joshua fell on his face to the earth, and did worship, and said unto him, What saith my lord unto his servant? And the captain of the LORD's host said unto Joshua, Loose thy shoe from off thy foot; for the place whereon thou standest is holy. And Joshua did so." Joshua 5:13, 15.

What made the ground that was just ordinary moments before these men's encounter with God holy? The answer is simple yet beautiful. The fact that God was present made even the ground holy. Is God present in your life? If He lives in your heart, you too are holy. Was the ground holy by nature? Just as the composition of the ground is ordinary by itself, we are as well. When God inhabits a person, place, or thing, it automatically becomes holy. Pray that the Lord will so permeate your life that you will be seen as holy in **God's** estimation. "But as he which hath called you is holy, so be ye holy in all manner of conversation; Because it is written, Be ye holy; for I am holy." I Peter 1:15, 16.

I AM THAT I AM

Exodus 3:14
"And God said unto Moses, I AM THAT I AM: and he said, Thus shalt thou say unto the children of Israel, I AM hath sent me unto you."

When meeting someone for the first time, it is a matter of common courtesy to introduce oneself by simply stating your name. It seems simple enough, yet it can have great impact depending on who is being introduced. For instance, suppose you were in the United States capital, Washington, DC visiting a war memorial and noticed an African-American man in a military uniform. As you looked closely, his face seemed familiar. Later on, a very important friend of yours introduced you to the man you noticed earlier by saying, "Meet U.S. Secretary of State, Colin L. Powell." This name means many different things to many different people, but one thing is certain, unless you never watch the news, you would *at least* recognize it.

The Bible is full of names and each of them has particular significance. Most notable is the name of God. At different critical points in Bible history, He has identified Himself using different names to communicate spiritual lessons. When Moses was being called to ministry in Exodus chapter 16, he was concerned that he may not be equipped to do the important work God had commissioned him to do. When God told him to go to the children of Israel with a message and mission, Moses asked Him to identify Himself should they inquire about who sent him. God told Moses to tell his people I AM THAT I AM sent me unto you. This name, among other things, means the God who is with you. God was saying that the Lord God of your fathers, who is interested in your personal affairs, has sent a special message, mission, and deliverance to you. Isn't it wonderful to know that God is not only the all-powerful God way up in heaven that created all things, but He is also intimately interested and involved in the lives of weak human beings? This may be one of the most valuable lessons we can learn about God.

Many were the times when the ancient people of the Bible called on the name of the Lord to find strength, emotional stability, love, companionship, comfort, joy and even their own identities. Forgiveness of sins, guidance and peace were also revealed in the names of God. In the New Testament, healing was often associated with the name of God as in the book of Acts the fourth chapter, where Peter and John healed a man in the mighty name of Jesus Christ of Nazareth. Certainly, Jesus is God, therefore His name, too, is powerful (Revelation 22:12-16).

Knowing that God's identity reveals that He is involved in our everyday affairs and is interested in our well being, we will take a short journey through some of the ways He has revealed Himself in the Bible. If His name is interwoven into our everyday experience, we will be among those seen in Revelation chapter 20, verse one that will experience eternal bliss with God forever and ever. Amen.

LET MY PEOPLE GO

Exodus 8:1
"And the LORD spake unto Moses, Go unto Pharaoh,
and say unto him, Thus saith the LORD, Let my people
go, that they may serve me."

If you have taken time to read the story of the exodus from Egypt, you realize as I have that it was a saga of epic proportions. There was a constant contention between Pharaoh and Moses. Some of the contention involved the fact that God commanded that Pharaoh free His people so they would be able to worship Him without restrictions. Pharaoh was only interested in defying the God of heaven, demonstrating his might, and strength to resist the command of the God of whom he is unfamiliar. As far as he was concerned, he was the only one in control.

After many meetings between Moses, Aaron, and Pharaoh and several devastating plagues, it became clear that Pharaoh was an evil man indifferent towards doing what God commanded. His obstinacy grew with the passing of each plague. It was difficult for me to understand how a man could be so insolent. The Lord was making Himself known and no one could deny that they were dealing with a great big God. It occurred to me after reading the following verse; God was using Pharaoh's disobedience as an object lesson. "And in very deed for this cause have I raised thee up, for to shew in thee my power; and that my name may be declared throughout all the earth. As yet exaltest thou thyself against my people, that thou wilt not let them go?" Exodus 9:16, 17. Pharaoh represents the devil and his determination to keep people in spiritual slavery at all costs. The Lord allows the devil to run a course that shows his might in binding people, and that only by supernatural power can God's people be free of this bondage. "And it came to pass, that at midnight the LORD smote all the firstborn in the land of Egypt, from the firstborn of Pharaoh that sat on his throne unto the firstborn of the captive that was in the dungeon; and all the firstborn of cattle. And Pharaoh rose up in the night, he, and all his servants, and all the Egyptians; and there was a great cry in Egypt; for there was not a house where there was not one dead. And he called for Moses and Aaron by night, and said, Rise up, and get you forth from among my people, both ye and the children of Israel; and go, serve the LORD, as ye have said. Also take your flocks and your herds, as ye have said, and be gone; and bless me also. And the Egyptians were urgent upon the people, that they might send them out of the land in haste; for they said, We be all dead men." Exodus 12:29-33.

Have you ever felt the controversy being fought over your soul? Do you realize that the devil is willing to defy God to the bitter end to keep you under his control? Know that God is a spiritual technician who knows how to free people at a time when He will get the most glory. When He sets us free through Jesus Christ, we are free to worship Him in the beauty of holiness; we are free to tell others what great things the Lord has done for us. The world will know that only the God of heaven could have broken the bands of wickedness that the devil put upon us. Don't be discouraged when it seems that your freedom is far away. "If the Son therefore shall make you free, ye shall be free indeed." John 8:36.

SLAVE MENTALITY

Exodus 14:11, 12
"And they said unto Moses, Because there were no graves in Egypt, hast thou taken us away to die in the wilderness? wherefore hast thou dealt thus with us, to carry us forth out of Egypt? Is not this the word that we did tell thee in Egypt, saying, Let us alone, that we may serve the Egyptians? For it had been better for us to serve the Egyptians, than that we should die in the wilderness."

There are those that have been enslaved for such a long period of time that they cannot conceive of themselves being free. The burden of their captivity has broken their spirit, and it is nearly impossible to instill hope in them. After many years of hoping and being disappointed, they cannot be convinced that a change is possible.

People of color endured centuries of slavery in the United States. Their slave masters gave them inferior food, poor living conditions, attempted to take their religion from them, and promoted disunity amongst them. Now, many years later, many people whose ancestors endured the slavery still demonstrate a slave mentality. This defeatist mentality is apparent in limited aspirations, pessimism, violence, poor eating habits, consistently choosing bad relationships, and other life defeating circumstances.

As God delivered the children of Israel from Egyptian slavery, the road was rough. At every turn they opposed the process of liberation God had employed. When they experienced the slightest trials, they desired to go back into slavery. Instead of looking forward to the final stages of liberation, they envisioned themselves as content slaves. This was sad. The Lord gave them signs in the sky by day and night to let them know that He was with them. He amplified the seventh-day Sabbath so they could regain a grasp on God through acceptable religion. He provided them manna from heaven and water in the desert, yet they desired the debilitating meats of slavery. They, no doubt, would rather have drunk the wine of bondage than the fresh water of progressive freedom.

Today, many that have chosen to follow Jesus begin to become discouraged as they grow. Sometimes the difficulty that comes through sacrificing self and sin on the altar of liberation is overwhelming. They allow the enemy to coax them into yielding Godly religion, heavenly bread, that is, the Word of God, and the hope of complete freedom that comes at the second advent of Jesus. Let the Lord invigorate you. Allow Him to instill a victorious mentality within you. As we grow through the sometimes difficult processes of emancipation, not giving up, we may appreciate the ways in which God leads us. We grow in optimism and welcome the opportunity to lead others to spiritual freedom. We want to tell the whole world about our emancipator Jesus Christ. Do not cherish a slave mentality. Accept the freedom that comes from knowing Christ. "If the Son therefore shall make you free, ye shall be free indeed." John 8:36.

You Can Trust God

Exodus 14:22
"And the children of Israel went into the midst of the sea upon the dry ground: and the waters were a wall unto them on their right hand, and on their left."

What a spectacle of nature it must have been to see the Red Sea parted down the middle with a path of dry land for the Israelites to cross over. The idea of such a miracle is beyond comprehension. In spite of its inconceivability, it is true. God did use Moses to part the Red Sea down the middle, and dry land did appear. I suppose it makes sense on a higher spiritual level. The same God, who divided the waters from the dry land in the creation account, divided the waters so the Israelites could be led to freedom. Both cases separated the God of heaven from all false gods.

Would you have been able to trust God while walking that long seabed to freedom? Can you imagine the anxiety that might have overtaken you? Perhaps you would be perfectly cool, calm, and collected. I am not sure how I would have reacted. One thing is certain; the Lord had given His children sufficient evidence on which to hang their faith. The plagues that fell on Egypt that passed over the Israelites, while devastating the Egyptians, were definitely great evidence that God was with them. Certainly, there was still room for doubt; however there was also abundant evidence for implicit trust in God.

The children of Israel were being led step by step by the greatest, most compassionate and loving Being in the universe. Although they were the disloyal spouse in this spiritual relationship, God remained faithful. What a blessing it is to consider that even in their extreme circumstances, God was right there with them to lead, comfort, and cheer.

This portion of the story begins with a murmuring bunch

of faithless people (Exodus 14:12), but ends with a congregation of thankful worshippers (Exodus 15:1-21). I realize that they reverted to their faithless ways soon afterward, but the reality still exists that the Israelites knew, without doubt, that they could trust God.

What impassible sea separates you from true freedom and worship? What tendencies cause you to flip-flop between praise and doubt? Learn a lesson from the Exodus. God will always be faithful to us, even in our extreme situations. In fact, it is in our seemingly impossible situations that He triumphs most gloriously. Let the Lord part your Red Sea of sinful habits, doubt, sadness, pain, or whatever you face. Surrender your faith to Him and know that you can trust the Lord.

GIVE US OUR DAILY BREAD

Exodus 16:4
"Then said the LORD unto Moses, Behold, I will rain
bread from heaven for you; and the people shall go out
and gather a certain rate every day, that I may prove
them, whether they will walk in my law, or no."

Food is necessary for sustaining human life. We usually eat a few times everyday in order to absorb the vital nutrients that are needed to maintain healthy lives. With proper nutrition, we are energized with clear perceptions and the ability to make right decisions in performance of our daily routines. This is the ideal. When we eat what is necessary to receive these benefits without taxing our system with inferior foods or excessive portions, we are elevated, and we are better able to understand God's will for us. We must trust Him daily to provide our necessary food.

Have you ever attempted to function on yesterday's food? I do not mean leftovers from Thanksgiving dinner. I mean literally function on the energy you received from yesterday's meals. Outside of a deliberate, well-planned fast, we cannot subsist from day to day on the previous day's meals. We may become weak or irritable. We may experience headaches and dizziness as well. Yesterday's food is generally not good enough for today.

The Lord taught this to Israel, while they were in the wilderness. As they murmured because of their perception of the difficult journey out of Egypt, the Lord instructed Moses that He had heard their particular complaints concerning food. They accused the Lord of bringing them into the wilderness to die. They would rather have continued receiving food from the inferior fleshpots of Egypt. "Then said the LORD unto Moses, Behold, I will rain bread from heaven for you; and the people shall go out and gather a certain rate every day, that I may prove them, whether they will walk in my law, or no." Exodus 16:4. Daily, the Lord provided a certain portion of heavenly bread for each person. They were in a situation where they had to trust Him implicitly since additional portions would have spoiled if they tried to subsist on them the following day. They were given their necessary portions everyday. Sabbath was special though. "And it shall come to pass, that on the sixth day they shall prepare that which they bring in; and it shall be twice as much as they gather daily." Exodus 16:5. The Lord provided by means of miracle, a double portion on Friday, which would cover the Sabbath as well. All of this, the Lord did in order to test their fidelity and demonstrate His love.

Such is the case with our spiritual food. We must trust the Lord to provide His word and faith for each day. God does not encourage us to neglect Bible study and prayer on any particular day with the idea that our experience on the previous day would sustain us. This is where many lose focus. The Lord has fresh meals prepared for those who trust Him enough to receive them daily. As in the wilderness journey, the Sabbath is special for us. The Lord provides a double portion of His hidden manna for additional blessing. We are able to rest and worship God on His holy seventh day. He is available to teach us on a level beyond even the daily experience. By worshipping Him as Creator, through Christian fellowship, and special devotional time, God miraculously enhances our lives in order to prepare us for the new week.

It is a blessing to receive God's word and blessings everyday. It is our privilege to exercise faith, knowing that He will never let us starve spiritually as long as we cooperate with Him. He will give us our daily bread and we will be sustained by faith until Jesus returns to take us into the heavenly Promised Land.

THE MISSION BECOMES POSSIBLE

Exodus 19:4-6
"Ye have seen what I did unto the Egyptians, and how I
bare you on eagles' wings, and brought you unto myself.
Now therefore, if ye will obey my voice indeed, and keep
my covenant, then ye shall be a peculiar treasure unto me
above all people: for all the earth is mine: And ye shall be
unto me a kingdom of priests, and an holy nation. These
are the words which thou shalt speak unto
the children of Israel."

I can remember watching a television show while I was growing up, where a man named Mr. Phelps assembled several people to view a videotape of a mission they would need to accomplish. Each episode would invariably begin with a voice saying to them, "Your mission, should you choose to accept it is…." I can still hear the theme music in my mind that let us know that the mission, which seemed staggering and required extreme planning, insight, and sophisticated gadgetry, would not only be accepted, but possible. The odds were always stacked against their success, but with persistent effort, they accomplished their goal. They had the right tools at their disposal, therefore missions that came with many challenges, were surmountable. The missions to them became possible.

After the Lord demonstrated His power and determination to deliver His people, Israel, from Egyptian bondage, He began to reveal His will for their lives even more. He commanded Moses to prepare the people to meet with Him at Mount Sinai. He outlined the ways in which He had been working in their lives to give them a better experience, and how swiftly He delivered them that they might become a peculiar treasure. As they obeyed His voice and kept His covenant, they would be a holy nation and a kingdom of priests. As He began to reveal Himself, the people were in awe immediately and proclaimed that they would do whatever the Lord commanded. Not many days later, the Lord spoke His holy ten commandment law and engraved it in two tables of stone, signifying its significance and perpetuity.

Many people today, have read the miserable failures of God's ancient people and choose to believe that it was simply impossible for them to accomplish His will. They suggest that the Lord knew that they could not possibly obey Him, therefore He abrogated His law and extended the grace of the New Covenant. While it is true that in our own strength, we cannot please God, His biddings are truly enablings. The Lord made a point to reveal many Old Testament characters as His faithful followers. These people stood in contrast to the world around them. People like Ruth, Joshua, Caleb, Rahab, Enoch, Seth, and others like them are a testimony to God's ability to reform and consecrate sinners, making us into His peculiar treasure. With the Lord's power within us, we are able to come forth as conquerors over sin, self, and Satan. Jesus overcame the world, and has transferred His victory to every helpless, believing sinner willing to do His will. He is able to blot out our sins, deliver us from spiritual slavery, and lovingly bring us into conformity to His will. As with the mission mentioned above, it will not be without challenges, but the Lord will be with us every step of the way. The mission to follow the Lord implicitly, which left to our own power would be impossible, has become possible.

May the Lord elevate you to the point where you believe in His power and trust Him enough to fulfill His promise to make you holy. One day soon, Jesus will gather everyone who trusted in Him together and take us to paradise. He will appear in the skies for all of the world to see and this life will become a distant memory. I look forward to that day. "But without faith it is impossible to please him: for he that cometh to God must believe that he is, and that he is a rewarder of them that diligently seek him." Hebrews 11:6. "Now unto him that is able to keep you from falling, and to present you faultless before the presence of his glory with exceeding joy, To the only wise God our Saviour, be glory and majesty, dominion and power, both now and ever. Amen." Jude 1:24, 25.

I Brought You Out

Exodus 20:2
"I am the LORD thy God, which have brought thee out of the land of Egypt, out of the house of bondage."

The many years of slavery that God's people endured in Egypt are instructive for us even today. Slavery itself can be an object lesson about the slavery to sin that human beings endure from day to day. We are constantly bombarded with the insults and injuries of this world's pharaoh, the devil, who would rather endure the punishment of heaven than to let us be free from spiritual slavery.

One of the most encouraging aspects of the exodus from Egypt is that the Lord did not give up the process of liberating Israel because of Pharaoh's insolence. God did not allow even the people's complaints in the wilderness to intimidate Him into leaving them in captivity. The Red Sea, kingly armies, and impossible odds were no match for God. His purpose was to show the entire world that all things are possible with Him. He wanted His people to know that He would deliver them by any means necessary.

Are you bogged down with the unfortunate reality of sinful bondage? Does it seem that the Lord has brought you to a dry desert to die? Do you often feel that it was better when you served sin in you spiritual Egypt? The Lord is saying to your soul, "I have brought you out of bondage for a purpose." You see, God did not go through all of the twists and turns of leading the exodus only to allow the people to whither and die. The Promised Land was in view. If they had been faithful to Him, in His strength, they all would have entered.

When the temptation comes to believe the struggle with sin is too difficult to bear, just look up to heaven and reach out in faith to your deliverer. Look upon Jesus and live, knowing that that ole serpent the devil cannot harm you with his deadly venom if God is on your side. Look to Jesus and live!

POINT OF REFERENCE

Exodus 20:2
"I am the LORD thy God, which have brought thee out of the land of Egypt, out of the house of bondage."

The Lord patiently led the children of Israel out of Egyptian bondage. With tender love, He listened to their grumblings even though they should have been praising Him. He knew that they would not always follow His plans for them, yet He remained faithful. Part of His liberation plan included a written revelation of ten principles governing His will. After releasing them from the wicked bonds of Pharaoh, He wanted them to receive a level of freedom that they could not receive except from Him. He wanted them to be free to worship Him with all their hearts. How could they be certain that He was able to expand on their freedom? He gave them a point of reference. He identified Himself as the Lord that had just released them from Egyptian slavery. They knew without a doubt that it was only by the grace of God that they were free. God wanted to associate their physical freedom with the spiritual freedom they would receive as they lived within the safeguard of His law.

In the words following His proclamation that He released them from Pharaoh, God began to speak His *ten words*. As He etched His will in stone for all to see, He would write His laws on their hearts and in their minds if they were willing to have faith in Him. His ten commandments would then become ten promises. As He promised that He would free them from Pharaoh, He promised that if they loved Him, they would have no other gods before Him. He promised, if they loved Him that they would not kill or steal. Every commandment became a promise to those who chose to live for Him.

As the Lord brings the light of His will for our lives, we

may think that His way is too difficult, but we must learn from the Israelites. The deliverance from Egypt that they needed was no easy process. In fact, if it were left to the people, it would have been impossible, yet the Lord prevailed over their enemies. The blessing is that all of the inherited and cultivated tendencies toward evil that we have are obstacles that the Lord will surmount as well. As He demonstrated to His people of old, He is able to utterly vanquish the enemy. When we receive His power by faith, he enables us to satisfy Him. He empowers us with His Spirit and makes promises to us as well. As we remain in step with Him, we walk on from victory to victory. It does not come without struggle, but the Lord does keep His promises.

Remember that the same God, who delivered Israel and brought them through the Red Sea on dry ground, is able to make His commandments living principles in each of our lives. If we still need a point of reference on which to build our faith, we need look no further than Calvary. It was at Calvary that Jesus bore every one of our sins and died in our place. At Calvary, the beginning of His plan of redemption was revealed. He demonstrated His ability to bury past sins, and early on Sunday morning, when He arose from the tomb, He demonstrated His power to make us alive in Him. Praise the Lord for these blessed points of reference!

PRIORITIES

Exodus 20:3
"Thou shalt have no other gods before me."

Every responsible human being is faced with the task of prioritizing daily. Whether it is related to tasks at work, school, or in relationships, we all must make decisions about what is most important to us, and how to organize them.

God has said in His word in so many instances, that He demands to be number one in our lives. His purpose for this is not rooted in selfishness. He is not merely saying that He wants us for Himself for some shallow or arbitrary reason. His love says that He cannot live without us. He knows that if we do not keep Him in a position of preeminence in our lives, we will never live with Him eternally.

Sin has mixed up the intended order of things. We have been programmed to think that the first priority should be self-satisfaction. The pursuit of riches, notoriety, and lofty educational attainments has, in many cases, dethroned God in our soul temple. Closely associated with God's command to keep Him first is His resume' of gifts to us. He has made every provision necessary for our freedom from the power and presence of sin; therefore, it should be an act of gratitude to make Him Lord of our every detail.

In the practical things of life, we can begin to put God first by jumpstarting our day with Him. Through worship, prayer, and Bible study we can bring what really matters into focus. When we have the right focus from the very beginning of our day, the enemy has less access to our lives, and the Lord is able to fight our battles for us. When we meet with God in the morning, we give Him permission to support or change anything we have planned.

Make, and keep the Lord first in your days, and He will remain seated on the throne of your life.

GOD IS TOO BIG FOR THAT

Exodus 20:4-6
"Thou shalt not make unto thee any graven image, or any likeness of any thing that is in heaven above, or that is in the earth beneath, or that is in the water under the earth: Thou shalt not bow down thyself to them, nor serve them: for I the LORD thy God am a jealous God, visiting the iniquity of the fathers upon the children unto the third and fourth generation of them that hate me; And shewing mercy unto thousands of them that love me, and keep my commandments."

The only true God, the God of heaven is so big in terms of His character and beauty that nothing tangible can truly represent Him. The only perfect revelation He has given us in this world was the man Jesus Christ. "God, who at sundry times and in divers manners spake in time past unto the fathers by the prophets, Hath in these last days spoken unto us by his Son, whom he hath appointed heir of all things, by whom also he made the worlds; Who being the brightness of his glory, and the express image of his person, and upholding all things by the word of his power, when he had by himself purged our sins, sat down on the right hand of the Majesty on high;" Hebrews 1:1-3. "For in him dwelleth all the fulness of the Godhead bodily." Colossians 2:9. This is why the Lord commanded that *nothing* be fashioned or worshipped to represent God. Any attempt to represent God in any earthly form would bring our view of Him down to the level of the thing representing Him. God is bigger than cows. He is bigger than birds. He is bigger than furniture. He is bigger than images of dead human beings who were supposedly God's saints.

The command not to worship images is interesting, because unlike having other gods before Him, this addresses even those that supposedly have good intentions. People all over the world claim to revere the only true God of heaven and only have these representations in order to make His presence or essence more accessible. This is part of the reason the children of Israel erected the golden calf. They did not intend to replace God by it, but worship Him through it. They did not have faith enough to lay hold on the power of God without something tangible, whether by some human leader, or a graven image.

It is our privilege today to worship the Lord in the beauty of holiness. We do not need a tangible crutch of dead so-called saints, animals, pictures of how we think God looks, or anything else to elevate our minds to worship Him. God has given us His Spirit for that purpose. He is the One who connects us with the essence of God. He carries our consciousness heavenward unencumbered by some impotent, unholy catalyst. I thank God that our view of God does not have to be limited by our view of His creatures. We have access to Him through heavenly agencies and I praise Him for it.

THAT NAME

Exodus 20:7
"Thou shalt not take the name of the LORD thy God in
vain; for the LORD will not hold him guiltless
that taketh his name in vain."

The name of God is holy. The ways in which He has revealed Himself throughout history, show us clearly, that He is no lightweight God. In His name judgments were pronounced, messages delivered, and vast armies defeated. In God's name kings, pharaohs, and governors were brought under subjection. In His name, diseases were cured, ailments sent to flight, and devils exorcised. The name of God is not to be treated lightly.

God's people have associated names of God with important junctures in their lives. In the case of Abraham on Mount Moriah, God was the Provider. In the case of Moses facing the charge to begin the exodus, He was the Lord; the one who is with you. In the creation, He was the Almighty One upon whom the worlds were established.

Looking closely at these realities gives us a view of why it is no small matter to misuse His name. Often I watch shows on cable that are good in general. I have noticed that even in the least offensive of them, the name of the Lord is treated lightly. One such example is in all of the home makeover shows that I have seen. Invariably, when home-owners see the great job the designer has done, they begin to repeatedly use God's name, not in worship or adoration, but in superficial surprise with no regard for His holiness. This neither pleases God nor does it bring Him glory.

Another way that may be more offensive is when we wear the name of God, and then chronically do things He disapproves of. Does He get any praise when we claim to be His, yet do not allow Him to control our lives? A whole world is watching even when we are not aware, and they blaspheme God when they recognize hypocrisy. Let us accept the name of God in our lives as it is our privilege to, and worship Him as He deserves. Many people will be won to the Lord if we would simply live as those that reverence His name.

GOD SAID REMEMBER

Exodus 20:8
"Remember the sabbath day, to keep it holy."

As time rapidly spirals into the future, our lives become cluttered with so much activity that many of us are completely burned out. We sometimes suffer from diseases related to overwork with far too many things competing for our attention. God knew that humans would be so bogged down with everyday life, that we would need a respite; a reprieve. Simply taking a vacation or several breaks throughout the day is just not enough for this machinery to be well rested and prepared to meet the rigors of everyday life. With wars and rumors of wars, fear of the unknown, and incurable diseases pressing in on our psyche, we need supernatural rest.

The Lord in His great wisdom devised a plan to give us the rest that we need. Jesus bought our salvation on Calvary and is now putting the finishing touches on the gift in the way of intercession in heaven in order for us to enter the salvific rest of God. We do not labor for our salvation. Rather, we rest in the perfect work of Jesus Christ.

In order to remind us of the great work of creation and re-creation, God has a commemorative time, week after week, for us to rest. The command to rest says that we are to labor for six days and on the seventh, which is Saturday, we rest. This rest is worshipful in nature. This rest recognizes God as the only Creator and Savior of the universe. This rest is for the people of God to consummate their growing love and relationship with God. No other time than the time the Lord has set aside will satisfy that need, because no other time was specifically blessed and sanctified by Him. We daily worship the Lord during the week leading up to the only day that God has sanctified as holy when we can focus on His goodness;

uninterrupted by the mundane chores of life.

Isn't it wonderful that God has the answer to our need for spiritual and physical rest? Please do not forget what God said to remember. Enter into God's rest.

HONOR YOUR PARENTS

Exodus 20:12
"Honour thy father and thy mother: that thy days may be long upon the land which the LORD thy God giveth thee."

I must be honest. This commandment seems very difficult to follow sometimes. We know of people whose parents are not the holy, spiritual parents that the Lord has called them to be. It almost seems as if the Lord forgot to qualify His statement. Surely, He must have meant to honor only honorable parents, right? How can we honor parents who gave us up for adoption? How can we honor parents that abused us physically, mentally, and sexually? How can we honor parents who do not care whether we live or die? How can we honor parents who, by their own actions or inactions do not honor themselves? I do not claim to have the answer to any of these questions. I do know however, that when the Lord commands us to do a thing, He give us the power to do it.

The New Testament recounts the commandment. "Children, obey your parents in the Lord: for this is right. Honour thy father and mother; which is the first commandment with promise; That it may be well with thee, and thou mayest live long on the earth." Ephesians 6:1-3. The Lord has said by this command, that they occupy a special position. It is right to give parents the respect and obedience that they are due. It is a shame that sometimes our parents do not live up to the standard of righteousness that God enjoins upon them, however, that has no bearing on our responsibility. We must honor them in every way inasmuch as it is lawful according to God's word. The promise for those that are obedient is to live long in the land that God gives. One day soon, we will inherit the land untainted by sin. In many cases Godly parents, by their righteous examples will be the reason why many of us receive the inheritance. We should praise the Lord for holy parents, and the opportunity to obey Him in spite of the poisonous influence of unholy parents. In either case, the Lord is pleased when we follow Him and do His will.

It's Murder

Exodus 20:13
"Thou shalt not kill."

In the news these days, there is often talk about disarming our enemies in other countries. Success is viewed as being able to locate and destroy weapons of mass destruction. On our streets police officers combat the presence of all types of weapons intended to cause harm. We are bombarded on the television and silver screen with scenes of senseless killings and mass murders. Our society is one big oxymoron, in that we do not want our loved ones hurt, yet we entertain ourselves with movies and video games that glamorize the hurting and killing of people.

The command not to kill has many implications. One such implication is that God is against murder. There are so many views of what murder actually is. Is it murder to take the life of an unborn baby when the Lord said of Jeremiah that He knew him when he was conceived in the womb? Is it murder to destroy the body that God has entrusted us with by intemperance, eating forbidden foods, and drinking forbidden drinks? Is it murder to practice promiscuity instead of faithfulness to your marriage? Is it murder to be angry with someone for selfish reasons? Is it murder to verbally destroy someone in order to make him or her feel bad? Is it murder to refuse to help those in need? Is it murder to neglect those who do not know the Lord when it is our privilege to introduce them to Him? Is it murder when we deliberately and habitually sin after we have tasted of the heavenly gift, seeing that we crucify unto ourselves Christ afresh and put Him to open shame (Hebrews 6:6)? We must answer these questions if we intend to be obedient according to the spirituality of this command.

Only the Lord can reveal to us where we have been, and

where we are murderers in His estimation. Only the Lord can teach us how to support life rather than diminish it. Pray that He will share His life-giving qualities with you and make you an agent of salvation and life. Remember, not supporting life and salvation actively is murder; spiritually speaking.

FIDELITY

Exodus 20:14
"Thou shalt not commit adultery."

Adultery is perhaps one of the most practiced sins. For millennia people have been unfaithful to their spouses. Kings and rulers have collected many intimate partners like trophies. Many women have chosen to earn a living by selling their sexuality for the love of money. It is a pity that our children see on television and on movies that infidelity can be considered romantic. As long as someone is doing what makes them feel their best it does not matter whether the Lord approves or not.

Our view of adultery in many instances needs to be broadened. "Ye have heard that it was said by them of old time, Thou shalt not commit adultery: But I say unto you, That whosoever looketh on a woman to lust after her hath committed adultery with her already in his heart." Matthew 5:27, 28. As we can see, adultery begins in the mind. If we never commit the outward act, it is still possible to be guilty in our deepest thoughts.

The Bible teaches that our relationship with God is like a marriage and unfaithfulness is considered adultery. "And I saw, when for all the causes whereby backsliding Israel committed adultery I had put her away, and given her a bill of divorce; yet her treacherous sister Judah feared not, but went and played the harlot also." Jeremiah 3:8.

As we grow in relationship with God and our spouses, we need certain safeguards in place in order to remain faithful. We need obviously to begin our day with worship. During this time, while we seek a solid relationship with God, we also seek for power to resist temptation. Oftentimes, we can steer clear of the pitfalls set by the devil to entrap us. If we commit our plans to God and sincerely ask for His protection and Guidance, He will surely deliver. Let the faithfulness of Jesus inspire you to the same. God is our greatest cheerleader for success. His desire is that we actively pursue fidelity.

DO NOT STEAL

Exodus 20:15
"Thou shalt not steal."

The command not to steal has a huge impact on relationships in every society. Often due to covetousness, people take it upon themselves to take things belonging to some else, without permission. Think about it. Would we need car alarms if people chose to abide by this commandment? Would we need home alarms with twenty-four hour monitoring services? Would women clutch their purses or rethink the route they choose to take while walking somewhere if we would simply obey the Lord? The impact stealing has had on our society is not easily measured.

The concept of theft has become more high tech and complicated since God gave the command originally. We have laws of copyright infringement, trademarks, patents, etc., to prove it. We need so many safeguards so others will not steal even intellectual property. Think about the number of people you know personally that use software that they purchased, on more than one computer, or share the program with friends when the end user license agreements clearly state that that is breaking the law? How many times have you shared copies of music or movies with friends, yet only purchased one original copy? How many times have you or your friends photocopied or scanned material from books or on the Internet, which clearly state that doing so without express written consent is illegal? How many times have you heard of college students simply rewording the works of others and submitting them as their own? Think about the number of coworkers you may have who spend time doing personal things rather than doing the work they are paid to do. How many times has someone you know taken supplies like pens and pads from work because the employer has an abundance? This overwhelming barrage of examples will help us think of how far reaching this commandment can be, even on surface levels. We have not even mentioned stealing the good reputation of people by crucifying their character falsely or other intangible examples.

Only the Lord can teach us not to steal. It is very easy to be a lawbreaker in this area, even if we are not doing it intentionally. Even if we are not waiting for someone not to be paying attention while we take their wallets out of their purse, we sometimes steal in more subtle ways. Perhaps the most important of all these things is being certain not to steal the Lord's worship and glory from Him. If we do not honor and respect the Lord enough to give Him quality time in worship and devotion, we steal His ability to receive glory through our lives. Let us pray that the Lord will teach us not to steal. Our entire society will be the better for it.

Do Not Lie

Exodus 20:16
"Thou shalt not bear false witness against thy neighbour."

Lying is a prevalent issue of society. Our criminal justice system is bogged down with innumerable cases based on deliberate, erroneous information. The sole purpose is to mislead the courts in order to win a case. Many murderers have gone free, divorces validated, and child custody cases won, all because of well-constructed lies. It is unfortunate in some ways that in these instances human beings cannot read minds, because all we have to work with is evidence, and the need to believe or disbelieve one side over another based on that evidence.

More than it just being an issue in court, lying pervades our lives in relationships. Oftentimes, people form a relationship, and sometimes eventually marry because one potential partner represented themselves as being one way, and are later found to be another way entirely. Lies have been at the center of spousal disputes, parent-child relations, and other interpersonal relationships, almost from the beginning of time.

It is the privilege of God's people to live transparent lives. I have heard a man on the radio say this many times, and it has stuck with me. When we do not tell untruths overtly, or attempt to deceive in more subtle ways, life is much easier. We do not have to remember what we said from one moment to the next if we maintain integrity. All we need to know is what is true. We do not need to worry about whether what we have said, or not said will be investigated more closely, because truth can stand up to the closest scrutiny. More than this, it is a blessing when we can build people up rather than destroy areas of their lives by lying or misrepresenting the truth. We are able to share in one of the most incredible attributes of God's character when we abide in the truth.

I like the idea of living according to truth on the highest of all levels, because it leads to life. When we love the Lord, His word, and His ten-commandment law, we are preparing for eternity with God, which no power in the universe can take away. Why not practice this love for truth by simply abiding in it? Everyone is better off when truth prevails.

DO NOT COVET

Exodus 20:17
"Thou shalt not covet thy neighbour's house, thou shalt
not covet thy neighbour's wife, nor his manservant,
nor his maidservant, nor his ox, nor his ass,
nor any thing that is thy neighbour's."

I heard one pastor say that the command not to covet is perhaps the most broken of all the Ten Commandments. I do not know about that, but I do know that it is near the top.

Coveting, which is the passionate desire for someone else's possessions, is rooted in discontent. Paul said, "But godliness with contentment is great gain. For we brought nothing into this world, and it is certain we can carry nothing out. And having food and raiment let us be therewith content. But they that will be rich fall into temptation and a snare, and into many foolish and hurtful lusts, which drown men in destruction and perdition. For the love of money is the root of all evil: which while some coveted after, they have erred from the faith, and pierced themselves through with many sorrows. But thou, O man of God, flee these things; and follow after righteousness, godliness, faith, love, patience, meekness. Fight the good fight of faith, lay hold on eternal life, whereunto thou art also called, and hast professed a good profession before many witnesses." I Timothy 6:6-12.

While all covetousness is not necessarily related to money, it may be the most overwhelming form. Think of the number of television shows that have to do with showing off the homes, jets, yachts, vehicles, wardrobes, and jewelry of the wealthy. The most influential genre of music and culture in the entire world today also perpetuates a lack of contentment. It perpetuates in music videos and lyrics, the need to have on hundreds of thousands of dollars worth of jewelry, or to ride in a chauffeured $400,000 car while sipping champagne poured from a $350 bottle. When people watch these things on a regular basis, it inspires envy, a covetous spirit, and in many cases, at any cost, an unhealthy pursuit of such things.

It is a blessing to be content in the Lord and what we have been blessed with. We have the privilege of thanking Him everyday for the spouses He has given us. We can thank Him for the material things He has blessed us with, and not covet the things of others. My prayer is that I will not look at *anything* that others may possess, in an unhealthy way, but thank the Lord for what He is doing for me daily on an individual basis. How about you?

A CHEERFUL GIVER

Exodus 25:2
*"Speak unto the children of Israel, that they bring me an
offering: of every man that giveth it willingly with his
heart ye shall take my offering."*

The Lord had delivered His people from Egyptian slavery
with a mighty hand. With a show of power, after leading His
people through the Red Sea on dry land, He overthrew
Pharaoh's armies. As they wandered in the wilderness, daily
and without fail, He provided them bread from heaven.

The time had come for God's liberated people see to the
eternal law etched in tables of stone, representing the perpetuity of the law. As He gave the tables to Moses in the mount,
He also gave him the blueprints for the sanctuary that would
serve as a tutor on the plan of salvation. The sanctuary was to
be used as a symbol of God's love for them and as a place for
them to be cleansed and their sins forgiven.

In the beginning stages, God said, "Speak unto the children of Israel, that they bring me an offering: of every man
that giveth it willingly with his heart ye shall take my offering." Exodus 25:2. They were to bring the precious bounty
that they had brought with them from slavery. What they
had adorned themselves with and what they had used as
sweet fragrances, they were to willingly give for the building of the sanctuary. All of these were to be worked into the
very structure of the building. "And this is the offering
which ye shall take of them; gold, and silver, and brass, And
blue, and purple, and scarlet, and fine linen, and goats' hair,
And rams' skins dyed red, and badgers' skins, and shittim
wood, Oil for the light, spices for anointing oil, and for
sweet incense, Onyx stones, and stones to be set in the
ephod, and in the breastplate. And let them make me a sanctuary; that I may dwell among them." Exodus 25:3-8.

Notice again, that they were to bring them with willing hearts; otherwise, they would not be acceptable.

This is a familiar process even in our day. The principle reason for the sanctuary was that God wanted to be close to His people and He chose this means to accomplish it. Does God want to be close to us today? He wants us to see the benefit of having a good relationship with Him and surrendering our all to Him. All that is precious should be dedicated to His service. This offering of self, as represented in offering our treasure is only acceptable when given cheerfully (II Corinthians 9:6, 7). Our offering of self should not be out of guilt or given half-heartedly. Rather, we should recognize the blessing from God of delivering us from the bondage of sin, by yielding ourselves to Him. When we do this, God's will can be realized. There will be no separation between us, and God; He will truly be able to dwell among us. Thank the Lord for His willingness to dwell with us.

WELCOME FROM BETWEEN
THE CHERUBIMS

Exodus 25:22
"And there I will meet with thee, and I will commune with thee from above the mercy seat, from between the two cherubims which are upon the ark of the testimony, of all things which I will give thee in commandment unto the children of Israel."

In the ancient Israelite sanctuary, an apartment called the holy of holies represented the throne room of God. This is where the Ark of the Covenant was housed. The ark had a lid on it called the mercy seat. The Ten Commandment law was kept inside of it under the seat, and there were two cherubs made of gold, one on either side, facing one another. This is where the Lord's visible presence rested.

When the Lord told Moses that He would commune with him and the children of Israel, from above the mercy seat, between the cherubim, He was communicating something very important. This position was to be understood as a position of power and holiness. Only God Himself dwelt between the cherubim. In the heavenly sanctuary, God's throne is between the cherubims. It was an honor to have God meet with His people from this exalted position.

God is still willing to meet with us today. He still dwells between the cherubims on His exalted throne (Isaiah 6). Instead of God using a human mediator like Moses, the man Jesus Christ is our only way into the God's presence. Through the veil, which is Christ, we have access to the throne of God. "Having therefore, brethren, boldness to enter into the holiest by the blood of Jesus, By a new and living way, which he hath consecrated for us, through the veil, that is to say, his flesh; And having an high priest over the house of God; Let us draw near with a true heart in full assurance of faith, having our hearts sprinkled from an evil conscience, and our bodies washed with pure water. Let us hold fast the profession of our faith without wavering; for he is faithful that promised," Hebrews 10:19-23. Through Christ, the Father says, "Welcome from between the cherubims."

THE LIGHT

Exodus 25:31, 37
*"And thou shalt make a candlestick of pure gold: of
beaten work shall the candlestick be made: his shaft, and
his branches, his bowls, his knops, and his flowers, shall
be of the same. And thou shalt make the seven lamps
thereof: and they shall light the lamps thereof, that they
may give light over against it."*

Revealed in the furniture of the ancient Jewish tabernacle
was a precious truth. This truth would change the face of the
world if fully realized. If world leaders understood it and
those who lived in each country lived by it, all wars would
cease. No crime would be able to thrive in any of our neigh-
borhoods. Love would abound and strife would always give
way to peace and safety.

The Lord instructed Moses to make a single golden
candlestick with seven lamps. The candlestick would have
three lamps on each side and one in the center. This candlestick would be beautiful and give light to all that was in its
presence. This was a simple article of furniture, but the truth
surrounding it is astounding.

Candles give light—that's obvious. Did you know that
the Bible reveals that the word of God is light? "Thy word is
a lamp unto my feet, and a light unto my path." Psalms
119:105. The Bible also says that Jesus Himself, called the
Word of God in John chapter 1, is the ultimate light. "And
the city had no need of the sun, neither of the moon, to shine
in it: for the glory of God did lighten it, and the Lamb is the
light thereof." Revelation 21:23. "Then spake Jesus again
unto them, saying, I am the light of the world: he that
followeth me shall not walk in darkness, but shall have the
light of life." John 8:12. Notice too, that the lamp was in the
holy place of the Jewish tabernacle. This holy place was a

symbol of the house of God and more importantly, the hearts of God's people. When Jesus, as revealed in the word of God is present in the church and His people, many incredible things begin to happen. His people are converted fully to God. Because of this miraculous conversion, we also teach others of the light that they too might live in harmony with God. "Ye are the light of the world. A city that is set on an hill cannot be hid. Neither do men light a candle, and put it under a bushel, but on a candlestick; and it giveth light unto all that are in the house. Let your light so shine before men, that they may see your good works, and glorify your Father which is in heaven." Matthew 5:14-16.

The blessing that we must find in the golden candlestick is that God has given us the light of Jesus Christ as revealed in His word. As we receive that light ourselves, we allow it to emanate from us in order to lead others into right relationship to God. It is a blessing to partake in heavenly light. It changes our lives for the better.

SWEET INCENSE

Exodus 30:1, 6
"And thou shalt make an altar to burn incense upon: of
shittim wood shalt thou make it. And thou shalt put it
before the vail that is by the ark of the testimony,
before the mercy seat that is over the testimony,
where I will meet with thee."

Have you ever been in the room with someone and found that they had an offensive odor? I don't mean as though they had not bathed, but something was not quite right. You could detect a sweet scent, but then another conflicting scent passed your nose. It occurred to you that this person decided that if one great scent was good then three or four must be even better. They chose to shower with one type of perfumed soap, moisturize with another, and then add yet another type of cologne. Somehow, the three did not blend to produce the fresh scent they had hoped and it was offensive to all present in the room.

In the earthly sanctuary of the Old Testament, God instructed Moses to make an altar of burnt incense. The priests were to use a specific mixture on the altar at specific times. "Ye shall offer no strange incense thereon, nor burnt sacrifice, nor meat offering; neither shall ye pour drink offering thereon." Exodus 30:9. When this command was obeyed, the incense ascended above the veil and covered the stench of the burning flesh on the altar of burnt sacrifice in the outer court. Ultimately it represented the perfect sacrifice of Jesus Christ as a sweet smelling savor (Ephesians 5:2). Although this sacrifice was represented by the altar of burnt sacrifice, it was as sweet as incense before the nostrils of God. It also represented the prayers of God's people (Revelation 8:4). Let us put the symbols together. The incense offered on the altar represented the prayers of

God's people sweetened by their faith in the perfect righteousness of Jesus.

When human beings racked with sin choose to approach the throne of God without faith in the Lord Jesus, their prayers are like mixing several different scents together. It is offensive to God. "He that turneth away his ear from hearing the law, even his prayer shall be abomination." Proverbs 28:9. The consequences are tremendous. "And Nadab and Abihu died, when they offered strange fire before the LORD." Numbers 26:61.

The benefits of receiving the Lord as the only acceptable incense to sweeten our prayers are inestimable. In His name, all of the bounties of heaven are released into our lives. In His name is liberty and peace. Do not settle for the strange incense of self-righteousness. Offer only the blessed fragrance of faith in Jesus and heaven will always be open to you.

THE OPPOSING SIDE

Exodus 30:6
*"And thou shalt put it before the vail that is by the ark of
the testimony, before the mercy seat that is over the
testimony, where I will meet with thee."*

The Bible is full of overwhelming truths that lead us closer
to God. Some of them are right on the surface and others are
deeply buried for only serious spiritual miners. Those who
spend time seeking the Lord diligently as for hidden treasure will be richly rewarded (Proverbs 2:4, 5).

A careful, comparative study of Exodus chapters 25-40
will give insight into one of the amazing, yet subtle ways in
which God chose to distinguish Himself from the false gods
surrounding the children of Israel. One way He chose to do
this was in the placement of each article of furniture in the
sanctuary. The gate through which all bearing a sacrificial
offering must pass was situated in the east. This symbolized
the singular way of salvation being through Jesus Christ.
The altar of burnt sacrifice was in front of the gate. This
symbolized the perfect sacrifice of Christ. The laver was
situated between the altar of sacrifice and the veil into the
holy place. This represented the law of God being a mirror
in which to gaze and the power of Jesus Christ to cleanse us
from all sin in preparation to commune with God. The
golden candlestick with its oil and seven lamps was situated
in the south. This symbolized Jesus being the light of the
world and the anointing power of the Holy Ghost. The table
of shewbread with the grape juice was situated in the north.
This represented the broken body and spilled blood of Jesus,
the Living Word of God who cleanses us from all sin. The
altar of incense was situated before the veil into the holiest
of all. This represented the sweet smelling savor of Jesus'
sacrifice covering the stench of sin, making the prayers of

the saints acceptable to God. The ark of the testimony was situated in the west. This represented the throne of God whose foundation is the unchangeable holy law covered by His mercy.

The critical issue of the arrangement of all of this furniture is the ark being in the west. As you may know, most of the pagan religions of the world bow themselves toward the rising sun, that is, the east. This has been the case for thousands of years. The pagan religions of old immortalized the sun and made it a god. Today, there are forms of paganism that have renamed their gods, but fundamentally continue the same practices.

God distinguished His people by situating the symbol of His throne and visible presence in the opposing direction. His visible presence hovered in the west. When the Bible says that God's people worshipped toward the direction of God's glory, they had their backs turned to the worship of false gods.

This is what God would have us do spiritually, even today. When God is enthroned within, we worship Him. No matter what the majority of people are doing, no matter the religious practices they have adapted, we will turn our backs and worship the only true God from hearts of gratitude.

THE LORD WHO SANCTIFIES

Exodus 31:12, 13
"And the LORD spake unto Moses, saying, Speak thou
also unto the children of Israel, saying, Verily my
sabbaths ye shall keep: for it is a sign between me and you
throughout your generations; that ye may know that I am
the LORD that doth sanctify you."

As the Lord communed with Moses in the mount, He outlined His will for His people. He shared very detailed instructions concerning the commandments, judgments, and the building of the sanctuary. The sanctuary was of particular interest, because it was to become a catalyst by which the people of God would look to the coming Messiah as their only way into the presence of God. They were to see clearly through rites and ceremonies, how God would save them. It was the gospel preached to them in the wilderness for many years (Hebrews 4).

As God continued speaking to Moses, He unfolded a brilliant truth to him. God did not do it as though Moses was oblivious, but He *did* put emphasis on the matter. "And the LORD spake unto Moses, saying, Speak thou also unto the children of Israel, saying, Verily my sabbaths ye shall keep: for it is a sign between me and you throughout your generations; that ye may know that I am the LORD that doth sanctify you." Exodus 31:12, 13. In order to distinguish the Sabbath to which He referred from those ceremonial days instituted because of sin, He continued. "Six days may work be done; but in the seventh is the sabbath of rest, holy to the LORD: whosoever doeth any work in the sabbath day, he shall surely be put to death. Wherefore the children of Israel shall keep the sabbath, to observe the sabbath throughout their generations, for a perpetual covenant. It is a sign between me and the children of Israel for ever: for in six days the LORD made heaven and earth, and on the seventh day he rested, and was refreshed." Exodus 31:15-17. In Ezekiel chapter 20, the same truth is shared and is associated with the deliverance of God's people from Egyptian slavery.

God's seventh day Sabbath sign is a blessing, because it demonstrates His power. The One that sanctifies us is also the One who created everything. The One who created everything demonstrated His ability to deliver us from the bondage of sin in the exodus from Egypt. If God can create the worlds from nothing, He can certainly sanctify His people by delivering us from the slavery of sin.

Another great blessing is that all of the rites and ceremonies, including ceremonial sabbaths were completely erradicated at the cross of Jesus. He was the fulfillment of all of these things. He is the genuine article. Just as we are able to receive the blessings of the New Covenant made with the house of Israel, we are blessed to receive the sanctification demonstrated in God's eternal seventh day Sabbath. You see, as we have faith in Christ, we are heirs according to the promise God made to Abraham. "And if ye be Christ's, then are ye Abraham's seed, and heirs according to the promise." Galatians 3:29.

The sign of God's exclusive power to create, sanctify, and deliver from sin is still in tact. He is calling people all over the world to worship Him in spirit and in truth. Will you receive His sign? Will you be known in these last days as one who believes He still sanctifies? Pray that the Lord will teach you what His sign means and why it is important in these days.

DIRECTED BY GOD

Exodus 40:38
"For the cloud of the LORD was upon the tabernacle by day, and fire was on it by night, in the sight of all the house of Israel, throughout all their journeys."

There are wonderful lessons concerning the leading of God in the Bible. He has been faithful in giving specific direction to His people so they know exactly what He would have them do.

God told Abraham to leave his kindred and go to a place He would reveal later, and Abraham followed. God told Noah to build an ark on dry land to prepare for a flood during a time when rain had never fallen upon the earth before, and he listened. The Lord called out to young Samuel in the quiet of the night, and he said, "Speak Lord, your servant heareth." God told the prophet Nathaniel to go to King David with a corrective message, and again, God's man followed His direction.

The Lord wants us to follow wherever He leads, even when we do not understand what He is doing. When God directed Moses to build a dwelling place for Him to tabernacle with the people, He gave them a visible sign of His guidance. A pillar of cloud by day and fire by night were, in a sense, God's signals of leadership. "And when the cloud was taken up from over the tabernacle, the children of Israel went onward in all their journeys: But if the cloud were not taken up, then they journeyed not till the day that it was taken up." Exodus 40:36, 37. They knew that the only way for them to know where the Lord intended to lead them and to be protected from the elements, was to move only when the Lord signified in the sky, that they should.

We may not have clear signs in the sky like clouds and fire. We may never hear an audible voice tell us exactly what we must do, but we do have a way to know God's will for our lives. When we want to know the will of God, we can find it by prayerfully studying His word. "If any man will do his will, he shall know of the doctrine, whether it be of God, or whether I speak of myself." John 7:17. "Wherewithal shall a young man cleanse his way? by taking heed thereto according to thy word. With my whole heart have I sought thee: O let me not wander from thy commandments. Thy word have I hid in mine heart, that I might not sin against thee. Blessed art thou, O LORD: teach me thy statutes." Psalms 119:9-12. When we seek the Lord diligently through His word, the Holy Ghost will reveal the will of God to us. It is a blessing to know that the Lord is still leading His people today. It is indeed a blessing to be directed by God.

FREE WILL

Leviticus 1:3
"If his offering be a burnt sacrifice of the herd, let him offer a male without blemish: he shall offer it of his own voluntary will at the door of the tabernacle of the congregation before the LORD."

All that was related to the sanctuary services had specific applications. These rites and ceremonies were to be understood in light of the coming Messiah. Every element of the sanctuary structure, as well as each sacrifice, pointed to Jesus. Every minister and sacrifice represented an aspect of Christ's ministry on our behalf.

The sanctuary services, when examined closely, are not just a bunch of dry ceremonies with strict guidelines. These services reveal in great detail, the lengths to which God would go in order to save us. God truly sacrificed everything in order to have us live with Him forever.

One of the key role players, in these blessed services, was the sacrifice. Whatever the acceptable sacrifice and for whatever purpose it served, it was to be given freely by the sinner. In the case of a burnt offering, it makes sense that a sinner, of his own conviction, brought the acceptable sacrifice signifying his faith in Messiah. It also makes sense that the sinner needed to be willing to accept the fact that salvation only came by the means of God's power and not his own.

The aspect of this particular process that intrigues me is that "...if his offering be of the flocks, namely, of the sheep, or of the goats, for a burnt sacrifice; he shall bring it a male without blemish." Leviticus 1:10. Isn't it amazing that even the sacrifice itself must be without blemish because Christ was the perfect Lamb of God?

Let's bring this all together. Since I am a sinner, I need

the Savior. Without Him, there is no way I would be saved. If I accept responsibility for my sin, confess, and in heart turn from it, I am on the right road. The ultimate blessing is that I can accept the perfect righteousness of Christ of my own free will. God does not force Himself upon us like the devil. He lovingly draws us, representing Himself in the best light possible, and empowers us to choose to love Him.

All of this and more are tied into the sanctuary services. Thank the Lord for His willingness to accept our offerings. Why not offer Him your entire being today?

IMPERFECT

Leviticus 1:12
"And he shall cut it into his pieces, with his head and his fat: and the priest shall lay them in order on the wood that is on the fire which is upon the altar:"

Of the few acceptable sacrifices for different situations and people, God accepted sheep, goats, and bullocks. According to the law, these were to be offered for atonement. One thing that was striking to me as I studied this is how they were to be handled by the priests after the sinner killed them. Among the many steps he had to complete, was the separation of parts. They cut the sacrifice into pieces, with its head and fat. After the priest washed the innards and legs with water, he brought it back to the altar, assembled it as closely as possible to the form of a whole animal and the offering was made.

Consider the true Lamb of God. When Jesus Christ was offered for our sins, He did not need to be washed with water. He is the water of life (John 4). In fact, while He hung on the cross, water poured from His side (John 19:34). His body was to remain whole on the cross, symbolizing the completeness of His sacrifice. "Then came the soldiers, and brake the legs of the first, and of the other which was crucified with him. But when they came to Jesus, and saw that he was dead already, they brake not his legs: But one of the soldiers with a spear pierced his side, and forthwith came there out blood and water. And he that saw it bare record, and his record is true: and he knoweth that he saith true, that ye might believe. For these things were done, that the scripture should be fulfilled, A bone of him shall not be broken. And again another scripture saith, They shall look on him whom they pierced." John 19:32-37.

Although the sacrifices offered in the Old Testament

sanctuary were to be without blemish or spot, they were incomplete. Though they were acceptable to God before Christ died, they were only symbols pointing forward to the superior sacrifice of Christ. Their validity was centered in Him. Without Him the sacrificial system would have been without effect. "For the law having a shadow of good things to come, and not the very image of the things, can never with those sacrifices which they offered year by year continually make the comers thereunto perfect. For then would they not have ceased to be offered? because that the worshippers once purged should have had no more conscience of sins. But in those sacrifices there is a remembrance again made of sins every year. For it is not possible that the blood of bulls and of goats should take away sins. Wherefore when he cometh into the world, he saith, Sacrifice and offering thou wouldest not, but a body hast thou prepared me: In burnt offerings and sacrifices for sin thou hast had no pleasure. Then said I, Lo, I come (in the volume of the book it is written of me,) to do thy will, O God. Above when he said, Sacrifice and offering and burnt offerings and offering for sin thou wouldest not, neither hadst pleasure therein; which are offered by the law; Then said he, Lo, I come to do thy will, O God. He taketh away the first, that he may establish the second. By the which will we are sanctified through the offering of the body of Jesus Christ once for all." Hebrews 10:1-10.

AT THE HANDS OF A SINNER

Leviticus 4:28, 29
"Or if his sin, which he hath sinned, come to his knowl-
edge: then he shall bring his offering, a kid of the goats, a
female without blemish, for his sin which he hath sinned.
And he shall lay his hand upon the head of the sin
offering, and slay the sin offering in the place
of the burnt offering."

Close your eyes and imagine the day that they took Jesus, now betrayed and falsely accused, to the place where they would crucify Him. Badly beaten, bruised, and forsaken by His fellows, Jesus patiently cooperates with His enemies while they nail Him to splintered wood that formed the shape of a cross. You hear the mocking and insults, but are paralyzed. You see the faces contorted with the devilish glee of a predator soon to make sure of its prey. You can almost smell the stench of imminent death, and the fear of those who would join Him. The heartless, calloused soldiers erect the cross and thrust it violently into a hole made especially for that purpose. How do you feel? What part do you play in the scenes that pass before you?

As I read some of the requirements of the ancient earthly system of sacrifices, these images became vivid to me. I considered the fact that the sins which require a sacrifice are mine. I am the cause of Jesus' death. Not only that, but the Bible says that those among the common people who sinned and the knowledge of that sin came to them, had to bring a sacrifice. They had to bring a female kid of goats without blemish or spot. As they entered the place where the sacrifice was to be made, you would think that it was transferred to the priest for an offering, but such was not the case. Each sinner had to bring their own sacrifice according to their economic situation, lay hands upon its head, and pray.

This act was symbolic of transferring the confessed sin to the innocent lamb. After that, the sinner had to cut the throat of the innocent, yet cooperative victim. *Then* the priest took over and began to apply the blood and make sacrifice according to the law.

Can you imagine laying hands on the Son of God, confessing your sins, and lowering the knife to cut *His* throat? When we sin, it is no small matter. It required the life of the only spotless Son of God. I wonder how prone I would be to deliberately transgress God's law if I was compelled to envision myself taking the life of Christ with my own bare hands. It is a sobering thought.

Praise the Lord for His willingness to bear our sins to the cross and give us the opportunity to be saved.

JOYFUL RECEPTION

Leviticus 6:4, 5
"Then it shall be, because he hath sinned, and is guilty, that he shall restore that which he took violently away, or the thing which he hath deceitfully gotten, or that which was delivered him to keep, or the lost thing which he found, Or all that about which he hath sworn falsely; he shall even restore it in the principal, and shall add the fifth part more thereto, and give it unto him to whom it appertaineth, in the day of his trespass offering."

In the days of sacrificial offerings, Moses was given strict guidelines pertaining to the way each type of sin, transgression, and iniquity was to be handled. The Lord told him exactly what sacrifices, in what condition, and any other necessary details he needed in order to teach the people. He also needed to understand so he could live according to the instructions himself.

When someone got something deceitfully, they were to restore it, add a fifth of the value in interest, and bring a trespass offering to the Lord through His appointed priests. By following these guidelines by faith, the sinner received atonement or peace with God.

One day Jesus passed through the city of Jericho. Zacchaeus, the chief tax collector, climbed into a tree to see Jesus pass through the streets. It was as though the Lord came to Jericho specifically to see him. He saw Zacchaeus in the tree and told him to come down quickly so they could go to his house together. "And he made haste, and came down, and received him joyfully. And when they saw it, they all murmured, saying, That he was gone to be guest with a man that is a sinner." Luke 19:6, 7. Jesus demonstrated His mission to the world in this one act. He came to this earth specifically to seek and save the lost (Luke 19:10).

The impact of Jesus' visit to the tax collector's house was evident by the way he joyfully received Him and by what he did next. "And Zacchaeus stood, and said unto the Lord; Behold, Lord, the half of my goods I give to the poor; and if I have taken any thing from any man by false accusation, I restore him fourfold." Luke 19:8. Zacchaeus more than fulfilled the law that God had given through Moses concerning ill-gotten gain. Zacchaeus was pleased to repent fully of His sin as a result of one encounter with the Master. "And Jesus said unto him, This day is salvation come to this house, forsomuch as he also is a son of Abraham." Luke 19:9.

How is it with you? When Jesus comes to you specifically to change your life, do you receive Him joyfully? May the Lord teach us all to accept His presence with thanksgiving and be thoroughly converted just like the former crook, Zacchaeus.

THE MERCY SEAT OF GOD

Leviticus 16:13-15
"And he shall put the incense upon the fire before the
LORD, that the cloud of the incense may cover the mercy
seat that is upon the testimony, that he die not: And he
shall take of the blood of the bullock, and sprinkle it with
his finger upon the mercy seat eastward; and before the
mercy seat shall he sprinkle of the blood with his finger
seven times. Then shall he kill the goat of the sin offering,
that is for the people, and bring his blood within the vail,
and do with that blood as he did with the blood of the
bullock, and sprinkle it upon the mercy seat,
and before the mercy seat:"

During the Day of Atonement that occurred once per year in ancient Israel, many wonderful things occurred. One of the most beautiful had to do with the mercy seat that was the lid on the Ark of the Covenant. The high priest was to appear in certain garments, at a certain time, and having certain things with him as he approached the visible presence of God in the holy of holies.

Without getting into too much detail, we will glean a small aspect of God's love for us. The Ark of the Covenant housed the Ten Commandments. Specifically, they were kept *under* the mercy seat. "And he wrote on the tables, according to the first writing, the ten commandments, which the LORD spake unto you in the mount out of the midst of the fire in the day of the assembly: and the LORD gave them unto me. And I turned myself and came down from the mount, and put the tables in the ark which I had made; and there they be, as the LORD commanded me." Deuteronomy 10:4, 5. When the high priest, who represented Jesus (Hebrews 7:22-28), came into the most holy place, he came at different times with sweet smelling incense, blood from a bullock, and blood from a goat. "And he shall take a censer full of burning coals of fire from off the altar before the LORD, and his hands full of sweet incense beaten small, and bring it within the vail: And he shall put the incense upon the fire before the LORD, that the cloud of the incense may cover the mercy seat that is upon the testimony, that he die not:" Leviticus 16:12, 13. The sweet incense represents the perfect sacrifice and righteousness of Jesus (Ephesians 5:2). Being covered by Christ's righteousness, the incense also represents the prayers of the saints (Revelation 8:4). "And Aaron shall bring the bullock of the sin offering, which is for himself, and shall make an atonement for himself, and for his house, and shall kill the bullock of the sin offering which is for himself:" Leviticus 16:11. "Then shall he kill the goat of the sin offering, that is for the people, and bring his blood within the vail, and do with that blood as he did with the blood of the bullock, and sprinkle it upon the mercy seat, and before the mercy seat:" Leviticus 16:15. The blood of these sacrifices all represent the blood of Jesus Christ, which takes away our sins (Hebrews 10:19; I John 1:7). All of these elements were in some way or another to be brought before the mercy seat, which was above the law of God.

It is a blessing to know that the law that we all have transgressed is covered by mercy. Not only that, but the mercy is sweetened by the perfect righteousness, and blood of Jesus Christ. If we did not have Jesus, the perfect high priest presenting Himself within the veil for us, we would be eternally lost. He presents Himself on behalf of those who love Him. His righteousness, for us is salvation. I praise the Lord for His ministry.

LOVING OTHERS

Leviticus 19:17, 18
"Thou shalt not hate thy brother in thine heart: thou
shalt in any wise rebuke thy neighbour, and not suffer sin
upon him. Thou shalt not avenge, nor bear any grudge
against the children of thy people, but thou shalt love thy
neighbour as thyself: I am the LORD."

I often think of a lofty relationship principle that can easily escape our attention. Imagine that you are in a room all alone with blank walls and no outside influences. You do not say a word. In fact, you have your eyes closed. As you sit and think, you ponder wicked things. In your own mind, you commit sin. When you open your eyes, you leave the room and never mention or act out the sin you conceived in your mind. Does this have an effect on those around you? Are others affected by your secret cognitive sin? It is an interesting thought.

Whenever we separate ourselves from the Lord through sin, we have an impact on all with whom we come into contact. In fact, if we are unrepentant, there may be people that could have been won for Christ that may not because we could not detect Him leading us to them for witnessing. All who do experience the atmosphere could be eternally influenced for good, but our witness is impaired. If I am to love my neighbor as the Lord commanded, I must first live in a love relationship with Him, knowing that a strong relationship with Him, equips us to do so. In that case, He is alive in us, empowering us to enfold others in our love. No human being is an island. All of our actions and inactions have an impact on the people around us.

The verses above and those preceding them teach an overwhelming lesson on relationships. They teach us not to lie. They teach us to provide for and respect the poor, and freely forgive others. All of these relationship principles are attainable only as we love the Lord. This is the lesson for today: "Jesus said unto him, Thou shalt love the Lord thy God with all thy heart, and with all thy soul, and with all thy mind. This is the first and great commandment. And the second is like unto it, Thou shalt love thy neighbour as thyself. On these two commandments hang all the law and the prophets." Matthew 22:37-40.

WHY SHOULD YOUR SOUL BE DRY

Numbers 11:6
"But now our soul is dried away: there is nothing at all,
beside this manna, before our eyes."

The Lord demonstrated His love and patience for the Israelites for many years. He heard their cry and sent a liberator through whom He would deliver them from slavery. Through the entire process, He was restoring their religion, dignity, and respect among those whom did not believe in God. All of this was done that they might know that God was desperately in love with them, and that the world would know that the God of heaven is the one true God who was worthy of worship.

All too often the children of Israel complained about the way God was choosing to effect their freedom. Murmuring became an intolerable habit that God hated. It is a blessing to know that in spite of the fact that God knew before He set them free, that they would behave this way, He still loved them.

One of the complaints they often related was their lust for the rich foods of Egypt. They were enslaved in their minds to foods that many people today are enslaved. The Lord gave them a miracle of provision while they wandered in the wilderness. "Then said the LORD unto Moses, Behold, I will rain bread from heaven for you; and the people shall go out and gather a certain rate every day, that I may prove them, whether they will walk in my law, or no" Exodus 16:4. In spite of this perfect food that God provided, they still cried for the fleshpots of Egypt. "But now our soul is dried away: there is nothing at all, beside this manna, before our eyes" Numbers 11:6. How could their souls be dried up when God Himself, knowing their need, gave them bread from heaven? This bread was an object lesson about the Messiah, the perfect provision for all of our needs (John 6:35).

Do we wander in our wilderness of life with dry souls? How can it be that God has given every provision for us and we still cry that our souls are dry? Eat and drink from the heavenly storehouse. God always supplies all of our needs (Philippians 4:19). Pray today, that the Lord will teach you how to accept His perfect provision and be satisfied. Why should your soul be dry?

MUST THE DONKEY SPEAK

Numbers 22:28
"And the LORD opened the mouth of the ass, and she said unto Balaam, What have I done unto thee, that thou hast smitten me these three times?"

God has revealed His unchangeable will in the Bible. Everything regarding salvation, that we need to know, is written there for us to study and do. It is curious that some people choose to grope in the darkness to find out what God's will is, when He has made such a wonderful resource available to us. It is also curious that sometimes those who have read and understood the will of God seek to find another interpretation of it. They pray to God hoping to find an answer to support some evil they intend to do. There will be no revelation that conflicts with God's word. "If any man will do his will, he shall know of the doctrine, whether it be of God, or whether I speak of myself." John 7:17. Anyone who wants to do the will of God will follow what He has already revealed. It is a blessing to search for clarity, but not to change God's will.

Balaam was a servant of God in ancient Israel. Balak, one of God's enemies, enlisted his services to curse the people of God because he was afraid of them. "He sent messengers therefore unto Balaam the son of Beor to Pethor, which is by the river of the land of the children of his people, to call him, saying, Behold, there is a people come out from Egypt: behold, they cover the face of the earth, and they abide over against me: Come now therefore, I pray thee, curse me this people; for they are too mighty for me: peradventure I shall prevail, that we may smite them, and that I may drive them out of the land: for I wot that he whom thou blessest is blessed, and he whom thou cursest is cursed. And the elders of Moab and the elders of Midian departed with the rewards of divination in their hand; and they came unto Balaam and spake unto him the words of Balak. And he said unto them, Lodge here this night, and I will bring you word again, as the LORD shall speak unto me: and the princes of Moab abode with Balaam." Numbers 22:5-8.

Why in the world did Balaam need to consult the Lord? There is no way God would have sanctioned such a request, yet Balaam sought the Lord anyway. The Lord specifically told Balaam that he should not curse the people because they were blessed. Balaam sent the message to Balak and he offered Balaam more riches in exchange for this favor. Balaam said that if he offered a house full of riches, he still could not do what the Lord forbade; yet he sought the Lord again, though His will was already made clear. "And Balaam rose up in the morning, and saddled his ass, and went with the princes of Moab. And God's anger was kindled because he went: and the angel of the LORD stood in the way for an adversary against him. Now he was riding upon his ass, and his two servants were with him. And the ass saw the angel of the LORD standing in the way, and his sword drawn in his hand: and the ass turned aside out of the way, and went into the field: and Balaam smote the ass, to turn her into the way. But the angel of the LORD stood in a path of the vineyards, a wall being on this side, and a wall on that side." Numbers 22:21-24.

This story has many other details but the question for today is, "Why must the donkey speak?" The Lord's will was abundantly clear to Balaam, yet he persisted in trying to find a way around it. He must have thought that if he asked enough, God's will might change somehow. Though an indictment of Balaam, God loved him so much as to give his donkey the ability to speak, just to get his attention. Why should God have to go to such great lengths to get our attention? Sometimes we ask the Lord whether it is fine for us to live with a lover we are not married to, even though He already said not to fornicate. Sometimes we ask the Lord whether we should marry someone that is not of like faith, even though He already said not to yoke with unbelievers. Sometimes we ask the Lord whether we should take a job that would require us to break His commandments, even though He said to *do* His commandments. Since God has revealed His unchangeable will in the Bible, it is a good idea to simply follow it. Let us not be so determined to do our own will that God must go to the extreme to get our attention. Why must the donkey speak?

WHY NEED WE SPIES

Deuteronomy 1:21, 22
"Behold, the LORD thy God hath set the land before thee:
go up and possess it, as the LORD God of thy fathers hath
said unto thee; fear not, neither be discouraged. And ye
came near unto me every one of you, and said, We will
send men before us, and they shall search us out the land,
and bring us word again by what way we must go up, and
into what cities we shall come."

The land of promise was before them. God's people had endured many years of toil and distress. The journey from Egypt that may have taken a short time was extended by years due to their lack of faith. Instead of receiving the power and determination that comes through trust in God, these wanderers chose the weakness that came from second guessing the way that the Lord chose to lead them.

The Lord made the way clear. His words to the children of Israel were, the land that He promised was set before them, and all they needed to do was move forward in faith to posses it. His will and intentions for them could not have been made any clearer. The promise was theirs for the taking. Why then did they need spies? Although Jesus had led them in a pillar of cloud and flame of fire in order to protect them throughout their journey, they found occasions to doubt. They often chose to contrive ways to distrust Him. It was almost like they were looking for a reason to lose faith and hope. The many miracles of the exodus, the parting of the Red Sea, manna from heaven, and the other tokens of God's care seemed not to impress the majority of His people.

The land was before them. Instead of simply moving forward as their children did later, when they took Jericho, they decided to send spies, who came back with a faith*less* report. All, with exception of Joshua and Caleb gave a false testimony. They all proclaimed God a liar. They said that what God promised to them was impossible. They said that there were giants in the land and there was no way that they could posses it. As a result, the adults who were freed from Egyptian slavery in order to worship the Lord, failed to receive the promise. All, with the exception of faithful Joshua and Caleb, died along the way because they did not trust God to deliver them.

So it is today. The Lord has proclaimed and demonstrated His ability to keep us faithful despite any temptation to do evil. Oftentimes, we see the giants of peer pressure, unholy entertainment, and ungodly relationships as insurmountable. Even though He said that He is able to keep us from falling, we often choose to be defeated and fail to fully enter the rest of God. The wilderness of sin encloses many and they do not receive the promise. We do not need the false testimony from the spies of faithlessness and discouragement. We *must* press on.

God has promised eternal life and immortality to those who diligently seek and love Him with their entire being. Let us all learn a lesson from Joshua and Caleb who said that if the Lord was with them, they could easily posses the Promised Land. We are on our way to heavenly Canaan. Let nothing obstruct our way. Let the lying witnesses of self-trust and faithlessness die in this earthly wilderness, while we move forward to the heavenly Promise Land.

OUR LORD IS ONE

Deuteronomy 6:4
"Hear, O Israel: The LORD our God is one LORD:"

The God of creation is beyond our human comprehension. He is all knowing, all-powerful, remarkably loving, and ever-present in our times of need. This great God is, most of all, worthy of our praise and worship. He is, "…The LORD, The LORD God, merciful and gracious, longsuffering, and abundant in goodness and truth, Keeping mercy for thousands, forgiving iniquity and transgression and sin, and that will by no means clear the guilty; visiting the iniquity of the fathers upon the children, and upon the children's children, unto the third and to the fourth generation." Exodus 34:6, 7. This God cannot be compared to any other. Concerning Himself He declared, "…for I am God, and there is none else; I am God, and there is none like me, Declaring the end from the beginning, and from ancient times the things that are not yet done, saying, My counsel shall stand, and I will do all my pleasure:" Isaiah 46:9,10.

One of the incredible aspects of God is the unity of God. In the creation of the world we see more than one distinct being at work. "In the beginning God created the heaven and the earth." Genesis 1:1. "And God said, Let *us* make man in *our* image, after *our* likeness: and let them have dominion over the fish of the sea, and over the fowl of the air, and over the cattle, and over all the earth, and over every creeping thing that creepeth upon the earth." Genesis 1:26. The term used for God in these verses comes from a plural, masculine noun, which denotes the Supreme Being. This agrees with the tenor of scripture concerning the triune nature of God and the creative work of Christ. "Hath in these last days spoken unto us by his Son, whom he hath appointed heir of all things, by whom also he made the worlds;" Hebrews 1:2.

When Jesus was in the flesh being baptized by John the Baptist, an amazing revelation occurred. First, the Lord Jesus condescended to be baptized in order to fulfill all righteousness (Matthew 3:15-16). Second, God the Holy Spirit descended upon Jesus revealing Him as the Anointed One of Old Testament prophecy (Daniel 9:25; Matthew 3:16). Third, the voice of God the Father was heard from heaven validating Jesus' ministry and identity (Matthew 3:17). This multifaceted revelation is wonderful. It shows us that all of heaven; Father, Son, and Holy Ghost works together for our ultimate salvation.

Just as the Lord our God is one, let us all be united in the spirit of love to cooperate with heaven to save a lost world from sin. Pray that the Lord will help us to this end.

MADE WHOLE

Deuteronomy 7:14, 15
"Thou shalt be blessed above all people: there shall not be male or female barren among you, or among your cattle. And the LORD will take away from thee all sickness, and will put none of the evil diseases of Egypt, which thou knowest, upon thee; but will lay them upon all them that hate thee."

From the very beginning of time, God intended that all of His creatures remain whole and free of all diseases. The blight of sin upon the earth was clearly seen when the intended plan was usurped by the choice of humankind to live contrary to God's commands. His commands were always in line with all of the laws that He instituted for our well being. Not the least of all of His laws is the law of nature. This law can be described from many different aspects, but every aspect must support productive and healthy living. Even in this world, following the inception of sin, God has bestowed grace to live free from many of the effects of disease and decay in our being.

The Israelites were, in many ways, to be trophy specimens of God's grace. Surrounding nations were to peer in on the lives of these chosen ones, and witness their prosperity and the protection of God on all of their possessions, and they, themselves, begin to worship Him. One of the promises God made was that if they followed all of His commandments, statutes, and judgments, He would insulate the Israelites from the diseases and barrenness of the heathens of that day. "He brought them forth also with silver and gold: and there was not one feeble person among their tribes." Psalms 105:37. While they followed the Lord implicitly, He made good on His promise. It was only when they violated natural, spiritual, and hygienic laws that they were diseased like the neighboring nations.

The Lord is in the business of making His people whole even today. "Bless the LORD, O my soul: and all that is within me, bless his holy name. Bless the LORD, O my soul, and forget not all his benefits: Who forgiveth all thine iniquities; who healeth all thy diseases;" Psalms 103:1-3. When it brings God glory, He answers the prayers of repentant sinners who seek diligently for healing. Many are sick today because of habits that violate the natural laws of health. If in these cases, we were turn to the Lord to receive forgiveness and full understanding of the bodies He has entrusted us with, He would make Himself available to forgive and heal our diseases.

Trust the Lord for everything, including good health. It brings Him joy to preserve those who trust Him from the disease and suffering that plagues the earth. He receives much glory when His obedient ones are able to show lost souls His way, so they too can be saved. They too can be healed even of physical ailments when they trust in the Lord and obey Him.

GOD IS JUST

Deuteronomy 25:2
*"And it shall be, if the wicked man be worthy to be beaten,
that the judge shall cause him to lie down, and to be
beaten before his face, according to his fault,
by a certain number."*

The justice of God is a subject of particular interest to many. Hence the question, "Why do bad things happen to good people?" Another interpretation of that thought is that it appears that God allows the wicked to prosper. King David often prayed about that. We can rest assured, knowing that God is indeed just.

In order to examine this a little more closely, we will look at an issue that is not pleasant. Even God does not enjoy talking about it, but since it is in His word, we cannot ignore it. First, let us establish one reality. God loves everyone and wants all of us to be saved. He has not selected a group to be saved and another to be lost. "The Lord is not slack concerning his promise, as some men count slackness; but is longsuffering to us-ward, not willing that any should perish, but that all should come to repentance." II Peter 3:9.

Think of the criminal justice system and how it should function. Let us say, for example, that a young child is caught stealing candy from a candy store in a western culture, immediately the police are notified and they come quickly. What kind of punishment should we expect this child to receive? Will they face a life sentence in prison? How about this? Let us say that a career criminal is caught after engaging in some type of terrorism that claims the lives of thousands of people. Should we expect that this person serve for ninety days in a minimum security jail cell with cable television and the internet? Either example would be unjust. Why is it that some people hold the world's systems to a higher standard than God's? Some of us believe that those who refuse to repent and are punished at the end of time, will burn in hell forever and ever. Would that be just? Should an individual who has lived a life of sin for seventy years experience eternal torment? Should that same person burn as long as those who spent eighty years of their lives murdering innocent children, or as long as the devil himself? God has a way to measure what each person deserves. Speaking of unfaithful servants, Luke says, "And that servant, which knew his lord's will, and prepared not himself, neither did according to his will, shall be beaten with many stripes. But he that knew not, and did commit things worthy of stripes, shall be beaten with few stripes. For unto whomsoever much is given, of him shall be much required: and to whom men have committed much, of him they will ask the more." Luke 12:47, 48.

When the Bible speaks of the wicked burning forever, it means until they are dead. There are several examples of this concept in the Bible. "And the angels which kept not their first estate, but left their own habitation, he hath reserved in everlasting chains under darkness unto the judgment of the great day. Even as Sodom and Gomorrah, and the cities about them in like manner, giving themselves over to fornication, and going after strange flesh, are set forth for an example, suffering the vengeance of eternal fire." Jude 1:6, 7. Is there some flame burning in the east where Sodom and Gomorrah once stood? Is the flame of their punishment still burning? The Bible writers used an idiom to make the point, not to say God will burn people without end. At the last day, God gives eternal life and immortality to those who love Him, not the wicked. They will not live forever in torment. Only the just will live forever.

All of this shows that the Lord is just. Quite honestly, none of us need be directly affected by this brand of justice. We can walk the streets of gold. We each can choose today to love and serve God because He has been so merciful. His balance of justice and mercy for us, is giving us the reward that Jesus is worthy of, instead of the punishment we are worthy of. Because of His great love, we have access to life everlasting. Take it—it's yours! "For all have sinned, and come short of the glory of God; Being justified freely by his grace through the redemption that is in Christ Jesus: Whom God hath set forth to be a propitiation through faith in his blood, to declare his righteousness for the remission of sins that are past, through the forbearance of God; To declare, I say, at this time his righteousness: that he might be just, and the justifier of him which believeth in Jesus." Romans 3:23-26. "And, behold, I come quickly; and my reward is with me, to give every man according as his work shall be." Revelation 22:12.

GET READY TO SHOUT

Joshua 6:15, 16
"And it came to pass on the seventh day, that they rose early about the dawning of the day, and compassed the city after the same manner seven times: only on that day they compassed the city seven times. And it came to pass at the seventh time, when the priests blew with the trumpets, Joshua said unto the people, Shout; for the LORD hath given you the city."

About forty years had passed since the Lord had delivered His people from Egyptian bondage. The parents of the Israelites who were now being lead by Joshua, all died in the wilderness, never experiencing the conditionally promised rest. They never entered into the Promised Land, or rest and victory, because of unbelief. Though the Lord demonstrated through convincing miracles and tender watch care, that He had their best interest at heart, and all things under control, they faltered. Though He never went back on a promise, or neglected to give them victories over their enemies when they were faithful, they were still a stiff-necked and disrespectful people.

The time had finally come. The Lord was about to reward the faith of the original former slaves' children, and they would soon receive the promise. They were about to enter the Promised Land. How must it have felt when they approached the walls of Jericho? Their fearless leader was one of two spies that reported many years ago that they could take the city with the Lord as their leader. He was not intimidated at all by the apparent might of their enemies, because he was well acquainted with, and convinced of the absolute power of God to vanquish all of His enemies.

After having an encounter with Christ and receiving explicit instructions on how to take the city, God's people were arrayed in the formation God had given. Each day, for six days, they were to compass the city one time. On the seventh day, they were to march around it seven times. "And it came to pass on the seventh day, that they rose early about the dawning of the day, and compassed the city after the same manner seven times: only on that day they compassed the city seven times. And it came to pass at the seventh time, when the priests blew with the trumpets, Joshua said unto the people, Shout; for the LORD hath given you the city. So the people shouted when the priests blew with the trumpets: and it came to pass, when the people heard the sound of the trumpet, and the people shouted with a great shout, that the wall fell down flat, so that the people went up into the city, every man straight before him, and they took the city. And they utterly destroyed all that was in the city, both man and woman, young and old, and ox, and sheep, and ass, with the edge of the sword." Joshua 6:15, 16, 20, 21.

This story is thrilling, because it is a symbol for us today. The Lord has been delivering people from sin for many years. He has proven His faithfulness to us by many miracles of His grace, and the Promised Land is in view. Unfortunately, some that had been formerly delivered will not enter in to the promise because of unbelief, but this need not be the case. We have the privilege to know, based on those who have viewed the land, like Enoch and Elijah that we can have it too. The Lord has empowered us to compass the walls of trials and tribulation to see them one day come crashing down. The Lord, the Captain of the heavenly hosts, will soon remove the enemy forever and we will inherit the land flowing with milk and honey. Momentarily, Jesus will descend with all of the angels. Those who remain faithful will shout with thanksgiving, "This is our God. He is finally here to rescue us. Praise the Lord!" Get ready to shout!

ACHAN IN THE CAMP

Joshua 7:25, 26
"And Joshua said, Why hast thou troubled us? the LORD
shall trouble thee this day. And all Israel stoned him with
stones, and burned them with fire, after they had stoned
them with stones. And they raised over him a great heap
of stones unto this day. So the LORD turned from the
fierceness of his anger. Wherefore the name of that place
was called, The valley of Achor, unto this day."

As I read the story of Achan, following the Israelite victory over the city of Jericho, I was distressed. The city of Jericho stood between the second generation of Israelites following the exodus, and entrance into the promise of God. They followed God's instructions concerning the way Jericho must fall. Thirteen times, they marched around the walls and shouted when the Lord commanded. With mighty triumph, the walls came crashing down as though heavenly angels had trampled upon them. The harlot Rahad and her family were saved alive for helping the Lord's people. God commanded that nothing be taken that should be destroyed, as an offering to the Lord.

After the things in the city were destroyed, Joshua received a report that their next conquest on the road to promise would not be difficult at all. In fact, all they needed were three thousand men for battle. Israel desperately lost, and Joshua sought the Lord in humility with other leaders. The Lord revealed that there was someone who did not follow the Lord's command concerning Jericho. That person kept back a portion of what the Lord had commanded that no one should touch. Using a process the Lord inspired Joshua with, they were able to find the culprit. Achan confessed that he was guilty of keeping clothes and precious metals, only when he had nowhere to hide. As a result of Achan's sin, he and his family were destroyed. "So Joshua sent messengers, and they ran unto the tent; and, behold, it was hid in his tent, and the silver under it. And they took them out of the midst of the tent, and brought them unto Joshua, and unto all the children of Israel, and laid them out before the LORD. And Joshua, and all Israel with him, took Achan the son of Zerah, and the silver, and the garment, and the wedge of gold, and his sons, and his daughters, and his oxen, and his asses, and his sheep, and his tent, and all that he had: and they brought them unto the valley of Achor. And Joshua said, Why hast thou troubled us? the LORD shall trouble thee this day. And all Israel stoned him with stones, and burned them with fire, after they had stoned them with stones. And they raised over him a great heap of stones unto this day. So the LORD turned from the fierceness of his anger. Wherefore the name of that place was called, The valley of Achor, unto this day." Joshua 7:22-26.

So it will be in the closing moments before we inherit the heavenly promise. There will be those that worked diligently for the cause of Christ; these people will have experienced many of the blessings of God until that point, yet at the end, they too will become *Achans*. They will become a hindrance to the work of God because of their disobedience, and the Lord will reserve them for judgment. They too, though they were formerly faithful, will be destroyed.

I pray that I will not be an Achan in the camp. I want to be faithful, by God's grace until the very end. By His grace, we all can be faithful. Don't be an Achan in the camp!

GOD'S PERMISSIVE WILL

Judges 14:3, 4
"Then his father and his mother said unto him, Is there never a woman among the daughters of thy brethren, or among all my people, that thou goest to take a wife of the uncircumcised Philistines? And Samson said unto his father, Get her for me; for she pleaseth me well. But his father and his mother knew not that it was of the LORD, that he sought an occasion against the Philistines: for at that time the Philistines had dominion over Israel."

The Lord's will is broader in its scope than most of us understand. His thoughts are far above our thoughts and His ways are above our ways. There is an aspect of His will that can be considered as the ideal. For example, God created humankind to live perfect lives and intended that Adam and Eve pass the test at the tree of the knowledge of good and evil. His purpose was that we never sin, and that we would live eternally. As you know well, based on your own experience, sin *did* enter the world; therefore, God's original intention was not met. If God were a human being, this would be the end of the story. Since He is not, this is where the arm of the Lord is revealed.

The Lord had a plan from eternity past that would immediately be enacted when humans chose to sin. We were not on an inevitable rollercoaster toward sin that we could not escape, but the Lord knew what choice *we* would make, therefore He had a plan. The Son of God would become a human being, live a perfect life, die a perfect substitutionary death, and rise again to minister for us in heaven. This plan, albeit beautiful, was only necessary because of the choice Adam made in Eden to defy His Lord. This fit more into God's permissive will, though He was active in orchestrating it.

There are different versions of the Lord's permissive will (as we understand it), which He allowed in order for His ultimate purposes to be realized. These versions would be painful for those involved, but if they accomplished their perfect work, the pain would drive God's people to Him. For instance, the Lord never intended for Israel to have a human king, but He allowed it. He never intended that human beings ever divorce, but under certain circumstances, though it may not be expedient, it is permitted. God never intended that we consume the flesh of dead animals for food (or living ones for that matter), but because of certain environmental issues after the flood, along with the griping and murmuring of His children in the wilderness, He allowed certain types for a season.

Such was the case with Samson. God told him at the beginning of his ministry what his plans for the Philistines were. He understood that Samson would be slow at carrying out his intended purpose; therefore, God figured it all into the equation. He wanted a wife that his parents disapproved of because of the clear counsel of God against marrying uncircumcised, ungodly people, yet the Bible says the Lord was leading him. God did not intend that he ever marry that woman, but knew what choice he would make, therefore the Lord allowed it so his ultimate purpose could be realized. In the end, through much turmoil and unnecessary pain, Samson fulfilled the Lord's will.

Here is the simple question for the day. Will you accept the Lord's will for your life? There are two ways for it to be accomplished, the second of which is long and painful. I personally like the idea of allowing the Lord to perform His ideal in my life, but He loves me enough to do *whatever* it takes to save me; even if I need His permissive will to be done.

ALL ALONE

Judges 16:20
"And she said, The Philistines be upon thee, Samson.
And he awoke out of his sleep, and said, I will go out as at
other times before, and shake myself And he wist not that
the LORD was departed from him."

This is a very sad story. The man whom God called from the womb to be a peculiar treasure, a Nazarite, found himself in a dire situation. Many times in spite of his vow to the Lord to be a special soldier for truth, Samson indulged his selfish passions, and misused the power God had given him to do well. He allowed the lust of the flesh and a daring thirst for power to rule him in the same way a ventriloquist controls a dummy.

One day, after having betrayed his mission and the trust of the living God, which gave him his extraordinary strength, he thought to shake himself awake and go on to presume upon the gift God had given to him. He did not realize that the Lord had departed from him. How did he move from being a chosen vessel, called specifically to bring Godly order, to anathema? How is it that the Spirit of God left him?

We can learn valuable lessons from the life of Samson. He decided many times to ignore the promptings of God to do right, and took for granted that God would always strengthen him no matter what he did. We see that God will not allow such presumption but for so long. Yes, the Lord is longsuffering, but He is not mocked (Galatians 6:7, 8). God allowed Samson the option of separating himself from Him to the point that the Spirit left him. It is a terrible thing to choose disobedience as a lifestyle.

Another lesson that can be learned is that although we sink to our lowest point spiritually, the Lord is able to raise us up. You see, Samson did not go to his grave having forsaken the Lord. In the closing scenes of his life, he allowed the chastening of the Lord to mold his character in such a way that his dedication was demonstrated even to the point of death. "And it came to pass, when their hearts were merry, that they said, Call for Samson, that he may make us sport. And they called for Samson out of the prison house; and he made them sport: and they set him between the pillars. And Samson said unto the lad that held him by the hand, Suffer me that I may feel the pillars whereupon the house standeth, that I may lean upon them. Now the house was full of men and women; and all the lords of the Philistines were there; and there were upon the roof about three thousand men, and women, that beheld while Samson made sport. And Samson called unto the LORD, and said, O Lord GOD, remember me, I pray thee, and strengthen me, I pray thee, only this once, O God, that I may be at once avenged of the Philistines for my two eyes. And Samson took hold of the two middle pillars upon which the house stood, and on which it was borne up, of the one with his right hand, and of the other with his left. And Samson said, Let me die with the Philistines. And he bowed himself with all his might; and the house fell upon the lords, and upon all the people that were therein. So the dead which he slew at his death were more than they which he slew in his life." Judges 16:25-30.

It is a blessing that the Lord is so merciful, but let us not take His kindness for granted. The story of Samson is a lesson about the grace of God and His forgiveness, but it is also a lesson about the benefits of obedience to God's will. Be faithful in all of your endeavors and receive the promise to God's people that He will never leave, nor forsake us.

A GOOD WITNESS

Ruth 1:16
"And Ruth said, Intreat me not to leave thee, or to return
from following after thee: for whither thou goest, I will
go; and where thou lodgest, I will lodge: thy people shall
be my people, and thy God my God:"

Naomi lost her husband to the cold hands of death, but her two sons and their wives remained. It seems that they had a relatively good relationship. Even the daughters-in-law loved Naomi. Eventually, tragedy struck her loving family again and both of her sons died. This distressed her deeply. She went to her daughters-in-law, Orpah and Ruth, to bid them farewell. She wanted them to leave her alone since her sons were dead. She said that if she were to remarry and have two more sons, they would not wait for them to come of age to marry again, so they should return to their families and to their own Moabite gods. Orpah kissed Naomi good-bye and went back to her family. Ruth, on the other hand, would not leave her. It may have been in part because she truly loved Naomi and did not want her to be alone, but there must have been more. She also must have experienced the blessing of Naomi's quiet witness. "And Ruth said, Intreat me not to leave thee, or to return from following after thee: for whither thou goest, I will go; and where thou lodgest, I will lodge: thy people shall be my people, and thy God my God: Where thou diest, will I die, and there will I be buried: the LORD do so to me, and more also, if ought but death part thee and me. When she saw that she was sted-fastly minded to go with her, then she left speaking unto her." Ruth 1:16-18.

How powerful is someone's witness to the glory of God, when as a result of it, a young woman refuses to go back to her own mother's house to possibly remarry, in order to be close to a widow? Ruth not only stayed with Naomi, but she chose to accept Naomi's God. The loving relationship they shared, inspired Ruth to convert to the God of heaven.

The question I must ask myself is whether my witness is so strong that others would rather choose my God, than to live a life of convenience. Is my experience with Christ so attractive that they would like to have a similar experience? It is a solemn thought. Allowing the love of God to shine through us is our duty. When we do this, others will want to know the Lord. "Let your light so shine before men, that they may see your good works, and glorify your Father which is in heaven." Matthew 5:16.

SPEAK LORD

I Samuel 3:10
"And the LORD came, and stood, and called as at other
times, Samuel, Samuel. Then Samuel answered,
Speak; for thy servant heareth."

As Hannah promised if God would make her womb fruitful, the young miracle child Samuel ministered to Him (I Samuel 1:11). He demonstrated attentiveness and a willingness to be faithful in serving God. Soon he would be introduced to a higher level of ministry. God would reveal Himself in a way that the child was not yet acquainted. God was about to speak.

As Samuel and his lord Eli were sleeping one night, Samuel heard a voice call out to him. He awoke and quickly went to Eli as any dedicated boy would. Eli told him that he should go back to sleep, because he did not call him. Samuel did as he was told and soon he heard the voice again. Samuel quickly went to Eli again, and once more Eli told him to go back to sleep because He did not call. Of course, Samuel did as he was told. Again, Samuel heard the voice. It was unmistakable. The voice said, "Samuel." Quickly Samuel went to Eli insisting that he called, and Eli knew that it was the Lord. "Therefore Eli said unto Samuel, Go, lie down: and it shall be, if he call thee, that thou shalt say, Speak, LORD; for thy servant heareth. So Samuel went and lay down in his place. And the LORD came, and stood, and called as at other times, Samuel, Samuel. Then Samuel answered, Speak; for thy servant heareth." I Samuel 3:9, 10. "And the child Samuel ministered unto the LORD before Eli. And the word of the LORD was precious in those days; there was no open vision." I Samuel 3:1.

Have you ever mistaken the voice of God? When unexpected situations have occurred in your life and the Lord was speaking through them, did you recognize His voice? As the Lord spoke to Samuel in the night, He speaks to us through the darkness of trials. As Samuel was bewildered going to his lord Eli, thinking it was he who called, sometimes we misinterpret our own life events, and become bewildered by our misapprehension of them. The blessing is that God persists. He gives us the Holy Spirit to make clear when it is God speaking to us. When we have that awareness, we like Samuel, can be still in the darkness and listen to the voice of God and say, "Speak, LORD; for thy servant heareth."

PERFECT PRACTICE

I Samuel 17:37
"David said moreover, The LORD that delivered me out of the paw of the lion, and out of the paw of the bear, he will deliver me out of the hand of this Philistine. And Saul said unto David, Go, and the LORD be with thee."

You have heard it said that practice makes perfect, but I say to you that *perfect* practice makes perfect.

Many rehearse music in order to become the best that they can be. They put their all into it. Just imagine if you were rehearsing for a piano recital and the musical piece was selected for you? You go to the music store to purchase the score and go to rehearse. Weeks have passed and the time has come to perform. You sit and prepare yourself, and suddenly you realize that the music you had been rehearsing was all wrong. You heard wrong and now you are completely unprepared. Now what do you do?

David was a little shepherd boy. One day he left his sheep behind to check on his older brothers. At once, he discovered that a giant Philistine stood in the valley blaspheming God near to where his brothers were. The giant openly defied God and the armies of Israel. David was filled with righteous indignation. "And David spake to the men that stood by him, saying, What shall be done to the man that killeth this Philistine, and taketh away the reproach from Israel? for who is this uncircumcised Philistine, that he should defy the armies of the living God?" I Samuel 17:26. David proposed that in the name of the Lord, he should fight the Philistine; everyone that stood by discouraged Him. Eventually, He had audience with King Saul and told him the same. "And Saul said to David, Thou art not able to go against this Philistine to fight with him: for thou art but a youth, and he a man of war from his youth. And David said unto Saul, Thy servant kept his father's sheep, and there came a lion, and a bear, and took a lamb out of the flock: And I went out after him, and smote him, and delivered it out of his mouth: and when he arose against me, I caught him by his beard, and smote him, and slew him. Thy servant slew both the lion and the bear: and this uncircumcised Philistine shall be as one of them, seeing he hath defied the armies of the living God. David said moreover, The LORD that delivered me out of the paw of the lion, and out of the paw of the bear, he will deliver me out of the hand of this Philistine. And Saul said unto David, Go, and the LORD be with thee." I Samuel 17:33-37.

There are many incredible details left in the story, but the short version is that David, armed with the might and determination of the Holy Ghost, defeated and removed Goliath's head using the Philistine's own weapon. In the end, the Lord was glorified, the Philistines had respect toward God, Israel realized their faithlessness, and young David saw his faith confirmed.

It is incredible to see the point of reference David used as assurance that he could defeat Goliath. He recalled the times that God had given him opportunity to exercise, or *practice* his faith. When he encountered other predators, he defeated them. With each victory, his resolve was strengthened. This is indeed a case of perfect practice making perfect. Many put their trust in self, others, and worldly strength. They experience what appears like victories, but when the crises come, they realize that their practice was not complete. They rehearsed the wrong sheet music, so to speak, and now they are at a loss as to what should be done.

As the Lord gives us opportunity to exercise faith, it is well that we do so. When the Goliaths of circumstance arise, we will be prepared and with God's power, we will be the victors. Remember; *perfect* practice makes perfect.

TRUE FAMILY

I Samuel 20:41, 42
"And as soon as the lad was gone, David arose out of a place toward the south, and fell on his face to the ground, and bowed himself three times: and they kissed one another, and wept one with another, until David exceeded. And Jonathan said to David, Go in peace, forasmuch as we have sworn both of us in the name of the LORD, saying, The LORD be between me and thee, and between my seed and thy seed for ever. And he arose and departed: and Jonathan went into the city."

King Saul harbored anger toward David and sought to kill him. The king followed him from place to place looking for an opportunity to kill him. At one point, he threw a spear at David trying to nail him to the wall, but he missed. On another occasion, the king sent his men to David's house. Michal, David's wife, told him to leave quickly because the king was looking for him. They decided to have an idol put in David's bed with some fake hair to fool the soldiers. The king found out that she tried to trick him and when asked why she treated him that way, Michal said that David threatened to kill her if she did not do what he said.

David went to his best friend Jonathan, who happened to be the king's son, to find out why the king was so adamant about killing him. Jonathan assured David that the king would not kill him, but as you might imagine, David did not believe him. Eventually, after conspiring together to find out the real intentions of the king, they came up with an elaborate plan. David would not be in his place at a feast the king was having. They said if the king asked where David was, Jonathan would say that he asked to go to Bethlehem as he always did at this time, and depending on the king's response, they would know whether or not he was truly planning to kill him. If the king became angry, they knew he was serious. On the second day of the feast, the king *did* ask where David was. All went according to plan and the king was furious. He was angry, and knowing that Jonathan was helping David, he tried to kill Jonathan too. Jonathan escaped and alerted David of his father's intentions, just as they had agreed before God. They left one another with an oath before God that they and their offspring would always be at peace.

This is a beautiful story about true loyalty, fellowship, and family. One would think that since Jonathan was the king's son, he would be on his side trying also to capture and kill David. Such was not the case. Jonathan demonstrated by his consistent actions that he and his earthly father were not truly family. He and his friend David, because of their Godly fellowship, were true family. This is a painful realization that all must come to at some point or another. When we choose to follow the Lord all of the way, some of our blood relatives will be against us and the Lord will give us true family according to Christian fellowship. In fact, this is what Jesus promised while He was here. "Then Peter began to say unto him, Lo, we have left all, and have followed thee. And Jesus answered and said, Verily I say unto you, There is no man that hath left house, or brethren, or sisters, or father, or mother, or wife, or children, or lands, for my sake, and the gospel's, But he shall receive an hundredfold now in this time, houses, and brethren, and sisters, and mothers, and children, and lands, with persecutions; and in the world to come eternal life." Mark 10:28-30. "While he yet talked to the people, behold, his mother and his brethren stood without, desiring to speak with him. Then one said unto him, Behold, thy mother and thy brethren stand without, desiring to speak with thee. But he answered and said unto him that told him, Who is my mother? and who are my brethren? And he stretched forth his hand toward his disciples, and said, Behold my mother and my brethren! For whosoever shall do the will of my Father which is in heaven, the same is my brother, and sister, and mother." Matthew 12:46-50.

In this time of widespread unfaithfulness, it can be discouraging when our blood families are against us, but we must not despair. We must do all within our power to lead them to Christ, that we may be in fellowship with them as well. Only the Lord can change hearts and we must cooperate with Him by patiently and lovingly praying for them. Whatever the outcome, thank the Lord every day for true family.

AMAZING REPENTANCE

II Samuel 12:12-14
*"For thou didst it secretly: but I will do this thing before
all Israel, and before the sun. And David said unto
Nathan, I have sinned against the LORD. And Nathan
said unto David, The LORD also hath put away thy sin;
thou shalt not die. Howbeit, because by this deed thou
hast given great occasion to the enemies of the LORD to
blaspheme, the child also that is born unto
thee shall surely die."*

King David allowed lust and being drunk with power get the better of him. He did not realize how far he had gone down the road away from the Lord. David sent Uriah, the Hittite, to the frontline in a war the Israelites were in the midst of because he had gotten Uriah's wife pregnant and could not find a way to cover it up. He thought he could make his sin go away by killing Bathsheba's husband. Of course this only made matters worse.

Since the Lord loved David so much, He sent the prophet Nathan to him to show him his sin. Nathan began speaking in a parable that described a rich man, with a lack of compassion, taking advantage of a poor man. This made David furious. "And David's anger was greatly kindled against the man; and he said to Nathan, As the LORD liveth, the man that hath done this thing shall surely die: And he shall restore the lamb fourfold, because he did this thing, and because he had no pity." II Samuel 12:5, 6. Nathan revealed the identity of the pitiless rich man. He said, "*Thou art the man.*"

Most people put in that same situation would become angrier, because the prophet exposed their sin. Jesus dealt with many of the leaders of Israel in His day, as did Nathan in this instance. The leaders invariably were angered and

163

tried to kill Him. This was not the case with David. Even after the Lord reproved him in detail, and told him of the judgment against his house, David had godly sorrow for sin, and in heart, turned from it. Though it was painful, he accepted his responsibility and punishment. He knew and agreed that God was just in His judgment. It seemed severe, but the Lord had to let all who observed, see that He was impartial. He knew that this would give His enemies occasion to blaspheme if He did not correct David's sin openly. It was a blessing that David's punishment was temporal. He had to endure extreme trials and watch strife overtake Israel because of his sin, but he did not lose eternal life, because he committed his ways to the Lord. He said, "Have mercy upon me, O God, according to thy lovingkindness: according unto the multitude of thy tender mercies blot out my transgressions. Wash me throughly from mine iniquity, and cleanse me from my sin. For I acknowledge my transgressions: and my sin is ever before me. Against thee, thee only, have I sinned, and done this evil in thy sight: that thou mightest be justified when thou speakest, and be clear when thou judgest." Psalms 51:1-4

This is the kind of repentance that God respects. Full heart repentance is the standard. God is ready, willing, and able to forgive us if we are ready and willing to turn from the sin. I want to have the humility of David and the willingness to follow the Lord all of the way. How about you?

THE LAST WORDS OF DAVID

II Samuel 23:2, 3
"The Spirit of the LORD spake by me, and his word was in my tongue. The God of Israel said, the Rock of Israel spake to me, He that ruleth over men must be just, ruling in the fear of God."

It is no light matter to be a leader in any capacity. Whether you are a parent, teacher, pastor, elder, mentor, monarch, or president, God holds you to a high standard of responsibility. With this responsibility should come an immense sense of humility. This was the last message of David before his death. Solomon demonstrated this self distrust when he said, "...Thou hast shewed unto thy servant David my father great mercy, according as he walked before thee in truth, and in righteousness, and in uprightness of heart with thee; and thou hast kept for him this great kindness, that thou hast given him a son to sit on his throne, as it is this day. And now, O LORD my God, thou hast made thy servant king instead of David my father: and I am but a little child: I know not how to go out or come in. And thy servant is in the midst of thy people which thou hast chosen, a great people, that cannot be numbered nor counted for multitude. Give therefore thy servant an understanding heart to judge thy people, that I may discern between good and bad: for who is able to judge this thy so great a people?" I Kings 3:6-9.

We live in a world where many leaders in various venues exhibit poor leadership. Many cities, states, and countries are burdened with the consequences of unwise leadership. What should we do in such a case? Should we criticize them? Should we allow anger to rule in our thoughts? Prayer is the key. When things seem hopeless and leadership goes astray, do not despair. The Lord sees everything and is always in control. Let it become a part of your daily worship to include prayers for those in authority. This is the beginning of constructive actions toward positive change. Our society is already too bogged down with disgruntled folks who never have a solution to the problems we face. Sharp words of criticism only fuel the rage of those already on the edge anarchy or retaliation. The sweet calming presence of God influences our prayers, and He will answer.

As you traverse the road not yet traveled, let God be your guide. May He help you to support leaders through prayer, into more responsible leadership.

THE LORD HE IS GOD

I Kings 18:39
*"And when all the people saw it, they fell on their faces:
and they said, The LORD, he is the God; the LORD,
he is the God."*

The prophet Elijah was sent of God to settle a score. God wanted all to know that He was the only true God, the God who created all of the earth. Elijah went to Obadiah, one of God's servants and told him to alert the wicked King Ahab that he was in town. Obadiah feared for his life because he had hidden two groups of fifty prophets from Jezebel who commanded that all of the prophets be killed. He was concerned about going into the presence of the wicked king to let him know that Elijah, whom they sought and could not find, was now here. He pressed through his fear, by God's grace, and did what he was told.

Now Elijah had come to the King and told him to assemble the four hundred and fifty prophets of Baal and four hundred prophets of the groves on Mount Carmel for a showdown. The purpose was to determine before all of the people, who the true and undisputed God was. It was done. "And Elijah came unto all the people, and said, How long halt ye between two opinions? if the LORD be God, follow him: but if Baal, then follow him. And the people answered him not a word." I Kings 18:21.

Notice the specific instructions Elijah gave for this spiritual showdown. "Let them therefore give us two bullocks; and let them choose one bullock for themselves, and cut it in pieces, and lay it on wood, and put no fire under: and I will dress the other bullock, and lay it on wood, and put no fire under: And call ye on the name of your gods, and I will call on the name of the LORD: and the God that answereth by fire, let him be God. And all the people answered and said, It is well spoken. And Elijah said unto the prophets of Baal, Choose you one bullock for yourselves, and dress it first; for ye are many; and call on the name of your gods, but put no fire under." I Kings 18:23-25. Though the unholy prophets danced, wailed, cut themselves, and many other strange things to invoke a response from Baal, nothing at all happed. "And it came to pass at noon, that Elijah mocked them, and said, Cry aloud: for he is a god; either he is talking, or he is pursuing, or he is in a journey, or peradventure he sleepeth, and must be awaked." I Kings 18:27. After a while, they prophesied that there was no answer or voice from Baal.

Elijah repaired the altar of the Lord, had men dig trenches around it, and completely drenched the altar, wood, and sacrifice. There was so much water that the trenches were full. "And it came to pass at the time of the offering of the evening sacrifice, that Elijah the prophet came near, and said, LORD God of Abraham, Isaac, and of Israel, let it be known this day that thou art God in Israel, and that I am thy servant, and that I have done all these things at thy word. Hear me, O LORD, hear me, that this people may know that thou art the LORD God, and that thou hast turned their heart back again. Then the fire of the LORD fell, and consumed the burnt sacrifice, and the wood, and the stones, and the dust, and licked up the water that was in the trench. And when all the people saw it, they fell on their faces: and they said, The LORD, he is the God; the LORD, he is the God." I Kings 18:36-39. Notice the way all the people responded. They recognized the power of God by the fire of heaven burning up the sacrifice, wood, dust, and water.

How will people know that God is true today? "I beseech you therefore, brethren, by the mercies of God, that ye present your bodies a living sacrifice, holy, acceptable unto God, which is your reasonable service. And be not conformed to this world: but be ye transformed by the renewing of your mind, that ye may prove what is that good, and acceptable, and perfect, will of God." Romans 12:1, 2. If we are fully dedicated to the work of witnessing, then the world will know that He is God. With the fire of the Holy Ghost upon us, as on the apostles on the day of Pentecost, we must lead others to the Lord. The Lord will show His acceptance of our offering by igniting us in truehearted service for Him.

Let us be fully yielded to the Lord's mission of salvation that those whom we reach will be able to say, "The LORD, he is the God; the LORD, he is the God." I Kings 18:39.

TAKE UP THE MANTLE

II Kings 2:12, 13
"And Elisha saw it, and he cried, My father, my father,
the chariot of Israel, and the horsemen thereof. And he
saw him no more: and he took hold of his own clothes,
and rent them in two pieces. He took up also the mantle of
Elijah that fell from him, and went back, and stood
by the bank of Jordan;"

The great prophet Elijah was approaching the end of his earthly journey. Word was circulated amongst the faithful students in the schools of the prophets that he would be translated into heaven without seeing death. His spiritual protégé, Elisha, followed him everywhere he went. When Elijah asked his son in the faith what he wanted from him, Elisha said, "A double portion of your spirit." Elisha recognized the mighty work that God had performed through his master and he wanted to be used on an even greater level. "And he said, Thou hast asked a hard thing: nevertheless, if thou see me when I am taken from thee, it shall be so unto thee; but if not, it shall not be so." II Kings 2:10.

Eventually, as they were speaking to one another, a chariot of fire came and took Elijah away. Elisha saw it; therefore, his master's promise was fulfilled. Elisha received a double portion of the Spirit of God that occupied Elijah. He then was fully prepared to do God's work. God's Spirit so attended Elisha, that even in his death, God showed His favor. He was dead in a sepulcher and a dead man was let down into the same place. The moment his body touched the bones of Elisha, he revived and stood on his feet (II Kings 13:21). The dead man whose body merely touched Elisha's dead bones was raised to live again.

Jesus Christ lived a perfect life on earth and promised that when He went to His Father in heaven, His followers would perform greater works than even He did. The ministry of Jesus Christ was all about saving souls. Those of us who claim to love Him will go about the same work. The same Sprit that attended Him is still available to those of us living in the last days. Take up the mantle of Jesus Christ. Experience the effects of a greater portion of power than was available even to His first apostles. Heal the sick, raise the dead, and restore sight to blind eyes. *This* is the will of God.

Pray that you will receive the power of the Holy Ghost without measure. Those, whom you touch, by having contact with the One who died to save us from our sins, will be restored to spiritual life. Take up the mantle; the mantle of Jesus Christ.

OH THAT WE MIGHT SEE

II Kings 6:15
"And when the servant of the man of God was risen early, and gone forth, behold, an host compassed the city both with horses and chariots. And his servant said unto him, Alas, my master! how shall we do?"

The enemies of God and His people conspired to overthrow them in a siege. They gathered many horsemen and chariots displaying their power. With the power of evil actuating them, they set their focus and prepared to make their move. As they were preparing, the servant of the prophet Elisha woke up early and saw their regal formation. In fear he exclaimed, "Look master! What should we do?" "And he answered, Fear not: for they that be with us are more than they that be with them." II Kings 6:16. Anyone with eyes and a reasonable ability to see would have been confused by his confidence. Where were those who supposedly outnumbered their enemies? "And Elisha prayed, and said, LORD, I pray thee, open his eyes, that he may see. And the LORD opened the eyes of the young man; and he saw: and, behold, the mountain was full of horses and chariots of fire round about Elisha." II Kings 6:17. The servant was given spiritual discernment to see the inner workings of God. He suddenly became aware of how the Lord always fought their battles. The heavenly hosts were arrayed against their enemies and would surely prevail.

Oh that we might see. Can you remember the last time that you were in a dire situation? Did you find yourself surrounded by the enemies of doubt, discouragement, poverty, or temptation? What was your response? Did you cry out to the Master, "What should I do?" Everyday of our lives, especially after we choose to serve the Lord, we are compassed with the agents of Satan sent with the express purpose of doing us harm, whether it be spiritual, emotional, or physical. His only goal is to steal, kill, and destroy. The Lord has not changed since the days of Elisha? He still gives His people faith enough to maintain composure in the crunch.

When you face trials and temptation, and feel overwhelmed, ask the Lord to open your eyes. Ask Him to show you that He is with you and concerned with your case. Whatever He chooses to show you, will strengthen your faith. Most of all, remember, "Ye are of God, little children, and have overcome them: because greater is he that is in you, than he that is in the world." I John 4:4.

ANSWERED PRAYER

I Chronicles 4:10
"And Jabez called on the God of Israel, saying, Oh that thou wouldest bless me indeed, and enlarge my coast, and that thine hand might be with me, and that thou wouldest keep me from evil, that it may not grieve me! And God granted him that which he requested."

Jabez is a name that most people are familiar with only because Bruce Wilkinson wrote a book highlighting principles related his prayer. His name is shuffled amongst many in the Chronicles. As you read through what seems like an endless list of names, his name suddenly stands out. Why? His name stands out because it is associated with answered prayer.

Jabez's name means sorrowful. In an era and culture where names were meaningful and indicative of something, this was not a name that promised a bright future. Perhaps this is why he ventured into holy territory with his God-given faith and asked God to do something special for him. Not allowing his name to dictate his demise, he lifted his heart to heaven and said, "Oh that thou wouldest bless me indeed, and enlarge my coast, and that thine hand might be with me, and that thou wouldest keep me from evil, that it may not grieve me!" I Chronicles 4:10. The Lord answered his prayer! I am not certain how you feel about this, but to me it is a big deal. There are so many who are limited by their circumstances, not willing to be elevated to a higher spiritual level. There are those who have loved ones who are living on a slippery slope of sin, and do not have sufficient faith to persist in prayer. There are those who also have not achieved any of their goals in life and are too fearful to aspire to greatness. To all, the Lord says, "Have you considered my servant Jabez?" Though his name is obscure in the record of scripture, it is well known in heaven. Heaven is familiar with him because he believed in God to the point where he expected his prayer to be answered. He believed God enough not to pray for selfish reasons, yet ask for a rich personal blessing. Only the Lord can give that kind of intelligent, balanced faith.

The prayer of Jabez should encourage us to pray diligently and never give up. This prayer should encourage us to seek God's face daily, believing that He will reveal Himself. "And I say unto you, Ask, and it shall be given you; seek, and ye shall find; knock, and it shall be opened unto you. For every one that asketh receiveth; and he that seeketh findeth; and to him that knocketh it shall be opened," Luke 11:9, 10.

THE LORD IS IN HIS HOLY TEMPLE

II Chronicles 7:1-3
"Now when Solomon had made an end of praying, the fire came down from heaven, and consumed the burnt offering and the sacrifices; and the glory of the LORD filled the house. And the priests could not enter into the house of the LORD, because the glory of the LORD had filled the LORD's house. And when all the children of Israel saw how the fire came down, and the glory of the LORD upon the house, they bowed themselves with their faces to the ground upon the pavement, and worshipped, and praised the LORD, saying, For he is good; for his mercy endureth for ever."

The temple of the Lord and the Ark of the Covenant were viewed as symbols of God's favor. The children of Israel felt secure when the ark was safe and the temple remained. Through consistent disobedience, there were several instances when these symbols were not present and God allowed their enemies to seemingly triumph over them. Certainly, the Lord used their enemies to bring them into conformity to His will.

During one of the times in which the temple lay in ruins, King David besought the Lord to allow him to rebuild it. God told him that is was well that it was within his heart to do such a great thing, but his hands were filled with too much blood. He promised that his own son Solomon would do it and God would be glorified. The time finally came. The temple was fully built and its magnificence was seen by all. It stood as a monument of the favor of God returning to His people Israel. The priests were arrayed in all of their pomp and majesty, the sacrifices were thoughtfully prepared, and the people of God awaited the glory of God as they all experienced the dedication of God's house.

Solomon prayed one of the most beautiful prayers recorded in the Bible. He recounted the incredible mercy of God, His love for Israel, and His awe-inspiring essence. Suddenly the Lord showed His acceptance of their worship with the signal fire from heaven that Elijah experienced on Mount Carmel. The glory of God so filled the temple that the priests could not even enter. It was surely the best day Israel had experienced, therefore they bowed themselves to the ground and continued to worship. All were pleased that the Lord saw fit to honor humankind with His presence.

Wouldn't it be wonderful if we put as much energy into inviting the Lord into our soul temples? For many years, the people of God longed to experience His presence in that special way. The king plead with God to allow him the honor of having a role to play in building this memorial to God. No expense was spared; no cost was too much for their Lord. I want the zeal of those who waited on the Lord in that day. I want to long to have Him occupy me, setting my soul ablaze with His spirit. I want to be able to say with all of those present at His grand display, the Lord is truly in His holy temple, my soul temple. This is where He most delights to dwell.

PRAYER AND HEALING

II Chronicles 7:14
"If my people, which are called by my name, shall humble themselves, and pray, and seek my face, and turn from their wicked ways; then will I hear from heaven, and will forgive their sin, and will heal their land."

At the dedication of the Lord's temple, that Solomon built, the Lord's presence was seen and felt by all. He made Himself unmistakably known. The children of Israel waited a long time to see this day. "And the LORD appeared to Solomon by night, and said unto him, I have heard thy prayer, and have chosen this place to myself for an house of sacrifice. If I shut up heaven that there be no rain, or if I command the locusts to devour the land, or if I send pestilence among my people; If my people, which are called by my name, shall humble themselves, and pray, and seek my face, and turn from their wicked ways; then will I hear from heaven, and will forgive their sin, and will heal their land. Now mine eyes shall be open, and mine ears attent unto the prayer that is made in this place." II Chronicles 7:12-15.

For many years, God's people had seen the ill effects of disobedience and the blessings of fidelity to God. Up and down they went. They had a problem with consistency. The Ark of the Covenant, which signified the throne and presence of God, had been captured and returned. The temple had been destroyed. The people had been in captivity. So many things occurred over a period of years, that all cannot be recounted here. One thing is certain. The Lord loved them, even though they were a stifnecked people.

During one of their good times with the Lord, He made a promise. "If my people, which are called by my name, shall humble themselves, and pray, and seek my face, and turn from their wicked ways; then will I hear from heaven, and will forgive their sin, and will heal their land." II Chronicles 7:14. The Lord responded to repentance and humility, and He still responds today. When we take the Lord at His word, healing and restoration comes to any situation that we find ourselves in.

HIDE AND SEEK

II Chronicles 15:15
"And all Judah rejoiced at the oath: for they had sworn
with all their heart, and sought him with their whole
desire; and he was found of them: and the LORD
gave them rest round about."

When we were children, we used to play a game called hide and seek. The objective was to hide from one person and do your best not to be found. When the seeker got tired or simply could not find those that were hiding, they would shout "Come out, come out, wherever you are!" It was a fun game. Would it have been fun if we were the ones seeking, and the Lord was hiding?

Unfortunately, some people feel like the Lord is hiding from them. The Bible is clear. The Lord wants us to find Him. The reason we must seek Him is not that He is lost, or hiding. We must seek Him because the pursuit of God *is* salvation. When we put all of our energy into pursuing the person and will of God, He will respond by revealing Himself to us. "Seek ye the LORD while he may be found, call ye upon him while he is near:" Isaiah 55:6. "And ye shall seek me, and find me, when ye shall search for me with all your heart." Jeremiah 29:13.

GOD'S FORGETFULNESS

II Chronicles 34:2
"And he did that which was right in the sight of the LORD, and walked in the ways of David his father, and declined neither to the right hand, nor to the left."

The Bible has a way of revealing the character of God that we would miss completely if the Holy Spirit was not with us. One of the characteristics of God that leaps from the pages is His ability to forgive and forget. Obviously, forgetting does not mean that He miraculously gives Himself amnesia. It does mean however that He does not hold forgiven sins against us while we remain in good relationship with Him. "I, even I, am he that blotteth out thy transgressions for mine own sake, and will not remember thy sins." Isaiah 43: 25.

I believe the Lord when He says that He forgives and does not remember, because God makes an interesting statement about young king Josiah. He said that he was right in the sight of the Lord just like His father David. Wait a minute! Is this a misprint? Did not David murder a man just to cover up his own lust and adultery? Did not David take the dead man's wife as his own? How in the world can God say that David was righteous?

As is the case with all repentant sinners, God honored His promise to forgive those who repent and confess their sin to Him. You see, God's accounting is not like ours. God's love for the repentant sinner does not allow Him to keep a record of wrong. The simple fact is that God answered David's prayer when he prayed, "Hide thy face from my sins, and blot out all mine iniquities." Psalms 51:9.

Are there sins that you have confessed for which you feel unforgiven? Take a lesson from David's experience with God. When he pursued God with his entire heart, all separation between them, including sin, was removed. Pray that the Lord will restore you through forgiveness, and you too will be called righteous. God's ability to forget gives us the ability to live on streets of gold. Be sure to thank God for this blessing.

FREEDOM TO WORSHIP

Ezra 6:14-16
"And the elders of the Jews builded, and they prospered
through the prophesying of Haggai the prophet and
Zechariah the son of Iddo. And they builded, and finished
it, according to the commandment of the God of Israel,
and according to the commandment of Cyrus, and Darius,
and Artaxerxes king of Persia. And this house was
finished on the third day of the month Adar, which was in
the sixth year of the reign of Darius the king. And the
children of Israel, the priests, and the Levites, and the rest
of the children of the captivity, kept the dedication
of this house of God with joy,"

Following their release from Babylonian captivity, God's people longed to rebuild the temple that was destroyed during Nebuchadnezzar's conquest. It was just as it was in the days of Moses. At that time, the children of Israel longed to be set free from Egypt so that, in the wilderness, they could offer sacrifices to the Lord their God. Over a period of years, many letters were sent out between various kings and governors, and eventually the building of God's temple took place uninterrupted. The Lord showed His people favor with the King Darius. "Let the work of this house of God alone; let the governor of the Jews and the elders of the Jews build this house of God in his place. Moreover I made a decree what ye shall do to the elders of these Jews for the building of this house of God: that of the king's goods, even of the tribute beyond the river, forthwith expences be given unto these men, that they be not hindered. And that which they have need of, both young bullocks, and rams, and lambs, for the burnt offerings of the God of heaven, wheat, salt, wine, and oil, according to the appointment of the priests which are at Jerusalem, let it be given them day by day without fail:

That they may offer sacrifices of sweet savours unto the God of heaven, and pray for the life of the king, and of his sons. Also I have made a decree, that whosoever shall alter this word, let timber be pulled down from his house, and being set up, let him be hanged thereon; and let his house be made a dunghill for this. And the God that hath caused his name to dwell there destroy all kings and people, that shall put to their hand to alter and to destroy this house of God which is at Jerusalem. I Darius have made a decree; let it be done with speed." Ezra 6:7-12.

When the Lord frees us from the bondage of sin, it is not merely for the sake of making us free. The liberty of God is freedom to worship. The emancipation proclamation from God for sinners saved by grace is, "I have delivered you to worship me with your lives. You are free to live with the power of the Holy Ghost motivating you to live according to all I have commanded. You are free to make disciple makers, that my name may be glorified. I have shown you favor, in order that you and those to whom you witness might be saved eternally." When the Lord gives us victory over sin, self, and Satan, it should not be treated lightly. No! The Lord has delivered us to bring glory and honor to His name. If we are still in bondage to sin, it is our privilege today, to diligently seek the Lord for deliverance and begin our lives anew with Him.

Repairing the Breach

Nehemiah 4:17-19
*"They which builded on the wall, and they that bare
burdens, with those that laded, every one with one of his
hands wrought in the work, and with the other hand held
a weapon. For the builders, every one had his sword
girded by his side, and so builded. And he that sounded
the trumpet was by me. And I said unto the nobles, and to
the rulers, and to the rest of the people, The work is great
and large, and we are separated upon the wall, one far
from another. In what place therefore ye hear the sound
of the trumpet, resort ye thither unto us:
our God shall fight for us."*

God's people were finally free from Babylonian captivity.
Through much opposition, they were also finally able to
rebuild the temple of God due to the favor the Lord had
shown them through king Darius. Nehemiah, the son of
Hacaliah considered the entire situation of those freed from
the captivity. He realized that the walls of the city were still
in ruins. The gates had been burned to the ground, and it
was a reproach. This is not what God intended for His city.
This is not what He intended for His people. They were to
be a light set upon a hill that could not be hid. They were the
repositories of light and through disobedience, their candles
flickered. This troubled Nehemiah. As Isaiah, Daniel, and
Moses had done on different occasions, Nehemiah began to
entreat the Lord, confessing his sins, and the sins of the
people. He wanted the Lord to reveal Himself and make
good on His promise to turn away their reproach, if they
would only repent and turn to the Lord.

God granted Nehemiah's prayer. He gave him favor with
King Artaxerxes, and the project to rebuild the wall of
God's city of peace began. The next fifty two days would

prove to be arduous. When some of Israel's enemies heard that they were attempting to repair the wall, they made fun of them, saying that if a fox stood atop the part of the wall they had completed up to that point, it would come tumbling down. Also, while there was yet a breach in the wall, they sought to ambush God's people to arrest their progress. What they did not understand was that the Lord blessed the work, and there was nothing they could do to stop it.

With godly wisdom, Nehemiah assembled every worker in a certain order. The workers were divided into two groups. One group would continue to build, while the others stood with weapons, ready for battle. Every man was prepared, whether he was building or guarding the work, each had weapons for battle.

"Now it came to pass, when Sanballat, and Tobiah, and Geshem the Arabian, and the rest of our enemies, heard that I had builded the wall, and that there was no breach left therein; (though at that time I had not set up the doors upon the gates;) That Sanballat and Geshem sent unto me, saying, Come, let us meet together in some one of the villages in the plain of Ono. But they thought to do me mischief. And I sent messengers unto them, saying, I am doing a great work, so that I cannot come down: why should the work cease, whilst I leave it, and come down to you? Yet they sent unto me four times after this sort; and I answered them after the same manner. Then sent Sanballat his servant unto me in like manner the fifth time with an open letter in his hand;" Nehemiah 6:1-5. In spite of their enemies attempts to stop their work, Nehemiah and the others successfully rebuilt the walls at Jerusalem. "So the wall was finished in the twenty and fifth day of the month Elul, in fifty and two days. And it came to pass, that when all our enemies heard thereof, and all the heathen that were about us saw these things, they were much cast down in their own eyes: for they perceived that this work was wrought of our God." Nehemiah 6:15, 16.

Do you know that there is a breach in the great wall of God's Ten Commandment law? He has given His people, those upon whom the ends of the world are come, the work of repairing it. When we draw near to Him in repentance as Nehemiah did, He will equip us with His whole armor that we may be able to stand against the attacks of Satan. With the Bible as our sword fully drawn and sharpened, we are to allow the Lord to defend against the enemy.

The breach in God's law is our forgetfulness of worship. It is our spiritual amnesia concerning the seventh-day Sabbath, which the Lord said to remember. His day is holy and cannot be transferred to another. Therefore, the Lord said if we return to the holiness of His word by feeding the hungry, giving clothes to the naked, and otherwise caring for the destitute and disadvantaged from our hearts, He will show us favor. "Then shalt thou call, and the LORD shall answer; thou shalt cry, and he shall say, Here I am. If thou take away from the midst of thee the yoke, the putting forth of the finger, and speaking vanity; And if thou draw out thy soul to the hungry, and satisfy the afflicted soul; then shall thy light rise in obscurity, and thy darkness be as the noonday: And the LORD shall guide thee continually, and satisfy thy soul in drought, and make fat thy bones: and thou shalt be like a watered garden, and like a spring of water, whose waters fail not. And they that shall be of thee shall build the old waste places: thou shalt raise up the foundations of many generations; and thou shalt be called, The repairer of the breach, The restorer of paths to dwell in. If thou turn away thy foot from the sabbath, from doing thy pleasure on my holy day; and call the sabbath a delight, the holy of the LORD, honourable; and shalt honour him, not doing thine own ways, nor finding thine own pleasure, nor speaking thine own words: Then shalt thou delight thyself in the LORD; and I will cause thee to ride upon the high places of the earth, and feed thee with the heritage of Jacob thy father:

for the mouth of the LORD hath spoken it." Isaiah 58:9-14. As in the days prior to the Babylonian captivity, the Lord never intended that His walls be broken down. His will has always been for His people to dwell in the light and live above reproach.

It is our privilege today to seek His face as did Nehemiah, and receive the light concerning our part in repairing the breach. As we return to honoring the Lord as the Creator of the universe by remembering His holy Sabbath, His favor will become evident in our lives. We will be instrumental in repairing the breach.

A MISUNDERSTANDING OF ROLES

Esther 1:22
"For he sent letters into all the king's provinces, into every province according to the writing thereof, and to every people after their language, that every man should bear rule in his own house, and that it should be published according to the language of every people."

One day King Xerxes gave a party with many important men in attendance. Vashti, his wife, gave a party for the women. The king ordered that everyone be given as much wine as they wanted, for as long as the party lasted. In a wine induced excitement, the king commanded that his beautiful wife, Vashti, be brought into his party so that he could parade her beauty before his guests. When the messengers took the command to her, she refused. This made the king angry. To know what he must do, he sought the counsel of members of his cabinet. His counselors told him that for the sake of his kingdom and for the order of every home ruled by husbands, he should replace her with an obedient wife. "For he sent letters into all the king's provinces, into every province according to the writing thereof, and to every people after their language, that every man should bear rule in his own house, and that it should be published according to the language of every people." Esther 1:22.

It is shameful that a similar misunderstanding of roles exist in many homes even today. Some have mistaken the counsel of God concerning men being the head in the Christian home, as a command to be the boss of chronically acquiescent wives. These men think that the Lord condones male domination. When we examine the record closely, we discover a very different reality. "Wives, submit yourselves unto your own husbands, as unto the Lord. For the husband is the head of the wife, even as Christ is the head of the church: and he is the saviour of the body. Therefore as the church is subject unto Christ, so let the wives be to their own husbands in every thing. Husbands, love your wives, even as Christ also loved the church, and gave himself for it; That he might sanctify and cleanse it with the washing of water by the word, That he might present it to himself a glorious church, not having spot, or wrinkle, or any such thing; but that it should be holy and without blemish. So ought men to love their wives as their own bodies. He that loveth his wife loveth himself. For no man ever yet hated his own flesh; but nourisheth and cherisheth it, even as the Lord the church:" Ephesians 5:22-29. With this counsel, the Lord gave the model for a well ordered home. How did the Lord Jesus love the church? The Bible says that He suffered and died in order to save us from our sins. This is very different from the picture of the tyrannical King Xerxes arbitrarily commanding that his wife bow to his wishes. A man of God follows the example of Jesus Christ and has the best interest of his wife at heart. Men are to stand daily as priests in the home carrying the needs of his family to the Lord in prayer.

Women are not to lose their identities in marriage. God has created each of us with unique roles and responsibilities. It is our duty to seek the Lord to understand His will for our relationships. I am certain that as we persist in seeking Him in this matter, He will make Himself clear and we will live in harmony with His divine will. Let us not perpetuate the misunderstanding of roles.

A HARD REVELATION

Job 3:2, 3, 25, 26
"And Job spake, and said, Let the day perish wherein I
was born, and the night in which it was said, There is a
man child conceived. For the thing which I greatly feared
is come upon me, and that which I was afraid of is come
unto me. I was not in safety, neither had I rest, neither
was I quiet; yet trouble came."

I cannot imagine Job's turmoil when he was faced with most difficult trial of his life. One day he received the news that all of his children, livestock, and earthly possessions were destroyed. While he yet grieved his loss, the Lord allowed Satan to afflict him with boils from head to toe. Job could not remember any unconfessed sin that he had committed, which made things even more difficult for him. If he could have, he would have repented with the hope that the judgment of God would be removed from him.

One of many depressing days, he loathed the day he was born and wished he could just rest in the grave. He was not suicidal, just weary. It seemed too much for him to bear, but the Lord was with him. The Lord was close by Job's side even though Job could not detect His presence.

After the many days of trial had finally passed, and after he had already endured the foul pessimism of his wife and so-called friends, along with the strong answer the Lord had given to his complaints, he praised the Lord. He said, "I have heard of thee by the hearing of the ear: but now mine eye seeth thee. Wherefore I abhor myself, and repent in dust and ashes." Job 42:5, 6. Though the Lord called Job righteous in the beginning of his ordeal, by Job's own admission, he was still lacking. After having experienced the trials that brought patience when their perfect work was done, he could see more clearly than ever before. He knew the mercy of God on a level beyond comprehension. He now could see what he could barely perceive before his trials. Because of this, he changed his mindset from the verses above. Instead, he praised the Lord.

Yes, it was a hard revelation for Job, but it was well worth it. He finally had a better relationship with God than ever before. When we face tribulations, we should read the words of brother Job to encourage us to be faithful. If he did it, being human, so can we.

Now I Know

Job 42:5
"I have heard of thee by the hearing of the ear:
but now mine eye seeth thee."

Job's ordeal was a long and arduous one. He was rich in every way. He was a servant of God, a good family man with a wonderful wife and many children, a great boss with many servants, and one who owned real estate and livestock extensively. Job had it all. One day the devil suggested to God that Job only served Him because of the blessings he received. He went further to say that if those things were taken from him, he would curse God to His face. All of this he suggested after God asked, "Hast thou considered my servant Job, that there is none like him in the earth, a perfect and an upright man, one that feareth God, and escheweth evil?" Job 1:8. The devil has always been averse to the thought that someone can live in harmony with God's law. In this accusation, he demonstrated his contempt for the holiness of God.

As the story continues, God allows the devil to plunder all that Job had, including his family and good health with one stipulation. Satan could not kill Job. It is a blessing to know that all that occurs in our lives must first pass through *the God filter.* It is also a blessing to know that God puts boundaries on what the enemy can do to us. He says to Satan, "This far you can go and no further."

As Job struggled through his extreme ordeal, covered from head to toe with painful putrefying boils, the people closest to him suggested that He curse God, and that these things happened because he sinned. Have you ever been down and your closest friends made your situation worse? Though Job was bewildered and confused, wishing that he had some mediator between himself and God, he remained faithful. He proved to the onlooking universe that God was more important to him than anything else. "And said, Naked came I out of my mother's womb, and naked shall I return thither: the LORD gave, and the LORD hath taken away; blessed be the name of the LORD." Job 1:21. "Though he slay me, yet will I trust in him: but I will maintain mine own ways before him." Job 13:15. Certainly, Job had questions and the Lord being as powerful and holy as He is, checked Job's questionings, yet Job still pleased God. (Job 38-41). "Then Job answered the LORD, and said, Behold, I am vile; what shall I answer thee? I will lay mine hand upon my mouth. Once have I spoken; but I will not answer: yea, twice; but I will proceed no further." Job 40:3-5.

It is curious to me how a man can be so highly spoken of by God, but he was. Even though Job was righteous before God and He demonstrated His favor by blessing Job with abundance, Job barely understood God. By the time his ordeal was over, Job had realized the limits on his relationship with, and view of God. It was through extreme experience with God through trials that he was able to say, "I have heard of thee by the hearing of the ear: but now mine eye seeth thee. Wherefore I abhor myself, and repent in dust and ashes." Job 42:5, 6.

In the end, God's character was vindicated before Satan, and Job's life was set back in order. "So the LORD blessed the latter end of Job more than his beginning: for he had fourteen thousand sheep, and six thousand camels, and a thousand yoke of oxen, and a thousand she asses. He had also seven sons and three daughters. After this lived Job an hundred and forty years, and saw his sons, and his sons' sons, even four generations. So Job died, being old and full of days." Job 42:12, 13, 16, 17.

IN THE MORNING WHEN I RISE

Psalms 5:3
"My voice shalt thou hear in the morning, O LORD;
in the morning will I direct my prayer unto thee,
and will look up."

Most of us have morning rituals. Some pray, exercise, eat breakfast, or have a cup of freshly brewed coffee. Others read the newspaper, watch the news, or set the VCR to record a favorite television show while they are out and about. Some of our rituals are helpful, while others are a hindrance.

Morning prayer is a practice that every household should be involved in. It is a good thing to pray with your family. Even if you have no family in your home, it is still absolutely necessary to weave prayer into the fiber of your morning practice. The Bible affirms this practice, and we gain a lot by doing so.

What kinds of benefits are there to talking with the Lord to begin our day? Just as with any relationship that is worthwhile, communication is critical in our relationship with God. Although He knows everything, He wants to hear what we have to say, and He wants to share His thoughts with us. Many of us forget the second half of this equation. God really want us to be attentive and listen for His voice. It is often in the stillness of the early morning devotional time, that God's voice is most distinct and clear.

Along with communication, we can enjoy the instructional aspect of prayer. When God makes Himself clear through His word, His still small voice, nature, providence, or any other means He chooses, He often instructs us on what we need to do or avoid, as the case may be. The instructions of God are always to steer us in the right direction. We can avoid many mistakes for the day if we simply listen for God's instruction.

We are able to receive therapy from God when we pray in the morning. I know this sounds weird, but it's true. Most therapists are very good listeners. What better person is there to share our likes, dislikes, wants, needs, and goals with than God? God is absolutely the best therapist in the universe. He helps us to daily manage our lives and make right decisions.

Not the least of all the benefits of prayer is God's blessing. We have the ability through our devotion and prayer to make God happy. This certainly makes sense. All good friends like to be affirmed periodically and God is no different in this. The aspect of this that is different is that affirming God is to praise Him for His matchless works in the universe. He is the only one truly worthy of affirmation and praise.

So there you have it. There are many benefits of beginning the day with prayer, even to the point of blessing God Himself. Every time you think of His goodness, breathe a word of prayer. I am positive that He will appreciate it.

EARLY MORNING BLESSING

Psalms 5:3
"My voice shalt thou hear in the morning, O LORD; in the morning will I direct my prayer unto thee, and will look up. For thou art not a God that hath pleasure in wickedness: neither shall evil dwell with thee."

As the darkness of the night slowly vanishes into the early morning mist, birds sing carols unto the Lord. As dim shadows give way to abundant rays of sunshine, all creatures are astir. They know the blessing of the Lord, though they cannot speak.

It is a privilege to awaken every morning, no matter how our night was or what we must face during the day. The fact that God cares enough to open our eyes to see a new day's dawning proves that He loves us. He has given us another opportunity to live for Him. He has blessed us with the pleasure of lifting our voices in praise to Him; for He is good.

While Jesus lived on earth, the Bible says that He woke up a great while before day and prayed in a solitary place (Mark 1:35). In the quietness of morning solitude, He was strengthened to do the work He came to do. He was braced for the temptations that would certainly come His way. It is our privilege to do the same.

David said that the morning hours would be greeted with the sound of his prayers. He understood the relationship between early morning devotion and protection from wickedness. This protection is not outward. It is an inner barrier against temptation. As long as we spend quality time with God and yield our wills to Him, we do not have to satisfy the urges of the flesh. David said that evil does not dwell with God. If we are fully enfolded in the presence of God, then evil must flee.

It is a blessing to know that the Lord awakens us daily

expecting to have a great time with us. He wants to teach us the mystery of godliness through His word, nature, and providence. He is pleased when we begin the day with Him. It makes sense not to disappoint Him.

WE NEED TO PRAISE HIM MORE

Psalms 9:1, 2
"I will praise thee, O LORD, with my whole heart; I will shew forth all thy marvellous works. I will be glad and rejoice in thee: I will sing praise to thy name, O thou most High."

Whenever we think of something that the Lord has done for us, we should praise Him. I know that I do not praise Him enough, and neither do many others. When we open our eyes in the morning, we should praise Him. When we drink our first glass of relatively clean water, we should praise Him. When we eat our first bite of food, we should praise Him. When we almost have a car accident, but don't, we should praise Him. When we do have an accident and come out alive, we should praise Him. The angels in heaven praise Him, and they are sinless. They do not know what it is to have the King of the universe become one of them and die the second death on their behalf, yet they praise Him all day long. If the angels praise Him, how much more should we upon whom the ends of the world are come? If we do not praise Him, inanimate nature will take our place. I do not want the rocks and trees crying out in my place. Make a list of the great things He has done. Go through them one by one, and praise Him.

When you are tempted to feel forsaken of God, remember these words: "My God, my God, why hast thou forsaken me? why art thou so far from helping me, and from the words of my roaring? O my God, I cry in the daytime, but thou hearest not; and in the night season, and am not silent. But thou art holy, O thou that inhabitest the praises of Israel." Psalms 22:1-3.

NATURE GLORIFIES GOD

Psalms 19:1-3
"The heavens declare the glory of God; and the firmament sheweth his handywork. Day unto day uttereth speech, and night unto night sheweth knowledge. There is no speech nor language, where their voice is not heard."

"The fool hath said in his heart, There is no God. Corrupt are they, and have done abominable iniquity: there is none that doeth good." Psalms 53:1.

Although nature as we know it wears the blight of sin, it still speaks of an intelligent, orderly and loving God. It is what we can see. We can handle it day by day. If we look closely, we will definitely realize that there is a God in heaven that loves those that dwell upon the earth. Paul said, "For the invisible things of him from the creation of the world are clearly seen, being understood by the things that are made, even his eternal power and Godhead; so that they are without excuse:" Romans 1:20.

It is shameful that so-called scientists and philosophers have attributed the order of the universe to chance, a coincidental arrangement of circumstances. If they would just allow the Spirit of God to soften their hearts and fill in the gaps of their understanding, they too would see that the vast expanse of the universe, with all of its intricate laws and details, must be the work of God. More fascinating than nature itself is that the Lord manages this universe, yet is still interested in human beings. We are but a small speck in the scheme of things, but we are the object of God's love and care.

I thank the Lord that He has given us a window into knowing Him. I thank Him all the more that He revealed Himself to us through His Son; the perfect representative of heaven. If nature glorifies God just by existing, how much more should we, for whom Christ gave His life?

I WILL FEAR NO EVIL

Psalms 23:4
"Yea, though I walk through the valley of the shadow of death, I will fear no evil: for thou art with me; thy rod and thy staff they comfort me."

Fear is an emotion that we all experience from time to time. A mother notices that her child is face down in the crib and she fears losing it to SIDS. A father listens to the news as he awaits his young son's return from the battlefield of Iraq and hears that yet another group of soldiers has been killed. He fears that his son may not return home. A husband and wife have a turbulent argument and say things they wish they had not. In contemplation of the altercation, they fear an irreparable breach has been made in the relationship. Fear is normal, but human.

Did you know that God is able to give us such blessed assurance that we will fear no evil? David understood it well. Many of his enemies, whom he thought were friends, sought to take his life. Betrayal was something he had grown accustomed to. He existed under the constant shadow of death, yet he said that he feared no evil. Why? God was with him. He said that God's rod and staff comforted Him. The rod of a *good* shepherd protected his sheep from predators and the staff guided them along the right path. God protects and leads us much in the same way.

We do not have to be gripped by fear. If we love the Lord, He controls every aspect of our lives. Nothing can happen to us that He has not first measured and allowed. There is no need to face life's situations with trepidation. If we cannot add another moment to our lives, we do not gain anything by undue anxiety (Matthew 6:27-34).

Let us trust the Lord as did David, proclaiming that we fear no evil. There is nothing that comes our way that, in unison with God, we cannot handle. "Trust in the LORD with all thine heart; and lean not unto thine own understanding. In all thy ways acknowledge him, and he shall direct thy paths. Be not wise in thine own eyes: fear the LORD, and depart from evil. It shall be health to thy navel, and marrow to thy bones." Proverbs 3:5-8.

CLEAN

"Who shall ascend into the hill of the LORD?
or who shall stand in his holy place?"

God dwells in light unapproachable. If we were not restricted by time or space even in our humanness, and burst into the presence of God in all of His glory, we would immediately burst into flames. Perhaps this is overly descriptive, but we would certainly die. There is no human being that can stand in the direct presence of God and remain alive. He is holy and we are not. He is spirit and we are flesh. He is love and we are estranged from the womb. The contrast between God and us is astounding.

David asks the question, "Who shall ascend into the hill of the LORD? or who shall stand in his holy place?" Psalms 24:3. He answered, "He that hath clean hands, and a pure heart; who hath not lifted up his soul unto vanity, nor sworn deceitfully." Psalms 24:4. Only the pure in heart can approach God. This reminds me of the story of Moses. At a critical point early on in His ministry, He needed affirmation from God. His mission was too heavy to bear. "Now therefore, I pray thee, if I have found grace in thy sight, shew me now thy way, that I may know thee, that I may find grace in thy sight: and consider that this nation is thy people. And he said, I beseech thee, shew me thy glory." Exodus 33:13, 18. The Bible continues by saying that the Lord enfolded Moses into His presence, and there revealed His character through His name. He made His goodness pass before Moses while shielding him by His mercy. This is a clear example of one who ascended into the hill of the Lord with clean hands and a pure heart.

Did you know that God is still cleansing people today? He still gives the blessing of forgiveness and cleansing. "If we confess our sins, he is faithful and just to forgive us our sins, and to cleanse us from all unrighteousness." I John 1:9. When we receive the cleansing of God by faith, we have full access to the hill, or presence of God through Jesus Christ. "Let us therefore come boldly unto the throne of grace, that we may obtain mercy, and find grace to help in time of need." Hebrews 4:16. "Having therefore, brethren, boldness to enter into the holiest by the blood of Jesus, By a new and living way, which he hath consecrated for us, through the veil, that is to say, his flesh; And having an high priest over the house of God; Let us draw near with a true heart in full assurance of faith, having our hearts sprinkled from an evil conscience, and our bodies washed with pure water. Let us hold fast the profession of our faith without wavering; (for he is faithful that promised;)" Hebrews 10:19-23.

After receiving the faith of God for cleansing and forgiveness, we are granted access to His presence. David concluded his statement by sharing what the benefit of it all would be. "He shall receive the blessing from the LORD, and righteousness from the God of his salvation." Psalms 24:5. Thank the Lord for giving us the privilege of being clean.

Wait On the Lord

Psalms 27:13, 14
**"I had fainted, unless I had believed to see the goodness
of the LORD in the land of the living. Wait on the LORD:
be of good courage, and he shall strengthen thine heart:
wait, I say, on the LORD."**

Have you ever been in a situation that seemed hopeless and someone looked into your eyes and said, "Don't worry, just wait on the Lord?" What exactly does it mean to wait on the Lord? It sounds like a cliché. When you have an opportunity, read Psalms chapter 27. In this chapter, you will see many of the challenges David was faced with. Through his experiences, he decided that if he focussed on God, the light of his salvation, he would be complete. He wrote at the end of this chapter, "I had fainted, unless I had believed to see the goodness of the LORD in the land of the living. Wait on the LORD: be of good courage, and he shall strengthen thine heart: wait, I say, on the LORD." Psalms 27:13, 14. Through all of our difficulties, we can always count on the Lord being there to strengthen us for as long as we trust in Him.

In these verses, David wanted to communicate that we should trust the Lord to deliver us from despair. We should patiently wait for the blessings that He has promised to the faithful. To endure every trial, we must *expect* the arrival of God's strength. Is it possible that the Bible teaches another way to wait on the Lord?

When the Bible says wait on the Lord, I think about young Samuel who, at the beginning of his ministry, was listening for the voice of God in the night. (I Samuel 3). I think of Huldah, the prophetess, who instructed King Josiah to be faithful to God by following His word (II Kings 22). When I think of what it could mean to wait on the Lord, in my mind's eye I see a woman named Mary so filled with gratitude that she anointed Jesus' head with expensive perfumes and washed His feet with her hair (John 12; Mark 14).

Waiting on the Lord is a humble attitude of servitude and love. It is like a waiter or waitress at an upscale restaurant, available to satisfy the patron's every desire. When we assume this posture, wanting only to please the Lord as His servants, we are in truth waiting on Him. Solomon gives us a snapshot of waiting on the Lord. "Let us hear the conclusion of the whole matter: Fear God, and keep his commandments: for this is the whole duty of man." Ecclesiastes 12:13.

Simply stated, whenever we are tempted to focus on our own trials, we should ask the Lord to teach us how to please Him. When we become so consumed with making God smile and lose sight of things that would usually distract us, Jesus said that He would supply everything we need (Matthew 6:33). If you need peace, wait on the Lord. If you need love, wait on the Lord. If you need companionship, wait on the Lord. If you need financial help or even healing, wait on the Lord. Wait, I say, on the Lord!

SING WHEN THE SPIRIT SAYS SING

Psalms 33:2
"Praise the LORD with harp: sing unto him with the psaltery and an instrument of ten strings."

Singing unto the Lord is one of the greatest blessings we can enjoy. When we rehearse the great things He has done for us, our delight is to worship Him in song. We may not have the most beautiful sounding voices, or skillfully handle stringed instruments, but sincere worship is acceptable to God. "O my God, I cry in the daytime, but thou hearest not; and in the night season, and am not silent. But thou art holy, O thou that inhabitest the praises of Israel. Our fathers trusted in thee: they trusted, and thou didst deliver them. They cried unto thee, and were delivered: they trusted in thee, and were not confounded." Psalms 22:2-5. When we pour out our hearts before the Lord, and praise Him with our entire beings, the Bible says that He who inhabits praise will deliver us.

Many incredible things occurred for God's people when they praised Him. I will give two examples of God's power to deliver in the midst of His people's worship. (1)"And at midnight Paul and Silas prayed, and sang praises unto God: and the prisoners heard them. And suddenly there was a great earthquake, so that the foundations of the prison were shaken: and immediately all the doors were opened, and every one's bands were loosed." Acts 16:25, 26. (2)"And they rose early in the morning, and went forth into the wilderness of Tekoa: and as they went forth, Jehoshaphat stood and said, Hear me, O Judah, and ye inhabitants of Jerusalem; Believe in the LORD your God, so shall ye be established; believe his prophets, so shall ye prosper. And when he had consulted with the people, he appointed singers unto the LORD, and that should praise the beauty of holiness, as they went out before the army, and to say, Praise the LORD; for his mercy endureth forever. And when they began to sing and to praise, the LORD set ambushments against the children of Ammon, Moab, and mount Seir, which were come against Judah; and they were smitten." II Chronicles 20:20-22. They sang when the Spirit led them to, and the Lord showed favor on them. Let us learn how to praise Him as they did.

The Lord has shown us how willing He is to dispel darkness at the sound of sincere melodies of worship. He has also shown us how He will deliver us at the last day in the presence of spiritual music. This time it will be melodies uttered by God Himself. Can you imagine what a wonderful day it will be when the melodious voice of God is heard, and the dead in Christ rise? Imagine how beautiful the sound of His trumpet will be in that day of final deliverance (I Thessalonians 4:16, 17).

It is a great idea to enrich our worship expression with musical praise. The Lord enjoys expressions of praise and dwells with His people when we do so.

PERSONAL EXPERIENCE

Psalms 34:8
"O taste and see that the LORD is good:
blessed is the man that trusteth in him."

Perhaps the most passionate sales people in the world generate revenue based on personal experience with their products. I have sold many products and services over the years. The most dreaded question to hear is whether or not the seller is using the product or service, and if so, how they are enjoying it. I have been on both sides of the fence. I have been able to give a well reasoned, detailed response based on pleasurable experience, as well as only being able to offer silence when I had no experience. The latter was discouraging. Furthermore, I had no way of hanging complete faith in what I was selling, because of my ignorance. The potential buyer can detect that a mile away and often will not become a long-term client.

Have you ever been to a restaurant on one of those self-dates when you just wanted to be alone? Did you discover on any of those occasions that there was a wonderful dish on the menu that one of your friends would just love? How difficult would it have been to convince that friend that the dish was absolutely delicious and prepared in the most simple and appetizing way? Were the colors represented and the food presentation extraordinary? Were the flavors, textures, and aromas brilliantly blended to compose the perfect culinary symphony? If this was the case, there could be no question that your communication of that point would be inspirational. Your friend would probably imagine eating the dish for as long as it took, until they were actually able to go for themselves.

Just as it would not take any contrivance on our part, if we had positive experience with a product, service, or exquisite dish to convince a potential client or friend of its value, people can sense our zeal for the Lord. You see, David said, "O taste and see that the LORD is good: blessed is the man that trusteth in him." Psalms 34:8. This was clearly an invitation and not a bidding to go where he had not gone himself. Experience is the best inspiration. David had seen the hand of the Lord mightily deliver His people Israel in the face of incredible odds many times. He also had individual experiences when God did the impossible through him for the entire world to witness. His invitation was simple; taste and enjoy what was then enjoying himself. The Lord is good and you are blessed when you trust in Him.

Ask the Lord for a richer and fuller experience for yourself today so that your testimony will only become more compelling to those who themselves have no experience with God.

TASTE FOR YOURSELF

Psalms 34:8
"O taste and see that the LORD is good: blessed is the man that trusteth in him."

I remember being on a beautiful island off the coast of Honduras. One of the tours took us to a beautiful garden. This was not just any garden. It was rich with the aromas of many flowering and medicinal plants. Some of them towered over us like large trees. Amongst them were many fruit bearing trees. It was quite an enjoyable experience. Part of the garden tour included a naturalist guide who shared, in detail, the uses of these wonderful bounties. After finishing the learning portion, the guide told us to sit in a circle. In the center, on top of a small table, she had prepared a fruit-tasting feast on banana leaves. As others tasted the fruit profuse with color and overflowing with natural juices, it was difficult to concentrate while waiting your turn. Everyone was so pleased. We could not help but share what we had already tasted for ourselves.

Living the Christian life is much the same way. God prepares a table before us and begins sharing His rich bounties. In fact, that is what He meant when He gave His message to the church of Laodicea. "Behold, I stand at the door, and knock: if any man hear my voice, and open the door, I will come in to him, and will sup with him, and he with me." Revelation 3:20. The Greek rendering of Jesus supping with those who respond to Him, suggests that *He* would bring dinner. The Lord is the one who prepares the table before His receptive children and sets before us bounties untold. As we partake, we cannot help but share our experience with others. We want everyone to know the joy and rich experience that we have with Him. We are not satisfied with merely enjoying God for ourselves only.

As you go through the day, take time to enjoy the Lord. When we do so, we will invariably invite others to do the same. We will say to them, "Taste and see, that the Lord is good."

THAT'S WHAT I WANT

Psalms 37:4
"Delight thyself also in the LORD; and he shall give thee the desires of thine heart."

The idea of putting the Lord first in everything that we do is prevalent throughout scripture. When the Lord is our priority, He keeps all other things in proper order. "But seek ye first the kingdom of God, and his righteousness; and all these things shall be added unto you." Matthew 6:33. "And this is the confidence that we have in him, that, if we ask any thing according to his will, he heareth us: And if we know that he hear us, whatsoever we ask, we know that we have the petitions that we desired of him." I John 5:14, 15. It is wonderful to know that the Lord of heaven, who has an infinite number of things to manage throughout the universe, is interested in my well-being.

When I read that the Lord will give me the desires of my heart when I delight myself in Him, I see it from an interesting perspective. Many of us pray for various things, and at the end add a phrase, "If it's your will Lord." What many mean by this is that they want the thing prayed for, and if they end the prayer with the right phrase, the Lord will give them the very thing they asked for. They suggest that all you need is true faith and you can name it and claim it or blab it and grab it. What the Bible says to me is that I need an adjustment in desires. When the Lord delights us and we in Him, He changes our desires so that we are in rhythm with Him. We do not know what to pray for, so He helps His children to align ourselves with His perspective. The desires of Almighty God become our desires.

Praise the Lord for being willing to adjust our attitudes toward what He wants for us. If we love the Lord, He will give us holy desires; then He can answer our prayers according to His own divine will.

PEACEFUL DESTINATION

Psalms 37:37-39
"Mark the perfect man, and behold the upright: for the end of that man is peace. But the transgressors shall be destroyed together: the end of the wicked shall be cut off. But the salvation of the righteous is of the LORD: he is their strength in the time of trouble."

I can remember anticipating a cruise my wife and I were planning to take about a year ago. I could hardly wait, because we would soon be boarding a huge floating resort in Miami, Florida to cruise the deep blue seas. We were going to several peaceful destinations. We went to Isla Roatan, Cozumel, Belize, and Grand Caymen. The beaches were beautiful; the ocean breezes were calming, and the scenery relaxing. The trip was the best I had ever experienced. It was a reprieve from the stress and business of everyday life.

God has given us reprieve from the annoyances of wicked people and the devil. This reprieve comes only from choosing to have a love relationship with Jesus Christ. The relief we receive from loving Him stems from building a relationship with Him that was previously shattered by sin. When sin entered into the world, we became God's enemies, but Jesus fixed it all. Through His perfect gift of salvation, He made it possible for all to be at peace with Him.

It is wonderful to know that when trials threaten to destroy us, wicked men seek to do us harm, and everyday temptations wear us down, that God has the peaceful destination of His love prepared for us. We are able to listen for the calming breeze of His Spirit. We can be refreshed by the moist dew of His power. We can be filled with the satisfying bread of His word. As we grow in love with Him, our peace grows as well. We are not at peace with this world, but we do have peace of mind knowing that soon Jesus will return and rescue us. One day soon all wickedness shall cease and we will walk by the peaceful shore of the heavenly crystal stream. I cannot wait for that day.

THE GOD THAT HAS EVERYTHING

Psalms 50:12
"If I were hungry, I would not tell thee:
for the world is mine, and the fulness thereof."

Think about it. It is time to give your husband a present for his birthday. You realize that his closets and drawers are full, his car is beautiful and fully loaded, and he earns a substantial income. What do you give a man who has everything?

We all must ask this question in regard to the Lord. We read a lot in the Bible about bringing gifts to the Lord. We read a lot about giving Him sacrifices and dedicating our lives to Him but really, what do you give to God who has everything? He even said it. The earth is His and everything in it. Not only that, He owns all humanity.

Rather than leaving us to grope around in the darkness, He told us in the scriptures what He likes. Are you ready? "Offer unto God thanksgiving; and pay thy vows unto the most High: And call upon me in the day of trouble: I will deliver thee, and thou shalt glorify me." Psalms 50:14, 15. "By him therefore let us offer the sacrifice of praise to God continually, that is, the fruit of our lips giving thanks to his name." Hebrews 13:15. Praise! The answer is praise. What do you give the God who has everything? Give Him sincere, heartfelt, fervent praise. *This* makes Him happy.

"Praise ye the LORD. Praise God in his sanctuary: praise him in the firmament of his power. Praise him for his mighty acts: praise him according to his excellent greatness. Praise him with the sound of the trumpet: praise him with the psaltery and harp. Praise him with the timbrel and dance: praise him with stringed instruments and organs. Praise him upon the loud cymbals: praise him upon the high sounding cymbals. Let every thing that hath breath praise the LORD. Praise ye the LORD." Psalms 150:1-6.

WHEN GOD WRITES

Psalm 51:9
"Hide thy face from my sins,
and blot out all mine iniquities."

Mary Magdalene was taken to Jesus and thrown at His feet as some hypocritical men thought to do away with both her and Jesus in one encounter. They sought to entrap Him by saying that this woman was caught in the very act of adultery and asking what they should do. They said that Moses' law stated that she should be stoned, but wanted to know what He would suggest. They thought to either have Jesus unjustly punish someone in a society ruled by Rome or openly disagree with the Law of Moses. In either case, their purpose would have been served. Jesus would have been cast in a poor light. They also wanted to cover their own sins while punishing a woman whom some say the men fornicated with. If they were successful in their plotting, two of their enemies would no longer be with them.

Instead of Jesus responding to them directly, He began doing something that struck the men as odd. "But Jesus stooped down, and with his finger wrote on the ground as though he heard them not. So when they continued asking him, he lifted up himself, and said unto them, He that is without sin among you, let him first cast a stone at her. And again he stooped down, and wrote on the ground. And they which heard it, being convicted by their own conscience, went out one by one, beginning at the eldest, even unto the last: and Jesus was left alone, and the woman standing in the midst." John 8:6-9. By writing the sins of these accusers on the ground, Jesus demonstrated an important biblical teaching. "And I saw the dead, small and great, stand before God; and the books were opened: and another book was opened, which is the book of life: and the dead were judged out of those things which were written in the books, according to their works." Revelation 20:12. Soon the Lord will judge the wicked from His book of recorded evil deeds. If an individual does not have their sins blotted out through faith in Jesus, then the record of them will seal their condemnation. Conversely, if an individual has their name written in the book of life in the end, by faith in Jesus their salvation is sealed. What does this mean for Mary? If you notice, the Lord did not write anything down concerning her. In fact, Jesus said that He did not condemn her, and told her to go and sin no more. The fact that the accusers' sins were written means that they were unrepentant; therefore all they could do was leave the Lord's presence.

How is it with us? Do we accept the power of God to be forgiven and cleansed of our unrighteousness? Do we accept the power of God to live victorious lives? He says to those who accept His love, "Neither do I condemn thee: go, and sin no more." John 8:11. David said it well when he wrote, "Blessed are they whose iniquities are forgiven, and whose sins are covered. Blessed is the man to whom the Lord will not impute sin." Romans 4:7, 8.

Only in the Lord

Psalms 62:7
"In God is my salvation and my glory: the rock of my strength, and my refuge, is in God."

Only in the Lord do we find peace in the time of trouble. Only in the Lord do we find stability when all the ground around us is as the shifting seismic plates of the western U. S. Only in the Lord can we put our trust. He has demonstrated His faithfulness to human kind from the beginning, in the Eden of old. He created all things perfectly and when Adam sinned, He enacted His plan of salvation so that, one day, we could live with Him in paradise without sin unto salvation.

The blessing of all is that we do not need to search high and low for the best possible candidate for salvation and refuge. Jesus is the only one that provides ultimate protection, strength and salvation. All others are imitators. Only in the *Lord* can we place our trust. He will never disappoint those who love and worship Him.

UNQUENCHABLE THIRST

Psalms 63:1, 2
"O God, thou art my God; early will I seek thee: my soul thirsteth for thee, my flesh longeth for thee in a dry and thirsty land, where no water is; To see thy power and thy glory, so as I have seen thee in the sanctuary."

Until we long for the Lord just as an animal lost in the desert would long for water, we will not receive the blessing of living water. Until His presence is so vital to us that we would stop at nothing just to hear *a* word from Him, we will always hunger and thirst. Nothing else will satisfy. Until we have experienced the power and presence of God in our lives, we are not capable of beginning to understand how vitally important a relationship with God is.

In the Psalms, David often uses the imagery of water to describe various facets of a relationship with God. Here are two examples: "Blessed is the man that walketh not in the counsel of the ungodly, nor standeth in the way of sinners, nor sitteth in the seat of the scornful. But his delight is in the law of the LORD; and in his law doth he meditate day and night. And he shall be like a tree planted by the rivers of water, that bringeth forth his fruit in his season; his leaf also shall not wither; and whatsoever he doeth shall prosper." Psalms 1:1-3. "As the hart panteth after the water brooks, so panteth my soul after thee, O God. My soul thirsteth for God, for the living God: when shall I come and appear before God?" Psalms 42:1, 2. Since our bodies are made up of a high percentage of water, the relationship between our need for God and our need for water is apparent.

I long for the day when I will desire the Lord consistently, as a parched traveler who had nothing to drink for three days. I realize that the Lord supplies even our desire to have a closer relationship with Him. I trust that He will give that blessing to me because He never withholds good gifts from His children.

BE GLAD

Psalms 68:3
"But let the righteous be glad; let them rejoice before
God: yea, let them exceedingly rejoice."

It is a blessing to live before a holy God with a clear conscience. How many times have you known God's will in a particular situation and gone against it? In those instances, did God simply allow you to continue on your course or did He let you know that His will was otherwise? Those who continue to follow self rather than God eventually lose their ability to hear His voice, and at some point, He ceases to call. It is very difficult to get to that point, however, it should not be taken for granted that God will always be available. "Seek ye the LORD while he may be found, call ye upon him while he is near:" Isaiah 55:6. "And the LORD said, My spirit shall not always strive with man, for that he also is flesh: yet his days shall be an hundred and twenty years." Genesis 6:3. This principle is clearly seen in the story of Noah. The Lord always has a probationary period set for humankind. In some cases He reveals it, and in others He does not.

David wrote about the final vindication of God's character and cause. Often it seemed like the wicked were allowed to flourish. It seemed as though God would let wickedness overcome good. In David's praise to God, he looked forward to the day when God would settle all opposition. "Let God arise, let his enemies be scattered: let them also that hate him flee before him. As smoke is driven away, so drive them away: as wax melteth before the fire, so let the wicked perish at the presence of God. But let the righteous be glad; let them rejoice before God: yea, let them exceedingly rejoice. Sing unto God, sing praises to his name: extol him that rideth upon the heavens by his name JAH, and rejoice before him." Psalms 68:1-4.

One day soon, we will fully see the justice of God. He will vanquish His enemies. For many years He called to His enemies, yet they ignored and rejected Him. He gave His life for them that they might have eternal life, but they would not be convinced of their need. He fought for them, but they fought against Him in return. Soon they will see the cost of their error. He is not willing that anyone loses their souls, but some are resolute to be lost. Pray that we will choose to accept Jesus' righteousness. It is in true love and faith in God that we are made glad.

THE CLEANSING

Psalms 69:9
"For the zeal of thine house hath eaten me up;
and the reproaches of them that reproached thee
are fallen upon me."

The temple of the Lord is His dwelling place. Anywhere the Lord dwells is holy. If *we* are to be His dwelling place, it is reasonable for Him to expect us to be holy.

In the Old Testament, the Lord told Moses to have His people build a sanctuary so He could dwell among them. When Moses was summoned into the mount to commune with God, He gave him the blueprints for the sanctuary, which was to be built after the pattern of the heavenly sanctuary. Can you imagine how it must have affected the Lord when, on so many occasions, the sanctuary and its services were taken lightly? Can you imagine how it was for Him when Eli's sons offered strange fire on the altar, or when King Uzziah took it upon himself to offer incense though he was not a priest? These acts were unacceptable and the Lord dealt with them swiftly.

Jesus shared the zeal of the Father concerning His sanctuary. "And said unto them, It is written, My house shall be called the house of prayer; but ye have made it a den of thieves." Matthew 21:13. When He discovered the leaders of the people in the holy temple taking advantage of the poor and downtrodden, it inspired holy indignation within Him, and He chased them from the temple. The defilement of the temple was reprehensible to Him. It was never intended for common use.

"What? know ye not that your body is the temple of the Holy Ghost which is in you, which ye have of God, and ye are not your own? For ye are bought with a price: therefore glorify God in your body, and in your spirit, which are

God's." I Corinthians 6:19, 20. It is with the same zeal that God thinks of His people. We are to be His dwelling place. We are not our own. The Lord Jesus gave His life and risked eternity for us, yet sometimes we defile our soul temples. "Do not ye yet understand, that whatsoever entereth in at the mouth goeth into the belly, and is cast out into the draught? But those things which proceed out of the mouth come forth from the heart; and they defile the man. For out of the heart proceed evil thoughts, murders, adulteries, fornications, thefts, false witness, blasphemies." Matthew 15:17-19. It is because of these character flaws that Jesus died. When we accept the sacrifice of Jesus in our behalf, the process of cleansing us from sin begins. As we walk with Him daily, we become more like Him. The difference between our soul temples and the temple in Jerusalem is that Jesus will not come in to us uninvited. He will not throw over the tables of the moneychangers and chase them away without our consent. "Behold, I stand at the door, and knock: if any man hear my voice, and open the door, I will come in to him, and will sup with him, and he with me" Revelation 3:20.

Day after day, the Lord wants to cleanse us in every way. It is a blessing when we open the door of our hearts by His grace, and let Him in. When Jesus lives within us, the temple is complete. We are created to commune with God and He is pleased when we let Him in.

I NEED HIM

Psalms 73:25
"Whom have I in heaven but thee? and there is none
upon earth that I desire beside thee."

This text is powerful. I suppose it goes without saying; after all, it is the word of God, but this one is particularly powerful because it gives priority to Him. There is no one, anywhere, in heaven or on the earth that satisfies like God.

For thousands of years, the Lord has made a career, so to speak, of satisfying needy souls. He is more filling than the best food. He quenches the dry soul more than any spring or well of water. He gives more rest than the most comfortable bed. He is more loving than the most compassionate spouse. He is more understanding than the greatest mother. He is more of a blessing than one thousand greeting cards. He is God and I need Him. *I* need Him.

We all need to praise Him more. He has done great things. If we were to praise Him every hour of the day, He would still be worthy of more praise. If we had two thousand tongues, each telling a different story of His goodness, it would not be enough. Angels bow before Him. Devils tremble at the sound of His name. When He is in the room, diseases cannot continue to afflict people. It is no wonder that David said he did not desire any on the earth more than he desired God. When you have the best person in the universe as your friend, who can replace Him?

If we give the Lord more praise each day, the gloom of life's darkest midnights would completely pass away. There would only be light as He permeates our being. We are blessed in that, God is willing to make friends with us through the ministry of Jesus Christ. What would we do without Him? We need Him. He is our everything.

THE WAY

Psalms 77:13
"Thy way, O God, is in the sanctuary:
who is so great a God as our God?"

The Old Testament sanctuary was God's way of teaching the gospel of Jesus Christ to the children of Israel. Through this means, they were to understand the eternal weight of sin, the blessing of salvation, and the love of God. All of this would be taught by pointing forward to Jesus Christ.

The weight of sin was revealed, in that Jesus was not spared the punishment intended for sinners because He became sin for us (Romans 8:32). He took our sins to the grave and died the second death on our behalf.

The blessing of salvation is revealed, in that Christ alone could become the propitiation for our sins. He became our substitute, because the Father wanted to save us. The only way we could be saved was if someone greater than or equal to the law that was transgressed by humankind, took on the eternal penalty for our sin. Jesus fit the requirements and He decided to take our sins all the way to Calvary.

The love of God was revealed in the details of the sanctuary. God specified the exact path one must travel to be forgiven of sin and cleansed from all unrighteousness. If anyone faithfully followed His command, they were certain to be restored into right relationship with Him.

As you can see, the sanctuary message is important. Every sacrifice, material, and piece of furniture pointed forward to Jesus. The very sanctuary itself represented Him. He was the dwelling place of the Father therefore, He too was the temple of God (John 2:19-21).

For anyone to approach the presence of God in the sanctuary, they must pass through the veil into the holy of holies. The only way for that to happen was for someone to go in for us, or someone to come out to us. Jesus met the requirement perfectly. "Having therefore, brethren, boldness to enter into the holiest by the blood of Jesus, By a new and living way, which he hath consecrated for us, through the veil, that is to say, his flesh; And having an high priest over the house of God; Let us draw near with a true heart in full assurance of faith, having our hearts sprinkled from an evil conscience, and our bodies washed with pure water. Let us hold fast the profession of our faith without wavering; (for he is faithful that promised;)" Hebrews 10:19-23.

Even in the Old Testament, the way of salvation was through Christ. Today, let us hold fast to Jesus Christ. When we do so, we will know the way. "Jesus saith unto him, I am the way, the truth, and the life: no man cometh unto the Father, but by me." John 14:6.

HE IS MY REFUGE

Psalms 91:2
"I will say of the LORD, He is my refuge and my fortress: my God; in him will I trust."

The Lord is our help in times of trouble. When the enemy assails us with trials and temptations, it is important to remember that the Lord is our refuge and fortress. When we are hid in Him, the enemy cannot harm us. It is said of the Lord that, "Surely he shall deliver thee from the snare of the fowler, and from the noisome pestilence. He shall cover thee with his feathers, and under his wings shalt thou trust: his truth shall be thy shield and buckler. Thou shalt not be afraid for the terror by night; nor for the arrow that flieth by day; Nor for the pestilence that walketh in darkness; nor for the destruction that wasteth at noonday. A thousand shall fall at thy side, and ten thousand at thy right hand; but it shall not come nigh thee." Psalms 91:3-7.

The Lord is our refuge in the midst of trouble. He does not always deliver us from trouble, *but* He *will* always be with us *in* our trouble. The three Hebrew boys are a good example of this. God could have chosen not to allow the wicked Babylonians to throw three Hebrew boys into the fiery furnace; instead, He chose to allow it. The blessing of it all was that Jesus was in the fire with them, and not a flame was set upon them, nor was there the smell of smoke on their clothes.

In the end, if we choose to let the Lord be our fortress, He will protect us as He sees fit. Ultimately, He protects our souls from condemnation and prepares us for heaven. This is the most important. I thank God that He has not left me exposed and unprotected to the enemy's attacks. He is truly our refuge in times of trouble.

WORSHIP HIM

Psalms 95:6
"O come, let us worship and bow down:
let us kneel before the LORD our maker."

Worship is perhaps the greatest issue at the center of the controversy between God and Satan over the souls of humanity. Both powers desire worship. God gives the opportunity to everyone to worship Him based on His being Creator and Redeemer of the world (Revelation 14:7, Revelation 22:17). This is to be a voluntary worship based on love. On the other hand, the devil wants worship that does not belong to him. Rather than operating on the principle of love, he attempts to force it (Revelation 13).

If you had the opportunity to choose between two relationships—one that was based on love, the other based on force, which would you choose? I choose love. It is amazing that day after day, people turn away from the loving relationship of Jesus Christ, to the cold listless arms of an unnatural high with the devil. We sometimes choose evil entertainment, unholy partnerships, drugs, sex, and pride, above God. The devil makes incredible promises of fame, fortune, and a good time, only to leave you by the side of the road used and condemned. He is the master of abusive relationships. Constantly, he comes and molests those who choose him, and when things really get out of control, he attempts to quiet the conscience by promising a better tomorrow. Those under his spell often send the Holy Spirit away from the situation, just as many women send the police away after calling them to a domestic disturbance when the abusive man threatens them or promises to behave. This is not the way a worship relationship is supposed to be.

When we worship God from a heart of gratitude, He *adds* to our lives. He brings the peace of heaven and waters us, as refreshing rains water the parched earth. He does not make promises that He cannot keep. His word is reliable.

"For he is our God; and we are the people of his pasture, and the sheep of his hand. To day if ye will hear his voice, Harden not your heart, as in the provocation, and as in the day of temptation in the wilderness: When your fathers tempted me, proved me, and saw my work." Psalms 95:7-9. Let the overwhelming love and respect God has for you compel you to worship Him. In every aspect of your life, choose God. The devil will only use you and leave you to die.

ONLY THROUGH REVERENCE

Psalms 111:10
"The fear of the LORD is the beginning of wisdom:
a good understanding have all they that do his
commandments: his praise endureth for ever."

Many seek wisdom in places where it may not be found. Many years are spent studying the philosophies of self-proclaimed atheists. In order to instruct young preachers, even theologians often quote their words. Wisdom is sometimes sought from psycics and palm readers, who, equally, cannot offer the kind of wisdom that leads to life.

God gives us the simple key to wisdom. He said that the fear of the Lord is the *beginning* of wisdom. That is, the very first step in receiving godly wisdom is to reverence His holy name. "He sent redemption unto his people: he hath commanded his covenant for ever: holy and reverend is his name." Psalms 111:9. As we learn to appreciate the Lord, as did the wise king, Solomon, He opens our minds to the mysteries of heaven. We become acquainted with the *person* of wisdom, Jesus Christ Himself (I Corinthians 1:30). As long as we remain close to the Lord and accept the counsel of all of His commandments, we will not be short of understanding.

Thank the Lord today for His word and willingness to give us wisdom. Meditate on His character, seek Him with all of your heart, receive His counsel by faith, and you will prosper.

SIMPLY PRAISE THE LORD

Psalms 113:3
"From the rising of the sun unto the going down of the
same the LORD's name is to be praised."

It is a wonderful privilege for the people of God to render praise to Him. It is in our praise that we are able to tell Him how much we love Him. It is in our praise that we witness to others who do not know Him, that God is worthy of our respect and adoration. It is through our praise that we share with fellow believers the special aroma of complete satisfaction with the way God orchestrates our affairs. He loves us, and we honor Him by sharing our love with Him through praise.

The children of Israel sometimes rendered praise to God, and their enemies were vanquished. The three Hebrew boys praised the Lord with their strict obedience, and as a result, King Nebuchadnezzar saw one like the Son of God walking in the midst of the fiery furnace with them (Daniel 3:25). Praise to, and appreciation for God caused the apostles to rejoice. "And they departed from the presence of the council, rejoicing that they were counted worthy to suffer shame for his name." Acts 5:41.

Why should we praise Him? Is it because He created all things, and without Him was not anything made that was made? Should we honor Him because He gives us food and water in due season? Maybe we should praise Him because He saw fit to give us the great sacrifice of Jesus Christ as eternal payment for our sins. What ever we choose to praise Him for, He is certainly worthy. If He never performed another miracle, if He never bestowed another blessing, He is due our praise.

Think of Him all day long, and every time you remember how wonderful He has been, simply praise the Lord. He is worthy!

WALKING BEFORE THE LORD

Psalms 116:8, 9
"For thou hast delivered my soul from death, mine eyes from tears, and my feet from falling. I will walk before the LORD in the land of the living."

David, the apple of God's eye, had a way of seeking after Him with his entire heart (Psalm 17:8). Oftentimes, the circumstances that inspired David's zeal had to do with his enemies viciously assailing him. Even his mind was full of trouble, and sometimes betrayed him, as an enemy would.

David's passion causes me to marvel often. How could a man who saw so much suffering and death because of his own disobedience, focus his eyes on the Lord? I know many people seek the Lord when they encounter strait places, but often when the trouble passes, their pursuit of God ceases. This was not the case with David. It seems that he did not let a day pass without humbling himself before the Lord, and like Mary Magdalene pour himself out at Jesus' feet.

Did David understand something important that we all need to grasp? There must have been a reason for his unwavering pursuit of God. Certainly, the overwhelming motivator was his appreciation and love for God. Time after time, the Lord delivered him in spite of his errors. I believe that David understood that his enemies would ultimately be powerless before him when he was humble before God. The best position to be in while living on this wicked planet is at the feet of Jesus. The most glorified position to assume is humility before Him. If we live in constant connection with God, we become an impenetrable fortress against the fiery darts of Satan. We become partakers in the victories that Jesus won while living on earth. The devil aimed his most destructive temptations at Jesus, and He came forth from the midst of them a conquering King. The victory of Jesus becomes ours when we put implicit trust in Him. This, my friends, is what David understood. This is what stimulated his appetite for godly things. Let us follow the example of David, and walk humbly before the Lord.

SIMPLY REJOICE

Psalms 118:24
"This is the day which the LORD hath made; we will rejoice and be glad in it."

King David was a great example, perhaps the greatest example, of a thankful believer in the Old Testament. He wrote and sang a countless number of songs to God about His love and tender mercies. He remembered the great sin that he committed against God, Uriah, and Bathsheba. He realized that much of the trouble that he faced during his rule was a natural consequence of that sin. Because of his sin, he lost one of his sons to the cold hands of an early death. He was often in distress because of his sin, but He never gave up on the Lord. He realized that natural consequences did not have to bleed over into the supernatural. He knew that if he would just have faith in God and praise Him for all that He was doing, that everything would be fine.

In one of his Psalms, David spoke of this day being made by the Lord and it appears that he was saying that we should rejoice simply because God had made it. In the midst of his recounting the troubles that he was facing, he constantly referred to praising and giving thanks to God. "Thou art my God, and I will praise thee: thou art my God, I will exalt thee. O give thanks unto the LORD; for he is good: for his mercy endureth for ever." Psalms 118:28, 29. He did not allow the evil pursuits of his enemies to keep him down. Rather, he chose to see God as the most wonderful and just judge, worthy of worship.

David said to give thanks to the Lord because God made this day. God made this day as an opportunity for all to have faith in Him. God made this day, for all to love and enjoy His company, God made this very day, for all to forget about the trials that come our way, but focus on how good God has been. Go created this day, for all to rejoice and be glad in it. Rather than being downcast because of troubles, *simply* rejoice.

Only the Lord Can Teach Them

Psalms 119:33, 34
"Teach me, O LORD, the way of thy statutes;
and I shall keep it unto the end.
Give me understanding, and I shall keep thy law;
yea, I shall observe it with my whole heart."

When the Lord descended upon Mount Sinai to speak His famous ten words, His eternal commandments, He was revealing His character in a concise format. The commandments are a transcript, a window into the character of God. They are the only safe governing principles by which we may live. This is why it was curious when the children of Israel responded to Moses concerning God's laws, judgments, and statutes, by saying, whatever the Lord said, they would do. On the surface, it was a good response. It is good to do the Lord's will. When Moses came from communing with the Lord, the problem was obvious, they would attempt to keep the law in their own power. As we well know, it was not long before they failed miserably at keeping it.

As the nation of Israel progressed, different groups within their tribes became extreme in their attempt to follow the letter of the law, to the point of making over six hundred additional laws as an addendum to what the Lord commanded. They thought that if they could master good behavior, that it would make them worthy of salvation; therefore, they prided themselves in the observance of their rules.

Jesus came to clear up the misconceptions about God's character. He revealed a God that loves us so much as to sacrifice *all* in order that we might be saved. In His discourse in another mount, Jesus reframed the eternal ten-commandment law by focussing in on its spirituality. He said, "Ye have heard that it was said by them of old time, Thou shalt not commit adultery: But I say unto you, That whosoever looketh on a woman to lust after her hath committed adultery with her already in his heart." Matthew 5:27, 28. He brought to blinding light the fact that the law is not about external expression only, which in some ways may be performed regardless of spiritual commitment. The law is about our heart condition toward the Lord, expressed in the way that we live. *Now* it makes sense why David said, "Teach me, O LORD, the way of thy statutes; and I shall keep it unto the end. Give me understanding, and I shall keep thy law; yea, I shall observe it with my whole heart." Psalms 119:33, 34. He realized that only the Lord could teach what it means to keep His commandments. He understood that, "For we know that the law is spiritual: but I am carnal, sold under sin. Wherefore the law is holy, and the commandment holy, and just, and good." Romans 7:14, 12.

Without the Lord keeping the New Covenant within us, we are simply incapable of pleasing Him. We cannot begin to comprehend His law. Remember that it is a micro revelation of His character; therefore it is as high above us as the heavens are high above the earth. I pray with David that the Lord will teach me His law and that I will keep and observe it with my whole heart.

HIS COMMANDMENTS ARE TRUTH

Psalms 119:151
"Thou art near, O LORD;
and all thy commandments are truth."

It is important to note in a time of incredible injustice and blatant disregard for law, that David spoke volumes in few words regarding truth. He said that all of God's commandments are truth. We do not need to be confused by the prevalence of lies and deceit in society. We need not be taken in by the effort of many religious groups to make the law of God of none effect. All of His commandments are *still* truth.

The Bible gives us a view of God's will, which we must search out. As we do this, we become closer to Him daily. Every word, including the Ten Commandment law should be followed inasmuch as the Lord empowers us to do so. Jesus said, "Ye are my friends, if ye do whatsoever I command you." John 14:15.

The unfortunate reality of our day is that many would have us believe that God's will is ambiguous and vague. They would have us believe that it changes with the times. The great thing about truth is that it cannot be influenced by any outside agency. By its very nature, it must remain consistent otherwise it ceases to be truth. This means that when God gives us truth, we can rest on it. We can be certain that the only thing that will change is our understanding of it. As we grow in our knowledge of truth, the Lord gives us more grace to live by it. The simple message for today is that the truth of God's holy commandments, including the ten, are abiding principles even in the last days. As the character of God remains, so does His truth.

FAR BEYOND THE HILLS

Psalms 121:7, 8
"The LORD shall preserve thee from all evil:
he shall preserve thy soul. The LORD shall preserve thy
going out and thy coming in from this time forth,
and even for evermore."

Far beyond the hills is the holy mountain of God. His throne is heaven and His footstool is the earth. David opens his Psalm with this statement: "I will lift up mine eyes unto the hills, from whence cometh my help. My help cometh from the LORD, which made heaven and earth." Psalms 121:1, 2. Far beyond the hills of human devising, beyond the hills of trust in other gods, is the hill of the Lord, from whence comes our help. From His vantage point, He can see all of the events of our lives equally and at the same time. He is able to manage them in righteousness, while patiently bringing us into conformity to His will. He loves us; therefore, while we are asleep, He is wide awake. He loves us; therefore, the burning sun of affliction is not enough to deter God. It shall not scorch those who trust in Him. We shall come through the trials without even the odor of smoke upon us.

When we pray for guidance and strength, let us focus our prayers beyond the hills of this world to the holy mountain of God's throne and "The LORD shall preserve thee from all evil: he shall preserve thy soul. The LORD shall preserve thy going out and thy coming in from this time forth, and even for evermore." Psalms 121:7, 8.

A BLESSED GIFT

Psalms 127:3
"Lo, children are an heritage of the LORD:
and the fruit of the womb is his reward."

Can you imagine how many of our children would feel loved and appreciated if parents truly believed this verse? How many parents would be more submissive in seeking the Lord's face if they understood the immense responsibility of rearing the children that God has entrusted to them? The abortion issue would become a non-issue, if more people valued children as the heritage of the Lord, even in the womb. If we valued children more than we do, this world would be a better place.

Sometimes parents allow work and other activities to take up so much of their time that the children are neglected. They do not have family worship consistently because they are too busy running hither and yon. Our society is declining almost exponentially, because our children are often not treated as the precious gifts that they are.

You may wonder how children are mistreated as I described. After all, don't most people look out for children? Even if children are not overtly neglected, instead of spending quality time with them, far too often, the television is the babysitter. Violent and mystical video games are purchased and given to them to absorb their minds, and the Bible is scarcely taught or read. We serve fats and sweets in excess, and putrefying meats at the dinner table, while the children's growing minds and bodies need the proper nutrition of fruits, nuts, grains, and vegetables. Disrespect of children is not always related to overt malicious treatment, it creeps into our homes in the form of everyday actions that are not supported by God.

All of us, even those who have no children, can show

appreciation to God, by assuring them that they are valued with a kind word, loving hug, or quality time spent in relationship-building. A child is a blessed gift. If our children are our future, it is a good idea to treat them that way. It is a good idea to invest godly love into their lives. One day the fruit of our labor will be manifested as they make this world a better place.

PRECIOUS OINTMENT

Psalms 133:1-3
"Behold, how good and how pleasant it is for brethren to dwell together in unity! It is like the precious ointment upon the head, that ran down upon the beard, even Aaron's beard: that went down to the skirts of his garments; As the dew of Hermon, and as the dew that descended upon the mountains of Zion: for there the LORD commanded the blessing, even life for evermore."

Godly and biblical unity is an irresistible invitation to the Holy Ghost to dwell amongst us. He said, "Follow peace with all men, and holiness, without which no man shall see the Lord:" Hebrews 12:14.

Following His resurrection, Christ told His followers to wait in Jerusalem until the promise of the Holy Ghost came. When they were on one accord, the Bible says that the Holy Ghost gave them the gifts of diverse tongues. When the followers of Christ spoke, each person understood what was being said in their own language. The apostles preached Christ and Him crucified. The power that attended their work brought thousands of souls to God in one day. The power of the Holy Ghost that washed over the apostles was like precious ointment used to heal wounds. He used them in a way never before seen on this planet.

The Lord wants to use us mightily as well. For His glory, He would have us receive the power of the Holy Ghost even greater than that of the days of the apostles. I want the anointing power of God. How about you? He stands ready to give it in order to empower us to lead others to Jesus. "If ye then, being evil, know how to give good gifts unto your children: how much more shall your heavenly Father give the Holy Spirit to them that ask him?" Luke 11:13.

HE ALONE IS WORTHY

Psalms 138:1, 2
"I will praise thee with my whole heart:
before the gods will I sing praise unto thee.
I will worship toward thy holy temple, and praise thy
name for thy lovingkindness and for thy truth:
for thou hast magnified thy word above all thy name."

Not all roads lead to heaven. You may have heard it said, that it does not matter what you call God it is all the same. King David resisted that idea. He lived during a time when there were so many gods it was impossible to count them. The children of Israel were plagued with the disease of idolatry and the Lord had to correct them regularly. He even showed by means of miracles that He was the only true God in the universe.

In David's praise, we see a stark opposition to the idea that just any god will do. He praised the God of *heaven* as superior. He said that he would praise *His* name among the many gods. David knew of the times when Jehovah had to prove that He was superior to Pharaoh, Nebuchadnezzar, Dagon, Molech, Baal, and others. Those who worshipped these inferior gods were always disappointed. When God's people were obedient, those in the surrounding heathen nations took note. They recognized that the God of Israel had no match in the entire universe.

David said that he would worship toward the temple. The sanctuary was a monument to the creative and sustaining power of God. Through its services, He taught Israel the gospel of Jesus Christ. As they faithfully continued to honor the ceremonies, the picture of the coming Messiah became clearer. The signal of God's presence was the Ark of the Covenant located in the holy of holies. The ark was situated in the west. The heathen nations usually worshipped the rising sun, which was in the eastern direction. This means that even their physical posture in worship was opposite of their enemies.

At this time in earth's history, the true and correct worship of God through Jesus Christ is relevant and important to maintain. It is important to resist the idea that just any god will do. The Creator of us all is the *only* one worthy of our worship, and it is our privilege to honor Him in that way. "Hear, O Israel: The LORD our God is one LORD: And thou shalt love the LORD thy God with all thine heart, and with all thy soul, and with all thy might." Deuteronomy 6:4, 5. "I am the LORD: that is my name: and my glory will I not give to another, neither my praise to graven images." Isaiah 42:8.

WONDERFULLY MADE

Psalms 139:14
***"I will praise thee; for I am fearfully and wonderfully
made: marvellous are thy works; and that
my soul knoweth right well."***

The thought for today is more in the form of a personal
testimony. At the time of this writing, for three weeks, I
have been going through a physical cleansing. The discoveries I have made are quite humbling. My mind is lifted
toward God even as I sit and type.

I have been in good health for as long as I can remember, but I realized that the bodies God has entrusted us with
should often go through certain types of cleansing. With this
most recent one, I experienced a revelation into how merciful God is. I wonder, knowing what I now know, how it is
possible for God to create an organism that is so durable and
resilient. I have good habits of hygiene, rest, exercise,
eating, etc., yet I found that my body, even after more than
two weeks of raw and no food at all was holding all manner
of potentially dangerous matter. The blessing in all of this
is, God somehow allowed me to get vitamins, minerals, and
nutrients from the food I was eating. It is a wonder how I
derived any benefit from my food.

I know that this is a weird way for you to spend your
time, reading about someone else's experience, but isn't that
what it is all about? Isn't it encouraging when we hear
someone's testimony? The Bible says that God's people
overcome the devil by the blood of the Lamb, and by the
word of their testimony. I testify to the Lord's tender
mercies, and His willingness to preserve human life, even
when we sometimes diverge from the path of natural law.

If you get anything at all from this today, please know that
the Lord has been masterful in creating the bodies and minds

He has entrusted us with. It would be a good idea to treat His creation with respect and humility. Ask the Lord how to treat yourself and make you the spiritual vessel He intended you to be. I promise you that if you seek Him diligently, He will respond. "Whether therefore ye eat, or drink, or whatsoever ye do, do all to the glory of God." I Corinthians 10:31.

TRUST ONLY IN THE LORD

Psalms 146:3, 4
*"Put not your trust in princes, nor in the son of man,
in whom there is no help. His breath goeth forth,
he returneth to his earth; in that very day
his thoughts perish."*

There was a point during the time of ancient Israel, that they were not satisfied with God as their absolute king and ruler. They wanted to have a human being on the throne just as the heathens did, and God was not pleased. He gave them explicit counsel concerning the consequences of their desire through His prophet, but they did not heed the warnings. According to God's permissive will, though He did not intend it to be so from the beginning, He gave them kings, and the consequences were realized almost immediately. It is never a good idea to put our trust in the strength of men.

Many years had lapsed since God anointed the first king to rule over Israel. Uzziah ascended the throne, and reigned in Jerusalem for fifty-two years. "In the year that King Uzziah died I saw also the Lord sitting upon a throne, high and lifted up, and his train filled the temple." Isaiah 6:1. It must have bee discouraging for the people of God when king Uzziah died. For many years, he ruled under the favor and direction of God. "And he sought God in the days of Zechariah, who had understanding in the visions of God: and as long as he sought the LORD, God made him to prosper." II Chronicles 26:5. Who would not want a king to rule over them that had the favor of God? It appeared that under the leadership of this king, Israel would be invincible.

"But when he was strong, his heart was lifted up to his destruction: for he transgressed against the LORD his God, and went into the temple of the LORD to burn incense upon the altar of incense. And Azariah the priest went in after him, and with him fourscore priests of the LORD, that were valiant men: And they withstood Uzziah the king, and said unto him, It appertaineth not unto thee, Uzziah, to burn incense unto the LORD, but to the priests the sons of Aaron, that are consecrated to burn incense: go out of the sanctuary; for thou hast trespassed; neither shall it be for thine honour from the LORD God. Then Uzziah was wroth, and had a censer in his hand to burn incense: and while he was wroth with the priests, the leprosy even rose up in his forehead before the priests in the house of the LORD, from beside the incense altar." II Chronicles 26:16-19. After all of that, the great king Uzziah died. Understanding the reason this king died may have been even more discouraging to the people than the fact that he died. Like Lucifer, he allowed his pride to lead him down the path to destruction.

The Lord saw the need of His people during this time of sadness. They had lost the leadership that they had grown accustomed to putting their faith in. Who would lead them now? Would the next king bring them the protection and prosperity they desired? The Lord gave Isaiah a vision of the mighty God of heaven. He was taken into the bewildering presence of the only true potentate of the universe. Isaiah needed to understand that God was still on the throne and in control of the affairs of men. Isaiah recognized his own unworthiness and received the blessing, cleansing, and commission of God. He understood clearly now, beyond any other time, the importance of trusting only in the Lord. Israel would endure many hard years because of their distrust of God, and Isaiah would be His mouthpiece.

Learn form the experience of Israel. God alone is worthy of absolute trust. When we are faithful to Him, He is faithful to deliver us.

Just Say No

Proverbs 1:10
"My son, if sinners entice thee, consent thou not."

Solomon wrote some of the briefest, yet wisest words in the Bible. He said a lot with few words. If sinners try to persuade you to do evil, don't do it. Can an admonition be any simpler?

On television in the eighties, I remember hearing a slogan about staying away from drugs—"Just say no! Then go! And tell!" It was catchy and memorable. I think there is a lot of religion in those few words. If I had to apply them to my spiritual life, I would say when the temptation to sin arises, just say no. When the temptation to sin arises, then go. When the temptation to sin arises, just tell the Lord all about it. All of this may seem too elementary, but it is through faith and simplicity that we are able to remain in good relationship with God.

Have we lost the childlike faith that many of us had when we first accepted Christ? That childlike faith kept us far away from evil activities, and from indulging to please our friends? Peer pressure does not affect school-aged children only. It affects all of us in some way or another. The simple word for today is to let the Lord be you guide, and "Submit yourselves therefore to God. Resist the devil, and he will flee from you. Draw nigh to God, and he will draw nigh to you." James 4:7, 8.

THE BEGINNING OF KNOWLEDGE

Proverbs 1:7
"The fear of the LORD is the beginning of knowledge:
but fools despise wisdom and instruction."

Show me someone with minimal formal education, but loves the Lord with all of their heart, and I will show you one of the wisest persons on the planet. Conversely, show me an astrophysicist that has no regard for God, and I will show you a fool.

God's accounting of wisdom, knowledge, and understanding is far different than ours. He measures them by how much we love, honor, and respect Him. Righteous King David said, "O how love I thy law! it is my meditation all the day. Thou through thy commandments hast made me wiser than mine enemies: for they are ever with me. I have more understanding than all my teachers: for thy testimonies are my meditation. I understand more than the ancients, because I keep thy precepts." Psalms 119:97-100. It is only as we worship the Lord with everything that we are, that our striving for knowledge is worthwhile. In Him, we receive the understanding of our need to be brought closer to Him that we might become better people for His glory. The wicked would rather find comfort in their own competence and accomplishments. Sadly, because of their pride, they resist the knowledge of God. I pray that all of us will learn to submit ourselves to God and be humble enough to receive the understanding of His truth. He is willing to give it. Are you ready to receive it?

FINDING THE KNOWLEDGE OF GOD

Proverbs 2:4, 5
"If thou seekest her as silver, and searchest for her as for
hid treasures; Then shalt thou understand the fear
of the LORD, and find the knowledge of God."

Solomon was the wisest man living in his day, and his admonition is proof. He was a man, though plagued with sin, as we all are, who knew what it was to seek after God. Solomon is the one who said, "The fear of the LORD is the beginning of knowledge: but fools despise wisdom and instruction." Proverbs 1:7. It seems that he had a healthy obsession with godly wisdom.

Many are in hot pursuit of riches. Some spend almost all that they have on lottery tickets. Others invest large sums in the stock market and real estate. Still others dig in the earth with hopes of discovering some priceless artifact or precious gem. Solomon is saying that the tireless energy we expend seeking the riches of this world, can be better used seeking God's wisdom. It is in searching that we begin to understand reverence for God, and departing from evil. It is in seeking God with all of our heart, that we begin an intimate relationship with Him. Seek the Lord while he may be found. Search for Him and you will find the knowledge of God.

HE WILL DIRECT YOUR PATHS

Proverbs 3:5, 6
"Trust in the LORD with all thine heart; and lean not unto thine own understanding. In all thy ways acknowledge him, and he shall direct thy paths."

It is not easy to put implicit trust in people. Oftentimes, those whom we have trusted the most also disappoint us the most. When we let someone into our emotional space, we feel vulnerable, and because of past hurts, we sometimes wish we did not allow ourselves to trust again. This is an unfortunate consequence of sin.

The Lord says that we *can* trust *Him*. He has demonstrated His consistency by causing the sun to shine and the rain to fall without fail for thousands of years. He has sustained the very breath in our bodies. This, along with all of His mighty acts, shows us His proven track record and *that* should put us at ease. This should encourage us to be faithful to Him.

So many people think it is possible to make important decisions without consulting the Lord. Decisions about marriage, business partnerships, and other situations are made without regarding Him. People suffer through unnecessary pain because they do not first confer with God. He says that if we put our trust in Him first, and resist the temptation to rely on our own limited wisdom, He will direct us in the way we should go.

More than anything else, we must rely on the Lord concerning issues of salvation. We have nothing of value to contribute to our salvation; He must perform miracles beyond our abilities in order to fit us for heaven. We are never to aspire to holiness in our own strength. We must trust in the Lord with our whole heart. As we do this, He will make known the mysteries of godliness and will prepare us to meet Him in peace. Isn't it great that the Lord is willing to show us, step by step, the way we should go? Trust in the Lord and you will never be disappointed.

THOU ART GOD

Proverbs 8:23-26, 30
"I was set up from everlasting, from the beginning, or ever the earth was. When there were no depths, I was brought forth; when there were no fountains abounding with water. Before the mountains were settled, before the hills was I brought forth: While as yet he had not made the earth, nor the fields, nor the highest part of the dust of the world. Then I was by him, as one brought up with him: and I was daily his delight, rejoicing always before him;"

King Solomon had a particularly strong grasp on wisdom. When he was in the beginning stages of his role as king, he spoke to the Lord humbly and openly. He admitted that he was but a small child and lacked what was necessary to rule over God's people. The Lord asked him what He should do for Him, and Solomon requested wisdom. The Lord granted his prayer and beyond. His first test as king revealed that the Lord's wisdom had become a part of his life.

Proverbs chapter 8, it seems, is a letter from wisdom to all who would listen. Wisdom said, "Unto you, O men, I call; and my voice is to the sons of man. O ye simple, understand wisdom: and, ye fools, be ye of an understanding heart. Hear; for I will speak of excellent things; and the opening of my lips shall be right things. For my mouth shall speak truth; and wickedness is an abomination to my lips. All the words of my mouth are in righteousness; there is nothing froward or perverse in them." Proverbs 8:4-8. These are strong words. They point to a wonderful truth that many may not realize. Wisdom, even as depicted in the Old Testament, *must* be none other than Jesus Christ.

When you come to the closing verses, it becomes even clearer. "The LORD possessed me in the beginning of his way, before his works of old. For whoso findeth me findeth life, and shall obtain favour of the LORD." Proverbs 8:22, 35. Are not these words spoken of Christ? Does not the Bible also say that those who *have* Christ *have* life (I John 5:12)? Is it not true that those who have Christ have favor with the Father as well? Notice the way Paul describes Jesus Christ. "But of him are ye in Christ Jesus, who of God is made unto us wisdom, and righteousness, and sanctification, and redemption: That, according as it is written, He that glorieth, let him glory in the Lord." I Corinthians 1:30, 31. Jesus is, indeed, wisdom.

What does understanding that Jesus is wisdom mean for us today? Whenever the Lord gives wisdom, that is, the ability to resist evil and use the truths God has revealed unto salvation, *Christ* is present. "If any of you lack wisdom, let him ask of God, that giveth to all men liberally, and upbraideth not; and it shall be given him." James 1:5. He is the perfect gift of wisdom that we all need. As we listen to Him, as we welcome His counsel, we are brought into closer relationship with Him. This is Christ's purpose. He cries aloud in order to draw us closer to Himself. If I had to say something about wisdom, I would agree with David when he said, "LORD, thou hast been our dwelling place in all generations. Before the mountains were brought forth, or ever thou hadst formed the earth and the world, even from everlasting to everlasting, thou art God." Psalms 90:1, 2. Praise the Lord for giving us His Son Jesus Christ. *He* is made unto us wisdom. Amen.

Deliberate

Proverbs 11:19
"As righteousness tendeth to life: so he that pursueth
evil pursueth it to his own death."

Sometimes people think that they can just float along through life aimlessly, like a ship without a sail, hoping to attain an eternal reward. It is like driving a car without a steering wheel, or flying an airplane with no navigational controls. There is *no way* to arrive anywhere beneficial, spiritually speaking, without being deliberate. We are *not* saved by default. We must actively respond to the faith, love, and power to obey, which God has already deposited within us.

Living according to God's word is like running top speed toward our only chance at life. The Lord has already mapped out the absolute path to heaven, which is through a good relationship with Him. Choosing another route will *always* get us lost. We will never arrive at the right spiritual place unless we return to the right path.

Likewise, living outside of the Lord's word is like flying a stealth military jet as fast as we can into the ocean. Certainly, it would disintegrate on impact. Those who choose a path opposite that of the Bible, do so to their own demise. It would not be a temporary situation. No, the death of the wicked is the second death that comes as the consequence of the judgment of God.

Let us pursue the path of righteousness, trusting that the Lord will guide us in the right direction. Let us be deliberate in our pursuit of Him. "Seek ye the LORD while he may be found, call ye upon him while he is near: Let the wicked forsake his way, and the unrighteous man his thoughts: and let him return unto the LORD, and he will have mercy upon him; and to our God, for he will abundantly pardon. For my thoughts are not your thoughts, neither are your ways my ways, saith the LORD. For as the heavens are higher than the earth, so are my ways higher than your ways, and my thoughts than your thoughts." Isaiah 55:6-9

UNAPPRECIATED

Proverbs 11:25
"The liberal soul shall be made fat: and he that watereth shall be watered also himself."

In a world where the number one concern in the minds of many people is self, it is encouraging to know that the Lord operates on principles that are higher. There are many who are very generous, but are seldom rewarded. Some are tempted to think that it is not worth it to help from the kindness of their hearts when their efforts are not appreciated.

The Lord Jesus is the best example of one who was not appreciated, yet He continued giving. "He was in the world, and the world was made by him, and the world knew him not. He came unto his own, and his own received him not." John 1:10, 11. Even the Creator of the world, was regarded lightly by those whom He created, but His purpose was not abated. "Even as the Son of man came not to be ministered unto, but to minister, and to give his life a ransom for many." Matthew 20:28. If the Lord of life could press through the heaviness of being unappreciated when He came to save the world from eternal condemnation, we may do the same. Since He was our example, there is no doubt that He can enable us to exercise altruistic benevolence, just as He did.

Those who are more interested in the welfare of others, rather than themselves, are blessed abundantly. When we think of giving, it is natural to think that the more we give, the less we will have. In the natural world, this is true, but in the supernatural world, things are much different. When we give unreservedly to the Lord, He returns a hundred fold. When we yield our lives to Him, He gives us the imparted life of Jesus. When we share with others, He shares with us. "Then Peter began to say unto him, Lo, we have left all, and have followed thee. And Jesus answered and said, Verily I say unto you, There is no man that hath left house, or brethren, or sisters, or father, or mother, or wife, or children, or lands, for my sake, and the gospel's, But he shall receive an hundredfold now in this time, houses, and brethren, and sisters, and mothers, and children, and lands, with persecutions; and in the world to come eternal life. But many that are first shall be last; and the last first." Mark 10:28-31. Does this mean that the Lord can be bribed? No. The Lord can not be bribed or influenced in that way, but He does keep His promises that He made because of His own righteousness. "The liberal soul shall be made fat: and he that watereth shall be watered also himself." Proverbs 11:25.

When you are tempted to think that nobody appreciates you, just know that any sincere service is registered in the books of heaven. When Jesus comes, His reward will be with Him. He will bestow the ultimate blessing upon on those who love Him—everlasting life.

LOVING PARENTS

Proverbs 13:24
"He that spareth his rod hateth his son: but he that loveth him chasteneth him betimes."

Solomon speaks with astoundingly serious tones concerning the discipline of children. It almost reads as though he is deliberately exaggerating just to get a point across by using the word hate, but a careful study of the Bible as a whole would reveal otherwise.

"And ye have forgotten the exhortation which speaketh unto you as unto children, My son, despise not thou the chastening of the Lord, nor faint when thou art rebuked of him: For whom the Lord loveth he chasteneth, and scourgeth every son whom he receiveth. If ye endure chastening, God dealeth with you as with sons; for what son is he whom the father chasteneth not? But if ye be without chastisement, whereof all are partakers, then are ye bastards, and not sons. Furthermore we have had fathers of our flesh which corrected us, and we gave them reverence: shall we not much rather be in subjection unto the Father of spirits, and live? For they verily for a few days chastened us after their own pleasure; but he for our profit, that we might be partakers of his holiness. Now no chastening for the present seemeth to be joyous, but grievous: nevertheless afterward it yieldeth the peaceable fruit of righteousness unto them which are exercised thereby." Hebrews 12:5-11. Notice what verse eleven says: The purpose of good discipline is to bring about the peaceable fruit of righteousness.

Godly discipline, that is, overall discipline, incentivizes or encourages right doing, and deincentivizes or discourages wrongdoing. Any method of discipline used to correct our children must have the purpose of leading toward Christ and entire change inwardly, not merely a fear of wrongdoing.

Godly discipline communicates love and genuine concern.

The Lord, throughout the scriptures, has fully demonstrated His methods of corrective discipline. In the beginning, following Adam's first sin, the Lord barred him and Eve from the Tree of Life and the Garden of Eden; their sin would have become eternal had they eaten from the tree in their fallen condition. By having to leave paradise, they needed to see that the consequences of sin could not be measured. God's purpose was clearly seen as He covered them with coats of skins, which symbolized His gift of righteousness.

The Lord also demonstrated discipline when chastising Israel through their various captivities. When they would refuse, over periods of time, to listen to the Lord's guidance, in order to go their own way, He allowed circumstances around them to cause a certain level of grief and pain, so they would learn to appreciate the Lord, and become more willing to listen to Him.

The blessing of *good* discipline is, if the one being disciplined yields themselves to the process, in the end, they will be changed from *within*. The one being disciplined will also know, without doubt, that the one that chastened them has only their best interest at heart and loves them. I thank the Lord that *He* is willing to do whatever it takes to bring me into conformity to His will. Loving parents do not withhold holy chastening which leads to salvation, even if it is a little painful. In the end, everyone involved will be better for it.

ONLY ONE WAY

Proverbs 14:12
"There is a way which seemeth right unto a man,
but the end thereof are the ways of death."

It is very difficult for us, as human beings, to relinquish control of our lives to God. It makes us feel helpless and distrustful. It is especially difficult when we must follow a narrow road of requirements. God does *not* give us general guidelines to follow. He tells us specifically what is necessary to please Him. Some are resistant to the idea of God giving details, and requiring us to observe them. This was the problem with Cain, Abel's brother. He thought that when God required an offering, he should follow his own interpretation of what God required. "And in process of time it came to pass, that Cain brought of the fruit of the ground an offering unto the LORD. And Abel, he also brought of the firstlings of his flock and of the fat thereof. And the LORD had respect unto Abel and to his offering: But unto Cain and to his offering he had not respect. And Cain was very wroth, and his countenance fell. And the LORD said unto Cain, Why art thou wroth? and why is thy countenance fallen? If thou doest well, shalt thou not be accepted? and if thou doest not well, sin lieth at the door. And unto thee shall be his desire, and thou shalt rule over him. And Cain talked with Abel his brother: and it came to pass, when they were in the field, that Cain rose up against Abel his brother, and slew him." Genesis 4:3-8. Cain decided that he would choose his own way to satisfy God's requirements rather than following His command to bring an animal sacrifice.

Such is the case with so many today. God has clearly said that Jesus is the only way to access God, but many resort to others for salvation. Many avatars have passed on to the grave, yet many look to these dead men to bring about salvation. They pray in the name of idols that humans have erected, to no avail. The belief is, all roads lead to heaven, but *God* never said that. "Enter ye in at the strait gate: for wide is the gate, and broad is the way, that leadeth to destruction, and many there be which go in thereat:" Matthew 7:13. When we choose to ignore God's clear messages, we do so to our own destruction. On the other hand, we have the privilege of entering great relationship with Him through Christ Jesus.

Pray today that you will choose to follow God wherever He leads, even if you do not understand His methods. Jesus is, indeed, the *only* way.

IT IS AMAZING

Proverbs 20:1
"Wine is a mocker, strong drink is raging:
and whosoever is deceived thereby is not wise."

Many things are amazing. The fact that the sun is close enough to the earth that we do not freeze and far enough away that we do not burst into flames is amazing. The fact that the earth does not spin out of control and throw us all into outer space is amazing. The fact that human beings can build a transatlantic tunnel thousands of feet below the ocean for cars to travel between continents is amazing. The fact that we have computers that fit in a fourteen inch square space on a table, with more computing power than room-sized computer had when computers first became popular is simply amazing.

The things mentioned above are amazing in a good way, but some negative things amaze me too. The fact that human beings can have such disregard for human life that we would kill an unborn child is amazing. The fact that we sometimes think that more war begets peace is amazing. The fact that we have been taught by *some* so-called health gurus that eating more meat and fewer carbohydrates [which includes fruit, vegetables, and whole grains] is healthy for us is amazing. The fact that tobacco companies think that they are in no way responsible for the countless degenerative diseases people get from using their products is amazing. These are not all. The fact that people can see and experience the ill and sometimes fatal affects of drinking alcohol, in all of its forms and still think that it is OK to drink is amazing.

The drinking of fermented fruits and grains in the form of wine, beer, and other alcoholic beverages, has been glamorized almost since the beginning of time. Long before we had huge breweries and wineries, people allowed these precious crops to sit and decay to a less desirable state. Children are sometimes born with a predisposition to alcoholism, because their parents were bound to the bottle before and during the fetus' life in the womb. No amount of these beverages is safe for consumption. If consuming alcoholic beverages alters a person's perceptions and inhibitions, how does one really know the resulting affects as they occur? How does one know how much damage alcohol has caused to brain cells and internal organs? With every drink imbibed, damage is done internally.

The wisest man living in his day, Solomon said wine is a mocker, strong drink is raging and those who are deceived by it are not wise (Proverbs 20:1). Notice what else he said: "Who hath woe? who hath sorrow? who hath contentions? who hath babbling? who hath wounds without cause? who hath redness of eyes? They that tarry long at the wine; they that go to seek mixed wine. Look not thou upon the wine when it is red, when it giveth his colour in the cup, when it moveth itself aright. At the last it biteth like a serpent, and stingeth like an adder." Proverbs 23:29-32. I'm thinking, with words as strong as these, it is probably better to leave strong drinks alone. "As newborn babes, desire the sincere milk of the word, that ye may grow thereby:" I Peter 2:2. If you want something strong to drink, drink the word of God.

CONTROL YOURSELF

Proverbs 23:19-21
"Hear thou, my son, and be wise, and guide thine heart in the way. Be not among winebibbers; among riotous eaters of flesh: For the drunkard and the glutton shall come to poverty: and drowsiness shall clothe a man with rags."

The United States is full of all-you-can-eat buffets and bars that serve half-priced drinks during happy hour. This, in part, is because our society has become so enamored by excess. In terms of popularity, these buffets are doing great business. If people exhibited more self control on a regular basis, such businesses would not exist. After all, who would patronize them? Perhaps buffets are good when people choose not to overeat from them. Certainly, nothing good comes from bars or drinking alcohol.

The Bible gives good counsel about gluttony and drunkenness. If we are prone to either of them, it leads to poverty. While there are practical implications, the spiritual are even more astounding. Look at the imagery. Gluttony and drunkenness leads to sluggish minds in the natural world. In spiritual life, if we become drunk with the wine of self-gratification, and become gluttonous with the meat of living for pleasure, our experience with God becomes sluggish. As we continue in those paths, the righteousness that God gives the faithful as a covering is exchanged for the filthy rags of self-righteousness.

Let us feast on the word of God and drink freely of the water of life. The Lord is willing to give us all that we need for nourishment, that we might share it with others. As we continue doing this, all with whom we come into contact will benefit from our experience, and will potentially gain an experience with God of their own to perpetuate the same blessing. One day we will meet on the streets of gold.

LIVING IT UP

Proverbs 27:1
"Boast not thyself of to morrow; for thou knowest not what a day may bring forth."

I have been quite guilty of being covetous. When I was a child, I watched television shows like *Lifestyles of the Rich and Famous*, wishing in many ways that I were the one of the people featured there. Even today, while watching three episodes in particular, of Extreme Engineering, when they featured homes, yachts, and jets, I wanted to own many of them myself. Many of the people living in the so-called lap of luxury had little regard for God. Wine sipping, extravagant parties, and extreme vacations seemed to rule their lives. Although I did not covet that aspect, I did want to have access to the riches. They often made long-term plans to do all sorts of things that the Lord would not approve of. It occurred to me that tomorrow is not promised.

People all over the world, not just the rich and famous, make plans far into the future. On one hand, it is good to have goals and aspirations, but these should be tempered by the will of God. James said it this way: "Go to now, ye that say, Today or to morrow we will go into such a city, and continue there a year, and buy and sell, and get gain: Whereas ye know not what shall be on the morrow. For what is your life? It is even a vapour that appeareth for a little time, and then vanisheth away. For that ye ought to say, If the Lord will, we shall live, and do this, or that. But now ye rejoice in your boastings: all such rejoicing is evil." James 4:13-16.

As we prepare for the future, we must always consult the Lord. Covetousness often leads people to unhealthy aspirations without the consideration of God. Some seek to gain wealth and riches at any cost. I am blessed that the

Lord has kept me from that and teaches me contentment everyday. I now look forward to the coming of the greatest reward known to humankind. I look forward to the coming of Jesus Christ. If we constantly look forward to that spectacular event and allow God to prepare us, we will not be ruled by earthly devising. We will not foolishly prepare to make ourselves comfortable on this sin-cursed earth.

Pray that the Lord will give us the spirit of contentment. Pray that we will learn to arrange our plans to fit into God's will, rather than boasting on our great plans for the future.

NO NEED TO RUN

Proverbs 28:1
"The wicked flee when no man pursueth:
but the righteous are bold as a lion."

It is a blessing to be righteous before the Lord. Certainly, this is not a position that anyone of us can occupy on our own. None of us can stand in the judgment on our own merits. However, the Lord blots out the sins of those who love Him and remembers them no more.

Have you ever watched television shows about police officers being followed by television cameras recording their daily duties? Have you ever seen instances where an officer has been simply passing by someone and they began to run? I have seen such cases. When the officers finally caught up to the runner because of suspicion, they asked the question, "Why did you run?" The runner said, "Because I was scared." The officer was not paying attention to the person until they began running. It is a blessing to have a conscience free and clear of guilt. Those that are innocent of wrongdoing have no need to fear.

Such is the case with those who truly love the Lord. He has not given us the spirit of fear. We need not run away from the Lord when He comes near. "Herein is our love made perfect, that we may have boldness in the day of judgment: because as he is, so are we in this world. There is no fear in love; but perfect love casteth out fear: because fear hath torment. He that feareth is not made perfect in love. We love him, because he first loved us." I John 4:17-19. Although He is absolutely holy and we are not, His love for the faithful covers a multitude of sin. I thank the Lord that He has declared His people innocent. I praise Him because He has given us enough grace for us to be called by His name. "What shall we say then? Shall we continue in sin, that grace may abound? God forbid. How shall we, that are dead to sin, live any longer therein?" Romans 6:1, 2.

LISTEN UP

Ecclesiastes 5:1
"Keep thy foot when thou goest to the house of God, and be more ready to hear, than to give the sacrifice of fools: for they consider not that they do evil."

It is always a blessing to enter into the presence of God. He is always drawing and inviting us to spend time with Him. When we seek Him in sincerity He reveals Himself to us. We should ever be ready to heed His voice. What a terrible thing it is to enter into His courts without being willing to commune with Him. It is an insult to Him when we take His presence for granted. When we listen attentively for and to His voice, we begin to understand our deficiencies, and His matchless grace. When we listen attentively, we hear those blessed tones that say, "I love you!"

The sacrifices of time and treasure that we offer to God are so much sweeter when they come from the heart submitted to following the Lord wherever he leads. Sincere praise registers as appreciation in heaven, and empowers us with a willingness to do His will.

Let us seek the Lord daily, asking Him what He would have us do, and then our sacrifices will be acceptable to Him.

WHOLE DUTY OF MAN

Ecclesiastes 12:13, 14
"Let us hear the conclusion of the whole matter: Fear God, and keep his commandments: for this is the whole duty of man. For God shall bring every work into judgment, with every secret thing, whether it be good, or whether it be evil."

Solomon, the wisest man living in his time, gave many admonitions that are pertinent even until this time. He gave wise counsel regarding good stewardship and preparation. He warned against illicit relationships, abominable sins, and drinking strong drinks. Many times he referred to the things that some of us live our lives in pursuit of as vanity, and chasing the wind. He had many wives and concubines, and possessed beauty and wealth beyond our imagination, yet all of this in his view, was vanity.

Having discussed, in two of his books, many practical guidelines for living, he concludes by saying, all that he said can be summed up by keeping the Lord's commands, and respecting Him as the Creator of the universe. This, he said, is the whole duty of man. God will judge every deed and misdeed to determine whether it was holy or not. He will judge even the intents of the heart.

The whole duty of humankind is to please God. When we first submit to God, and then live our lives to please Him, we fulfill our duty as human beings. It is in this kind of commitment that we lead others to a richer and fuller experience, which will eventually lead to the salvation of their souls. It is when we do our best to please God that we are demonstrating our love for Him, thus fulfilling the greatest commandment (Matthew 22:36-38).

It is a blessing that God has put a mechanism in place to afford faulty human beings the privilege of pleasing Him.

Only blessings and security, in the trying hour of God's judgment can occur when our focus is fully fixed on bringing Him glory.

Pray that the Lord will empower you with the principle element of love which, when exercised properly, pleases God.

GOD SIMPLY ADORES US

Song of Solomon 4:1
"Behold, thou art fair, my love; behold, thou art fair;
thou hast doves' eyes within thy locks: thy hair is as a
flock of goats, that appear from mount Gilead."

The passion in Solomon's writing concerning his love for his wife is unmistakable. He speaks in clear poetic tones describing every feature as an artist would, in order to communicate a vivid mental picture. He is enamored by her. He absolutely adores her and wants everyone to know it. He showers her with the best gifts of beauty and fragrance. *Nothing* is too expensive for her.

God's people are depicted in Jeremiah chapter 6 as a beautiful woman. The Lord adores us even more than Solomon did his wife. Through the sacrifice of His dear Son, He gave us the ultimate gift of everlasting life. He showers us with all that is beautiful. The character He refines within us is full of beauty. It is a wonder to behold, considering all except Christ, were born as enemies of God. Through the miracle of grace, He has brought us into conformity to His will. Let all that experience the sweet fragrance of Jesus' sacrifice on our behalf, know that God is awesome.

I am so glad that right now, in heaven, we have someone who adores us and will stop at nothing to save us, and will give us the eternal inheritance promised to His servant Abraham.

PASSION FOR LOVE

Song of Solomon 5:9
"What is thy beloved more than another beloved, O thou
fairest among women? what is thy beloved more than
another beloved, that thou dost so charge us?"

Song of Solomon is one of the most passionate books of love ever written. I can really appreciate the way it is written. Solomon speaks in gentle tones of his love for his wife, and paints vivid pictures of their passion. The passion is not a worldly sentimentalism. It is the adoration of a man for his wife. Most of us men, who are married, could learn a lesson from this book. If we could receive the poetic expression that the Lord gave Solomon, our wives would be *overwhelmed* with love for us. It is obvious that the Lord gave him wisdom even in the area of intimacy. Though he often misused his gift, it was a gift, nonetheless.

One of Solomon's wives, who was so taken by his love, that when she saw that he had left her for a season, she searched for him feverishly. She found trouble and pain in the streets as she searched, but she did not give up. When she spoke to the daughters of Jerusalem, asking that they tell him that she is lovesick, they asked, "What is thy beloved more than another beloved, O thou fairest among women? what is thy beloved more than another beloved, that thou dost so charge us?" Song of Solomon 5:9. She responded with a heartfelt expression that would cause any man to be drawn to his wife. They wanted to know, so she told them. "My beloved is white and ruddy, the chiefest among ten thousand. His head is as the most fine gold, his locks are bushy, and black as a raven. His eyes are as the eyes of doves by the rivers of waters, washed with milk, and fitly set. His cheeks are as a bed of spices, as sweet flowers: his lips like lilies, dropping sweet smelling myrrh. His hands are as gold rings set with the beryl: his belly is as bright ivory overlaid with sapphires. His legs are as pillars of marble, set upon sockets of fine gold: his countenance is as Lebanon, excellent as the cedars. His mouth is most sweet: yea, he is altogether lovely. This is my beloved, and this is my friend, O daughters of Jerusalem." Song of Solomon 5:10-15.

As you may well know, God's people are symbolized in the Bible as a woman, a bride. When we are searching for a better relationship with the Lord and someone asks what makes our Lord so great, do we respond as passionately as did Solomon's wife? Do we welcome the opportunity to express, with the passion of love, what He means to us? If we would just spend quality time with Him and listen to His tender voice, being willing to do whatever He wants from us, our experience will surpass even hers. As the Lord reveals Himself to us daily, He becomes so irresistible that we would rather die, than sin against Him. I pray that my zeal for God will be inspired by this woman's love for her darling Solomon.

YOU MUST HAVE THAT TRUE RELIGION

Isaiah 1:16, 17
"Wash you, make you clean; put away the evil of your doings from before mine eyes; cease to do evil; Learn to do well; seek judgment, relieve the oppressed, judge the fatherless, plead for the widow."

It is unfortunate that so many people are afraid of the word religion. It seems that religion has been given such a bad reputation, that even the *word* has been dragged through the mud. Have you ever heard someone say, "I don't belong to a religion, it's a way of life?" This usually stems from a misapprehension of what religion really means.

Let us see what qualifies as authentic religion in the Bible. "Pure religion and undefiled before God and the Father is this, To visit the fatherless and widows in their affliction, and to keep himself unspotted from the world." James 1:27. Pure and true religion is based in godly relationships. When we are pure according to God's estimation, we have the best interest of others at heart, especially the downtrodden of society. If orphans, widows and the afflicted cannot receive the care and attention from those who claim to love the Lord, who *can* they count on? The religion of Christ was all about remaining undefiled by the world and relieving the suffering of others.

Today, ask the Lord how to exemplify pure and undefiled religion. There are many among us that can use spiritual encouragement and practical help. Many among us will only recognize Jesus as He shines through *us*. When all is said and done, we must have that true religion. We must be converted.

LET'S REACH AN UNDERSTANDING

Isaiah 1:18
"Come now, and let us reason together, saith the LORD:
though your sins be as scarlet, they shall be as white as
snow; though they be red like crimson,
they shall be as wool."

Have you ever been given an offer that you could not refuse? Did the other party involved, present their offer in such a way that you would have been unwise to refuse? I recently encountered a mortgage lender with a special program where they would refinance my mortgage for free, give me an interest rate that was slightly above the market rates, and every one hundred-twenty days for the life of the loan, if the interest rates went down at least a quarter percent, I would receive a refinance package without another home appraisal or credit check. The benefit in my view is that since the lender pays all of the closing costs and fees, I do not need to stay in my home for any period of time hoping to recoup the money I spent on the deal. I suppose this is their way of attracting mortgagees. In my case, it certainly worked.

God gives offers that are even more irresistible. He offers salvation as a totally free gift, and one of the catalysts is forgiveness. He pleaded with His children Israel, through the prophet Isaiah. He brought them a strong argument intending that they reach an understanding. Their sins had been noticed by heaven and could not be tolerated. God was in a situation where justice must be served. He chose to offer them a way of escape from the natural, spiritual consequences of their sins. The plan of salvation was clearly seen in the imagery. He would make their sins, though red like crimson, as white as snow. Their blood guilty sins were represented as crimson and scarlet, and the blood of the Lamb of God must be shed on their behalf. Through that transaction, which would take place in the future, they could receive absolute pardon and be seen as white as snow. "If ye be willing and obedient, ye shall eat the good of the land: But if ye refuse and rebel, ye shall be devoured with the sword: for the mouth of the LORD hath spoken it." Isaiah 1:19, 20. The offer was on the table. They could receive the gift of forgiveness for free or pay dearly the penalty for their own sins. In my view the only option was to extend the hand of faith and receive the gift of God.

Where are you on this? Is there anything that would cause you to choose the alternative to God's gift of forgiveness? It is a no-brainer. God's way is always better. Pray that He will make Himself irresistible in your experience and hopefully you too will reach an understanding

HE'S STILL ON THE THRONE

Isaiah 6:1
"In the year that king Uzziah died I saw also the Lord
sitting upon a throne, high and lifted up,
and his train filled the temple."

The people of God were in a dire situation. They experienced the faithful leadership of king Uzziah for many years. They witnessed how God proved faithful when their enemies sought to defeat them. They felt secure in the leadership of good King Uzziah.

After a time, the Bible says that the king became proud and eventually died under the judgment of God. He thought so highly of himself that he ventured into holy territory unprepared. He took upon himself the God given prerogatives of a priest, and attempted to burn incense in the holy place of the sanctuary. Consequently, the king lost his life.

This turn of events was actually a window into the state in which the people of God found themselves. Isaiah said that he and the people were of unclean lips (Isaiah 6:5). The people chose to be lead by their own passions rather than the Lord who had been faithful to them for so long, and He was displeased with them (Isaiah 6:10-13).

It is difficult to imagine the inner turmoil the prophet Isaiah was experiencing. He knew their history of inconsistent obedience. He understood the conditions of blessings God revealed through Moses (Deuteronomy 28). He knew that in their present state, Israel would not benefit from the blessings God intended for them. This was the case with every prophet sent to God's people. The prophets carried a burden for them that could not be uttered. They desperately wanted God to find favor in His people, and would give anything, including their own lives in some cases, to see them remain faithful.

Do you ever feel as though the world is out of control? Do you look around at the people you share fellowship with, and see that all of you need divine intervention if you are to receive the blessings of God's favor? I often have that burden. The story of Isaiah's vision encourages us that the Lord is still on His throne. He is the one controlling everything in the universe simultaneously. He sees when earthly rulers and presidents become proud and misappropriate their authority like king Uzziah. He understands, as well, His people's state of affairs. Do not be overwhelmed with discouragement, but look to heaven and by faith see the heavenly King sitting upon His throne. God is still in control!

SATISFIED

Isaiah 6:3
"And one cried unto another, and said, Holy, holy, holy, is the LORD of hosts: the whole earth is full of his glory."

Satisfaction is usually associated with having one's needs fulfilled. If an individual is hungry, and then has a plate of wholesome food, they should be satisfied. When a marriage is successful and each spouse feels complete and happy in one another, they can be considered as satisfied. When a child of God has food and clothing, that child should be satisfied, not ambitious for worldly riches or fame (I Timothy 6:8).

In my studies several years ago, I encountered an interesting facet of contentment. It was about the fulfillment that angels must posses when in the presence of God. David, the one beloved of God, understood this kind of satisfaction when he wrote, "Thou wilt shew me the path of life: in thy presence is fulness of joy; at thy right hand there are pleasures for evermore." Psalm 16:11. In the presence of God, we may find all that we need. There is abundance in His presence. There is peace in His presence. There is life in His presence. It is impossible to be proud while engulfed by His presence.

When Isaiah was in vision, he witnessed heavenly worship. "And one cried unto another, and said, Holy, holy, holy, is the LORD of hosts: the whole earth is full of his glory." Isaiah 6:3. The angels praised the Lord to the point that the very pillars of heaven shook (Isaiah 6:4). It occurred to me through further study, that although the angels are incredible specimens of beauty and power, they are so satisfied by the presence of God, that they lose sight of themselves. His splendor so overwhelms them, that they cannot recognize the light with which they are covered. Their greatest joy and pleasure is to adore *Him*.

The Lord is more than worthy of our praise. If sinless,

beautiful angels adore Him, what hinders us? "O come, let us worship and bow down: let us kneel before the LORD our make." Psalms 95:6.

SEEK THE LORD

Isaiah 8:19
"And when they shall say unto you, Seek unto them that have familiar spirits, and unto wizards that peep, and that mutter: should not a people seek unto their God? for the living to the dead?"

In the days of King Ahaz, as in other eras, the people of God often lost focus. When faced with dire situations, they may have sought the Lord for a season, but if He did not answer as quickly or in the way they desired, they sought other means. When Moses was in the mount with God longer than the people expected, they became impatient. "And when the people saw that Moses delayed to come down out of the mount, the people gathered themselves together unto Aaron, and said unto him, Up, make us gods, which shall go before us; for as for this Moses, the man that brought us up out of the land of Egypt, we wot not what is become of him. And Aaron said unto them, break off the golden earrings, which are in the ears of your wives, of your sons, and of your daughters, and bring them unto me. And all the people brake off the golden earrings which were in their ears, and brought them unto Aaron. And he received them at their hand, and fashioned it with a graving tool, after he had made it a molten calf: and they said, These be thy gods, O Israel, which brought thee up out of the land of Egypt." Exodus 32:1-4. Rather than waiting on the Lord, they resorted to idolatry.

King Saul was under an incredible amount of stress because of his own disobedience. Matters in his kingdom were spiraling out of control. "And when Saul saw the host of the Philistines, he was afraid, and his heart greatly trembled. And when Saul enquired of the LORD, the LORD answered him not, neither by dreams nor by Urim, nor by prophets. Then said Saul unto his servants, Seek me a woman that hath a familiar spirit, that I may go to her, and enquire of her. And his servants said to him, Behold, there is a woman that hath a familiar spirit at Endor." I Samuel 28:5-7. With an unrepentant heart, Saul inquired of the Lord. Because of his iniquities, the Lord did not answer him. Instead of repenting, he demonstrated his lack of faith by seeking a witch, which God forbade.

How often do we resort to evil in order to understand things that are going on in our lives? The Lord would have us to love and trust Him in all things. He is more than willing to reveal Himself to us in times of need, if we would simply trust Him. We need not consult horoscopes, fortune cookies, or obscure Bible codebooks for understanding. We need not resort to overeating, promiscuity, or unhealthy ambitions for comfort. When we ask Him in prayer, He is ready and willing to lead us, if we are willing to *be* lead. The Bible is our God-given resource for knowing His will. The Holy Spirit will guide all sincere seekers to truth. "Trust in the LORD with all thine heart; and lean not unto thine own understanding. In all thy ways acknowledge him, and he shall direct thy paths. Be not wise in thine own eyes: fear the LORD, and depart from evil. It shall be health to thy navel, and marrow to thy bones." Proverbs 3:5-8.

HIS NAME IS WONDERFUL

Isaiah 9:6
"For unto us a child is born, unto us a son is given: and the government shall be upon his shoulder: and his name shall be called Wonderful, Counseller, The mighty God, The everlasting Father, The Prince of Peace."

At a time when worldly kings and kingdoms had proven unstable and God's people could have no confidence in their rulers, the Lord sent them a message. It was a message that would change the face of history forever. When they did not have much reason to trust in their leadership, God encouraged His people to look to the future. He spoke directly to their situation in a few words. He inferred that it did not matter that King Uzziah lost focus after having received the blessings of God. It did not matter that King Ahaz made alliances with heathen nations in an attempt to preserve his kingdom, or that the people consulted wizards for guidance rather than God. He had great plans. He would give His Son whose name was Wonderful. His roles were Counselor, mighty God, everlasting Father, and Prince of peace. This child, upon whose shoulders the everlasting government would rest, could be no ordinary man. He would ascend the throne of David, yet he was greater that David. The names and longevity of this King indicate that this was none other than God in the flesh, Jesus Christ. He was the only God-man born of a woman, upon whom the government could rest in absolute justice.

It is interesting that the throne Jesus would ascend was usually a standard by which all other thrones were measured. Whenever a king was crowned, it seems that the Bible always referred to David. When Josiah and Hezekiah were made kings, the Bible says that they were faithful like their father David. Likewise, when Ahaz was crowned, the

Bible says also, that he did not like David. In the case of this child that would be born after David, yet existed before David, we find an oxymoron. Jesus was born of a woman in order to save us. He was crowned in a spiritual sense, the King of kings, yet his government was everlasting. Before David was ever born, Jesus was King of kings. Jesus, who was already the divine ruler, assumed human flesh and vanquished the self-proclaimed ruler of this world, the devil, and fulfilled the promise of peace that God made to the universe. True, the peace has not yet been fully realized, but the down payment has been made. One day, the one who was faithful before David, the human standard of righteous kings, will come in the clouds. The mighty Lion of the tribe of Judah, conquering King Jesus, will reign forever. He is coming with innumerable angels to deliver His faithful ones and return order to the entire universe. Why is He going to do this? He will do this because His very name is Wonderful. Wonderful King Jesus love us so much, He will soon burst the clouds and take His people home.

ULTIMATE FULFILLMENT

Isaiah 11:8-10
"And the sucking child shall play on the hole of the asp, and the weaned child shall put his hand on the cockatrice' den. They shall not hurt nor destroy in all my holy mountain: for the earth shall be full of the knowledge of the LORD, as the waters cover the sea. And in that day there shall be a root of Jesse, which shall stand for an ensign of the people; to it shall the Gentiles seek: and his rest shall be glorious."

We are looking forward to a day when the Lord Jesus will settle inequity for the last time. He will gather all of His people together, from every nation, kindred, tongue and people to the great reward of the righteous. For those who are in Christ, there will no longer be a distinction. There will be no male, female, bond, free, Jew, or Gentile. All will be united under the singular bloodstained banner of Jesus Christ (Galatians 3:26-29). Predators will cease to exist. Children will be able to play with snakes that were once deadly, without the possibility of being hurt. There will be absolutely no blight of sin present forever.

This is the ultimate fulfillment of the mission and ministry of Jesus Christ. When He bursts through the clouds of heaven at the last day, He will have fully accomplished His mission of salvation. His substitutionary death, which started the events for our salvation, will have been completed. The empty tomb, where Jesus once laid, will stand as a living memorial to the power He exhibited over hell, death, and the grave. It will prove that He is able to raise sinners to the level of saints in His sight. The judgment of His house and cleansing of His people will have already seen its end; therefore, when He returns, He will be able to bring His eternal reward with Him. In that day, the ultimate fulfillment of all prophecies, attributed to the prosperity of His people, will be apparent. It will be a wonderful day! It will be a great day! It will be a glorious day! I look forward to it, how about you?

UNDERSTANDING THE SCRIPTURES

Isaiah 28:9, 10
"Whom shall he teach knowledge? and whom shall he make to understand doctrine? them that are weaned from the milk, and drawn from the breasts. For precept must be upon precept, precept upon precept; line upon line, line upon line; here a little, and there a little:"

Have you ever had difficulty understanding the Bible? Do you want to know what the Lord wants from you, but it seems that the scriptures are full of hidden meanings, and the understanding of them eludes you? Think of this. If the Lord has a message for you, would it be fair of Him to hide it from your eyes? Certainly not, God's messages are for our learning and He has given us the keys that we need in order to be aligned with His will.

One of the keys that God has given for our understanding of the Bible has to do with submission. While He was here, Jesus taught in the temple. Many of the Jews were astonished because He knew so much, yet He was not trained in their schools. "Jesus answered them, and said, My doctrine is not mine, but his that sent me. If any man will do his will, he shall know of the doctrine, whether it be of God, or whether I speak of myself." John 17:16, 17. If we are willing to do whatever the Lord brings to our consciousness, we are well on our way to understanding the Bible.

Another key to understanding the scriptures is having the Holy Ghost teach us. If we do not have His Spirit by our side every step of the way, we cannot be truly willing to do His will, nor will we ever understand the intent of His words. "Howbeit when he, the Spirit of truth, is come, he will guide you into all truth: for he shall not speak of himself; but whatsoever he shall hear, that shall he speak: and he will shew you things to come." John 16:13. The Holy Spirit brings the

293

truth for our need to our understanding, and the blessing of His holiness, which converts willing hearts to the truth. If we have the Holy Spirit, we will know God's will. God is more willing to give us the Holy Spirit when we ask, than parents are willing to give good gifts to their children. "If ye then, being evil, know how to give good gifts unto your children: how much more shall your heavenly Father give the Holy Spirit to them that ask him?" Luke 11:13.

The last key we will discuss is using the Bible as its own interpreter. Many people look outside of the Bible for some commentary on what the Lord must have meant by this or that. Commentaries are useful as far as they go; however, the best way to understand a text is to search the scriptures for related themes. As we do this, the Lord brings a depth of truth to our awareness that no commentary can. "Whom shall he teach knowledge? and whom shall he make to understand doctrine? them that are weaned from the milk, and drawn from the breasts. For precept must be upon precept, precept upon precept; line upon line, line upon line; here a little, and there a little:" Isaiah 28:9, 10. When we study the Bible looking for other texts relating to the one we began with, and meditate on how they may all relate to our salvation, we are on the right path to understanding the scriptures.

There are a number of elements, not covered here, however, you have been given a good foundation for Bible study. If we are led by the Spirit through prayer, if we are willing to do what the Lord reveals, and use the Bible to interpret itself, we are well on the road to receiving the revelation we are so in need of.

WHAT HAVE THEY SEEN IN THINE HOUSE

Isaiah 39:4
"Then said he, What have they seen in thine house? And Hezekiah answered, All that is in mine house have they seen: there is nothing among my treasures that I have not shewed them."

King Hezekiah was sick and about to die. The prophet Isaiah was sent to tell him that the Lord said to get his life together or death was certain. As one might expect, this troubled the king greatly, and he began to seek the Lord in prayer and devotion. The Lord finally heard the king's prayer, and sent word to Him through Isaiah that his life would be extended fifteen years. Can you imagine the joy that must have brought to the king as he faced certain death? "And Hezekiah said unto Isaiah, What shall be the sign that the LORD will heal me, and that I shall go up into the house of the LORD the third day? And Isaiah said, This sign shalt thou have of the LORD, that the LORD will do the thing that he hath spoken: shall the shadow go forth ten degrees, or go back ten degrees? And Hezekiah answered, It is a light thing for the shadow to go down ten degrees: nay, but let the shadow return backward ten degrees. And Isaiah the prophet cried unto the LORD: and he brought the shadow ten degrees backward, by which it had gone down in the dial of Ahaz." II Kings 20:8-11.

The fame of Hezekiah's healing was spread even to Babylon. The Babylonians were skilled at marking the movements of the heavenly bodies, and would immediately take note of such a miraculous event as the sun moving backward ten degrees. As such, the king of Babylon, and his entourage eventually went to meet Hezekiah, whose God was able to command even the heavenly bodies to do impossible things. When the king received his visitors he could have been a great witness to them of God's goodness, and his ability to save souls from sin in the same degree that He was able to manipulate nature, but this is not the route Hezekiah chose. "And Hezekiah was glad of them, and shewed them the house of his precious things, the silver, and the gold, and the spices, and the precious ointment, and all the house of his armour, and all that was found in his treasures: there was nothing in his house, nor in all his dominion, that Hezekiah shewed them not." Isaiah 39:2. Instead of showing the goodness of the Lord to the heathen king, Hezekiah demonstrated that silver, gold, and material wealth were his gods. What a great impact he could have had on the entire heathen world if he had simply told his story of God's goodness.

Today we have the same opportunity. The Lord showers us with grace everyday. With this grace comes great responsibility. This is no ill burden by any means. It should be a pleasure to witness concerning the blessings of God. Let us learn a lesson from King Hezekiah. Instead of worshipping the blessing God has bestowed, we must worship the giver of all blessings.

The end of Hezekiah's story was sad. As a result of his failed witness, all of his material wealth was stolen, and his sons were castrated and became slaves to the Babylonians. Certainly this could have been avoided. The way of wickedness is hard, but the good witness of a righteous man brings joy, peace, and the favor of God.

MY SERVANT ISRAEL

Isaiah 49:3
"And said unto me, Thou art my servant, O Israel, in whom I will be glorified."

The Lord so identified Himself with His people Israel that Jesus, the Messiah, was called by the same name. As Isaiah describes God's servants throughout the book, he refers to the wayward people who would not listen to God's counsel, and would surely bear the consequences, as Israel. Because of His own righteousness, after a time, God would deliver them. Suddenly, the language shifts. The term Israel is still used, but instead of sin, shame, and judgment, God mentions glorification and faithfulness. God's mysterious servant Israel, would glorify Him through His ministry to the wayward tribes of Jacob, and be a light to the Gentiles.

God often opens our eyes to the mysteries of His love. The fact that God would clothe Himself in the garb of humanity, as in the person of Jesus Christ, is a mystery. It is a mystery that God would love Abraham and Lot so much that the preincarnate Christ would appear, along with two angels, to warn them of the things that would shortly befall Sodom and Gomorrah. It is a mystery that, in Christ, God would identify Himself as Israel. Jesus is the faithful Israel of whom Isaiah spoke.

Let us look at Him for a moment. The faithful Israel would be especially called from the womb. Jesus was especially called from the womb (Galatians 4:4). Faithful Israel's name would be mentioned from the bowels of His mother's womb. Jesus' name was mentioned from the time He was conceived (Matthew 1:20-23). Faithful Israel would serve to rise up and restore faithless Israel. He would also serve as a light to the Gentiles. This is how Jesus is described. "For mine eyes have seen thy salvation, Which thou hast prepared before the face of all people; A light to lighten the Gentiles, and the glory of thy people Israel." Luke 2:30-32. "And Simeon blessed them, and said unto Mary his mother, Behold, this child is set for the fall and rising again of many in Israel; and for a sign which shall be spoken against;" Luke 2:34.

Simply put, God has so identified Himself with His people that a revelation of Jesus Christ was given using the very name given to His people. All who decide to follow Jesus in truth are called by His name, the Israel of God. He has corrected our unfaithfulness. If we receive this blessing by faith, we become heirs according to the promise given to Abraham. "For ye are all the children of God by faith in Christ Jesus. For as many of you as have been baptized into Christ have put on Christ. There is neither Jew nor Greek, there is neither bond nor free, there is neither male nor female: for ye are all one in Christ Jesus. And if ye be Christ's, then are ye Abraham's seed, and heirs according to the promise." Galatians 3:26-29.

I WILL NOT FORGET YOU

Isaiah 49:15
***"Can a woman forget her sucking child, that she should
not have compassion on the son of her womb? yea, they
may forget, yet will I not forget thee."***

Mothers all around the world possess nurturing instincts for their children. This is true for species besides homo sapiens. For human mothers, the instinct is developed over the period the child is developing in the womb. Even the most attuned father cannot begin to understand the link between mother and child. Mothers generally have a protective instinct that allows them to understand, in most cases, the need of their babies although they cannot communicate their own needs. More than just a generic nurturing instinct, mothers are drawn even closer when they breast feed. When they are busy outside of the home and must be separated from their babies, they often utilize breast pumps in order to provide the milk needed while they are gone. It is with all of this and more, that God speaks to us regarding His commitment to us.

Our Lord says that a loving mother in the midst of the suckling period of their baby's life would sooner forget that baby than He would forget us. We know that it is nearly impossible for a mother in this situation to forget her baby, yet the Lord seems to exaggerate the point in order to make it clear to us. He keeps us always under His care and direction. Like a mother who would give all for her baby, God has given all for us because He loves us. He gathers us together and shields us like winged creatures gather their chicks. It is under His wings of protection that we may put our trust (Psalms 91:4).

As you traverse the road yet to be discovered today, remember that the Lord is always near His children and will never forsake us.

THANKSGIVING

Isaiah 51:3
"For the LORD shall comfort Zion: he will comfort all
her waste places; and he will make her wilderness like
Eden, and her desert like the garden of the LORD; joy
and gladness shall be found therein, thanksgiving,
and the voice of melody."

It is a blessing to consider the promises of God. His promises are sure. All too often, we make promises that we either cannot keep or never intended to keep. Some of the promises that we actually kept, were kept with the wrong motive. God is different. His motives are always pure, and He always comes through.

When we consider the promises made to specific people in the Bible, most of the time we can apply them to our own lives. It is not difficult to determine whether God was making a principle-based promise to someone, or a specific promise that only applied to them. If we meet the requirements of those based on principle, and depend upon conditions, we too may benefit.

A great example of a promise we can benefit from is the one outlined in the following text. Notice the implied condition. "Hearken to me, ye that follow after righteousness, ye that seek the LORD: look unto the rock whence ye are hewn, and to the hole of the pit whence ye are digged. Look unto Abraham your father, and unto Sarah that bare you: for I called him alone, and blessed him, and increased him. For the LORD shall comfort Zion: he will comfort all her waste places; and he will make her wilderness like Eden, and her desert like the garden of the LORD; joy and gladness shall be found therein, thanksgiving, and the voice of melody." Isaiah 51:1-3. When we are faithful to God by His grace, listen to Him, and follow after righteousness, He will comfort us, make our desert places like the fruitful Eden of God, give us joy, and teach us how to sing melodies of thanksgiving.

Faithful Abraham gave an example that all would do well to follow. The Bible says that his faith in God was accounted to him as righteousness. Even though Abraham did not always understand the commands of God, in the end, he was faithful. Abraham did not withhold obedience. This is why he is called the father of the faithful.

When your life seems to be as dry and lonely as desert places, remember to be faithful, seek the Lord, listen to the voice of God, and follow after righteousness, and God will fulfill His promise to all who obey Him. Be blessed and full of thanksgiving as you accept the promises of God.

WOUNDED

Isaiah 53:5
"But he was wounded for our transgressions, he was
bruised for our iniquities: the chastisement of our peace
was upon him; and with his stripes we are healed."

What love! This is the very first thought that comes to my mind when considering what Jesus endured for me. What kind of love leads God to take on human flesh and risk everything in order to save a sinner like me? It is incomprehensible to consider all that was at stake. All of heaven was focused on the lesson book of salvation, from which God was teaching us all the value of one soul.

Wouldn't it be wonderful if we sacrificed ourselves just a fraction of how He sacrificed Himself? How many wars would we have with one another if we could clearly see the love that God has deep within for us? How many arguments would we allow to pass our lips if we grasped the agony of soul Jesus endured to make eternal life available to us? How many times would we allow judgementalism to rule our thoughts when we see people struggling with sinful habits if we could see into the invisible spiritual battle being fought over us everyday? I think our perspective would change drastically if we focused on the love of God. Truly, Jesus was wounded because of our sins. Whatever pain He needed to go through as our heavenly substitute, in order to establish an eternal bond of peace between us and God, He did so patiently. He suffered the agony of becoming sin for us. He endured the long road of inner turmoil every step of the way to Calvary. He experienced the effects of eternal separation from His father in our place. The Lord of glory endured all of this and more, in order to save us. Through His suffering, we now have healing. Through His infinite sacrifice, we can receive eternal life. By His wounds, we are healed.

SILENCE IS GOLDEN

Isaiah 53:7
"He was oppressed, and he was afflicted, yet he opened
not his mouth: he is brought as a lamb to the slaughter,
and as a sheep before her shearers is dumb,
so he openeth not his mouth."

An incredible lesson can be derived from the example of Jesus' last moments before the cross. Isaiah prophesied that He [Jesus] would be oppressed and afflicted, yet not open His mouth. How is it that Jesus could be quiet while being spat on, beaten, stabbed, ridiculed, lied on, teased, and mocked? How could Jesus maintain His composure knowing that He created the people who, under the power of the devil, would soon kill Him? How could Jesus, who spoke into the darkness of nothingness and created the worlds, keep silent?

Jesus knew beforehand that He would meet with the most intense struggle ever waged on the earth. Jesus endured His severe test through absolute reliance on His heavenly Father. It seems like a cliché to simply state that Jesus trusted His father for strength, but there is no other way to say it. It was through all night prayer meetings, deliberate separation from sinful practices, dedicated Godly service for His fellow men, that Jesus was able to stand composed with dignity, as evil men dared stretch forth a defiled hand to cause Him pain.

As we meditate on His perfect example of holiness and self-distrust, we too can be silent when the trials of life threaten us. When people falsely accuse us, or seek to cause us pain through gossip, we can lay hold on the power of God. When it is necessary for us to remain silent, we can. All of the benefits of Jesus' victory are available to us today. When God gives us an awareness of our relationship to Him, we, with Jesus, can demonstrate to the watching world that silence indeed is golden.

GREAT DAY IN THE MORNING

Isaiah 55:1
"Ho, every one that thirsteth, come ye to the waters, and he that hath no money; come ye, buy, and eat; yea, come, buy wine and milk without money and without price."

There is a restaurant in downtown Washington, D.C., that my wife and I like very much. When we were dating, it was the first one that she took me to for my birthday. There was a good selection of vegetarian items, and the food was well prepared and well seasoned. The interesting thing about this restaurant which is characteristic of many large, affluent cities, is that it is located in the heart of commerce and government, yet directly across the street is a park where homeless people gather daily. It makes one wonder how such poverty can exist so close to the White House and United States Capital Building. This is a disease infecting many large cities. The rich own property beautiful where others beg for their next meal.

While reading today's verse, it occurred to me that it would be a great day in the morning, if the restaurant opened with the owner announcing, into a megaphone, that all water, juice, and food was free today. Can you imagine the disbelief that would mark the faces of those in the park? Do you think there would be any question as to whether they would be interested?

God has made a similar call. He has thrown open the doors of salvation to everyone who is hungry for it. He has thrown open the cisterns of His grace to anyone dehydrated by a lack of acceptance with God. All that they can eat and drink is free. Now, it is free to them, but to God it was a great investment. Through Christ, the penalty for sin was completely satisfied; therefore, salvation can be made available to anyone willing to receive it. It is just that simple.

God gives us the ability to choose Him and then opens the door of opportunity. All we need to do, initially, is say yes.

Let's change the scenario a little. Suppose the same offer in Washington, D.C. was extended to the homeless in the park, but some whose bellies were distended by hunger said that they were not really hungry and passed on the opportunity? Suppose they refused the clear refreshing water and freshly squeezed fruit juice? Would that make sense? Most people do that with salvation. Spiritually parched and exceedingly hungry people refuse salvation everyday. These souls expend all of their energies grasping at things that do not satisfy. To such ones, God says, "Wherefore do ye spend money for that which is not bread? and your labour for that which satisfieth not? hearken diligently unto me, and eat ye that which is good, and let your soul delight itself in fatness. Incline your ear, and come unto me: hear, and your soul shall live; and I will make an everlasting covenant with you, even the sure mercies of David." Isaiah 55:2, 3. Receiving the bounties of God today would make it a great day in the morning.

THE SAVIOR IS WAITING

Isaiah 55:7
"Let the wicked forsake his way, and the unrighteous man
his thoughts: and let him return unto the LORD,
and he will have mercy upon him; and to our God,
for he will abundantly pardon."

There was a man with two sons. One son came to his dad and asked if he could receive his inheritance money now, in spite of the fact that his dad was still alive. The father consented. "And not many days after the younger son gathered all together, and took his journey into a far country, and there wasted his substance with riotous living. And when he had spent all, there arose a mighty famine in that land; and he began to be in want. And he went and joined himself to a citizen of that country; and he sent him into his fields to feed swine. And he would fain have filled his belly with the husks that the swine did eat: and no man gave unto him. And when he came to himself, he said, How many hired servants of my father's have bread enough and to spare, and I perish with hunger! will arise and go to my father, and will say unto him, Father, I have sinned against heaven, and before thee, And am no more worthy to be called thy son: make me as one of thy hired servants. And he arose, and came to his father. But when he was yet a great way off, his father saw him, and had compassion, and ran, and fell on his neck, and kissed him." Luke 15:13-20.

In this parable, the father is seen waiting for his son to return. The text did not say that when the wayward son returned, a servant alerted his father about his son's arrival. It says that the father saw the son a great way off. It is clear that the father was *waiting* for the day when his son would return.

The Lord waits for us much in the same way. We often squander the wealth of God's mercy and when we become completely destitute, and have nowhere else to go, we seek the Lord. Ashamed and feeling unworthy to be called God's children, we go to Him confessing our sins, willing to occupy any place He gives us in His kingdom. As we come to ourselves, the Lord reveals our need of Him; otherwise, we would not know that we need Him. Patiently He calls us, awaiting our response. With tender love, He longs for us to return to Him so He can welcome us home. When we finally go to Him, he treats us as honored kings and queens, and *not* as servants. In that moment, He abundantly pardons, and never brings up the record of our faults again. The Savior is waiting to enter your heart. Please let Him in.

Thank the Lord for being so willing to bless His people.

FREE ACCESS

Isaiah 56:6, 7
*"Also the sons of the stranger, that join themselves to the
LORD, to serve him, and to love the name of the LORD,
to be his servants, every one that keepeth the sabbath from
polluting it, and taketh hold of my covenant; Even them
will I bring to my holy mountain, and make them joyful in
my house of prayer: their burnt offerings and their
sacrifices shall be accepted upon mine altar; for mine
house shall be called an house of prayer for all people."*

Many times, ancient Israel, the people of God, became
overwhelmed with the idea that they were the chosen of
God. As they saw the favor of God poured out upon them
in spiritual knowledge, the exodus from Egypt, and victory
after victory over their enemies, many mistook that as a
reason to be religious bigots. True, the counsel was clear.
God had chosen them as the royal priesthood to be set
apart for a holy use. He did instruct them to remain separate from all others because their religion was pure and
undefiled. They worshipped the only true God and looked
forward to the Messiah coming to reveal God to the earth.
Somehow, in all of this, many had forgotten the reason
God had chosen them. They lost sight of the fact that He
wanted them to evangelize the world. He wanted them to
show, because of God's favor on them, that there are benefits to turning from sin and serving the Lord. Some misin-
terpreted this sanctification as an exclusive club of saved
people barring all others from salvation. This was not the
case.

God revealed a wonderful truth through the prophet
Isaiah. "Neither let the son of the stranger, that hath joined
himself to the LORD, speak, saying, The LORD hath
utterly separated me from his people: neither let the eunuch

say, Behold, I am a dry tree. For thus saith the LORD unto the eunuchs that keep my sabbaths, and choose the things that please me, and take hold of my covenant; Even unto them will I give in mine house and within my walls a place and a name better than of sons and of daughters: I will give them an everlasting name, that shall not be cut off." Isaiah 56:3-5. He revealed that although salvation was of the Jews, the purpose of their favor was to bring others of all nations into knowledge of the truth. Their express purpose for living was to lead others to a relationship with the God that they knew so well. All, who by the power of God, saw their need for Him and accepted Him as their Lord and Savior, were accepted.

There are those today, who have the same elitist view of their own religious group, as did God's ancient people. What does God have to say about this? "And other sheep I have, which are not of this fold: them also I must bring, and they shall hear my voice; and there shall be one fold, and one shepherd." John 10:16. Those who worship God in spirit and in truth, who have the testimony and faith of Jesus, do not fall into the same trap. Resist the temptation to think you are the only ones eligible for salvation. Rather, accept the charge that God has always given to His people to evangelize the world. The fact that He has chosen you to gather all of those who love Him is reason *enough* to be humble. It is a reason to stay connected yourselves, in order to know His will that you might execute it faithfully. "For ye are all the children of God by faith in Christ Jesus. For as many of you as have been baptized into Christ have put on Christ. There is neither Jew nor Greek, there is neither bond nor free, there is neither male nor female: for ye are all one in Christ Jesus. And if ye be Christ's, then are ye Abraham's seed, and heirs according to the promise." Galatians 3:26-29. All who can hear the voice of God have free access to all of His promises. "And the Spirit and the bride say, Come. And let him that heareth say, Come. And let him that is athirst come. And whosoever will, let him take the water of life freely." Revelation 22:17.

DELIGHT THYSELF IN THE LORD

Isaiah 58:13, 14
"If thou turn away thy foot from the sabbath, from doing thy pleasure on my holy day; and call the sabbath a delight, the holy of the LORD, honourable; and shalt honour him, not doing thine own ways, nor finding thine own pleasure, nor speaking thine own words: Then shalt thou delight thyself in the LORD; and I will cause thee to ride upon the high places of the earth, and feed thee with the heritage of Jacob thy father: for the mouth of the LORD hath spoken it."

In the days of Isaiah the prophet, God's people Israel were in a needy condition. They needed the Lord to bring what He deemed as important, to the forefront of their minds. In some ways, they understood proper outward behaviors, like fasting for example, but the practical godliness that springs from within was lost. Because of their lack of commitment to God, they simply could not understand His will. This is why God often sent special messages. If they had been diligent in seeking the Lord for themselves, they would not have needed such pointed messages to come through the prophets. It is a blessing to know, that whatever the needed spiritual supplementation is, God is willing to give it.

Fasting, an outward sign of piety was apparently respected highly by God's people. Often they associated it with holiness, regardless of their inner spiritual state. They wore fasting like a badge of honor. God was not satisfied with most of their fasts. He desired a greater level of inner commitment to match their outward piety. "Is not this the fast that I have chosen? to loose the bands of wickedness, to undo the heavy burdens, and to let the oppressed go free, and that ye break every yoke? Is it not to deal thy bread to the hungry, and that thou bring the poor that are cast out to thy house? when thou seest the naked, that thou cover him; and that thou hide not thyself from thine own flesh? Then shall thy light break forth as the morning, and thine health shall spring forth speedily: and thy righteousness shall go before thee; the glory of the LORD shall be thy rereward." Isaiah 58:6-8. Great promises were associated with true-hearted, godly commitment.

God revealed to them that along with relieving the suffering of others and bringing them the light of salvation, they were to return to true worship through Sabbath commitment. They were to return to God's intended use of His holy time. They were to reserve the seventh-day as God's special day to commune with them on a level greater than on any other day. In this way they would delight themselves in the Lord. In this way He would cause them to ride upon the high places of the earth. Great promises were associated with true and godly observance of the seventh-day Sabbath.

If we seek to be called by God's name in the last days, His admonitions to the ancient children of Israel are to be heeded (Galatians 3:29). When we return to practical godliness by relieving suffering, and remembering His holy time, we stand only to benefit. We are aligning ourselves with the King of the universe and He is pleased. Do not sell yourself short on God's blessings. Return to practical godliness and watch the Lord work in new ways in your life.

NOTHING BETWEEN

Isaiah 59:1, 2
"Behold, the LORD's hand is not shortened, that it
cannot save; neither his ear heavy, that it cannot hear:
But your iniquities have separated between you and your
God, and your sins have hid his face from you,
that he will not hear."

At many hotels in the swimming pool area, signs are posted with the opening and closing times. During the open times, there are families and others enjoying the water. They play pool volleyball, dunk one another, and swim laps. During these open times, they have lots of fun. In the event that someone begins drowning, someone is available to help. They can throw out a life-saving device and call for help. In the event that someone ventures into the pool area after hours and decides to swim, that protection is not there. If they encounter the same difficulty, it is likely that no one will be available to help. There is a door between the unwise swimmer and the outside world; therefore, the odds of being heard are slim.

This is an analogy of how it may be if an individual decides to ignore the posted signs of good relationship with God. God is perfectly capable of hearing and saving sinners. Some people ignore the promptings of God's Spirit, and when they have chosen to continue in sin, a door of separation exists. God cannot hear the voice of those unwilling to turn to Him in repentance. It is not that God is unwilling to save. He is available to all who are willing to follow Him. He said, "If we confess our sins, he is faithful and just to forgive us our sins, and to cleanse us from all unrighteousness." I John 1:9. This means that the door of separation does not have to remain.

In our analogy, suppose the swimmer ignored the posted

hours of operation, but a hotel employee that is accustomed to people doing so, checked the pool after hours? In this case, the employee sees the swimmer in trouble and throws that person a lifeline. God also sees people in trouble that should know better, and continues for a time, to pass their way. At some point, some turn from their arrogance and accept the help God offers. The door between them and God is now ajar and He can hear their plea.

It is wonderful to know that God does not merely sit by while we drown in sin. Although we often choose separation, God does all that He can to make Himself available to us. Pray for the faith necessary to have nothing between your soul and Jesus.

HEAVENLY UNIFORM

Isaiah 61:10
"I will greatly rejoice in the LORD, my soul shall be joyful in my God; for he hath clothed me with the garments of salvation, he hath covered me with the robe of righteousness, as a bridegroom decketh himself with ornaments, and as a bride adorneth herself with her jewels."

In most every nation of the world, certain people are distinguishable by their uniforms. The police, military, foodservice employees, medical staff, etc., are all clothed in such a way as to clearly show their purpose. The uniforms they wear tell a story about their duties and goals.

The children of God have a uniform as well. It is a heavenly uniform that distinguishes us from everyone else. This uniform demonstrates to anyone looking, that we have a particular purpose. This uniform demonstrates our duties and goals. The uniform issued by the heavenly courts is Christ's righteousness. While it may not have a particular color outwardly, inner light emanates from those who have it. The power of God is evident in those wearing the heavenly uniform.

As with those wearing earthly uniforms, our spiritual uniforms manifest God's duties and goals. Those with the righteousness of God are determined to lead others to a right relationship with Him. Our goal, because of our influence, is to lead as many people to heaven as possible. We desire to make an indelible impression on as many people as God sends to us.

As you prepare for the day ahead, be certain that you have on your heavenly uniform, pressed and clean. Remember that *you* represent the company whose insignia you wear. Represent it well. It may be that those, with whom you come into contact, will have just one encounter with the heavenly kingdom, through you. Pray that it will be a fruitful one.

MORE THAN JUST A RESTORATION

Isaiah 65:17
"For, behold, I create new heavens and a new earth: and the former shall not be remembered, nor come into mind."

The end of all things is at hand. The Lord will soon fulfill His promise to return and receive His people unto Himself, that where He is, there we will be also (John 14:1-3). Soon we will see the sign of the Son of man in the heavens and say, "this is our God and we have waited for Him." Our hearts will soon quicken with pulses of joy as we see Him descend, knowing that in a moment, in a twinkling of an eye, we shall be changed. We shall be like Him and see Him as He *really* is (I Corinthians 15:50-58; I John 3:1-3). After we have lived with the Lord in heaven for one thousand years, we, with the New Jerusalem of God, will descend to the new earth, following the complete destruction of all wickedness. Then, there will be no more tears, suffering, death or pain. (Revelation 20:4-10; Revelation 21:7). We look forward to that day.

From our limited perspective, it would be wonderful if God were to restore the entire universe, especially the earth, to a pre-sin state. There would be no more predators, no fluctuations in climate, and no more sin. Notice what the Bible says. "And he that sat upon the throne said, Behold, I make all things new. And he said unto me, Write: for these words are true and faithful." Revelation 21:5. Notice, God did not say that He was going to merely reset the sin clock so the earth would be as it was before sin. Follow me. Before earthly sin, God tested Adam and Eve on the issue of obedience at the tree in the midst of the garden. They failed the test, although God had given them the power to succeed. If we were to be merely restored to the state at which the holy pair existed prior to their test, we would be incomplete.

318

Imagine where they would have been had they passed the test. They would have been forever sealed in a state of sinless bliss, having triumphed, in love, over the devil's temptations.

The human race has endured severe testing for thousands of years. Our fidelity or unfaithfulness is being proven. One day, in the end, those who love the Lord will be exalted to the state of perpetual growth that Adam and Eve would have entered had they passed their test. Soon, those who are filthy will remain that way until they are destroyed. Those who are righteous will remain that way forever and ever. Sin shall never rise again (Revelation 22:10-14; Nahum 1:9). The re-created human race now has something else that exalts us. Jesus Christ occupies the same glorified bodies we do. The plan of salvation required Him to become a human. Having been victorious over hell, death, the devil, and the grave, Jesus ascended to heaven as our representative. He carried His glorified body into the heavens.

Do not settle for the idea, albeit decent, that we are simply going to be restored. No! We look forward to an even better existence with God than Adam and Eve had prior to their fall. Praise the Lord for this glorious truth!

NOURISHED

Jeremiah 17:7, 8
"Blessed is the man that trusteth in the LORD, and whose hope the LORD is. For he shall be as a tree planted by the waters, and that spreadeth out her roots by the river, and shall not see when heat cometh, but her leaf shall be green; and shall not be careful in the year of drought, neither shall cease from yielding fruit."

I can remember when I was a child, learning in science class that green leaves do not burn. The teacher told us, in not so many words, that the nourished leaf is evidenced by how green it is. Trees, plants, and all kinds of bushes draw their nourishment through their roots much like the way veins and arteries carry blood throughout our bodies.

Dry leaves, we were taught, easily burned because the moisture had already been removed. This is why, during the dry season, we hear about so many wildfires in the western portion of the United States.

Jeremiah and David understood this science. They equated the righteous to green trees and those who did no not trust in the Lord to dry leaves. "And he shall be like a tree planted by the rivers of water, that bringeth forth his fruit in his season; his leaf also shall not wither; and whatsoever he doeth shall prosper. The ungodly are not so: but are like the chaff which the wind driveth away." Psalms 1:3, 4. The Lord consistently nourishes those who love Him with the refreshing waters of His grace, and they will always bear fruit. To the degree that we remain connected to the Lord, we are nourished. "I am the vine, ye are the branches: He that abideth in me, and I in him, the same bringeth forth much fruit: for without me ye can do nothing. If a man abide not in me, he is cast forth as a branch, and is withered; and men gather them, and cast them into the fire, and they are burned." John 15:5, 6. "Jesus answered and said unto her, Whosoever drinketh of this water shall thirst again: But whosoever drinketh of the water that I shall give him shall never thirst; but the water that I shall give him shall be in him a well of water springing up into everlasting life." John 4:13, 14.

It is a blessing to be nourished by the revitalizing rains of God's Spirit so that we may continue bearing fruit. "But the fruit of the Spirit is love, joy, peace, longsuffering, gentleness, goodness, faith, Meekness, temperance: against such there is no law. And they that are Christ's have crucified the flesh with the affections and lusts. If we live in the Spirit, let us also walk in the Spirit." Galatians 5:22-25.

THE MASTER POTTER

Jeremiah 18:3, 4
"Then I went down to the potter's house, and, behold, he
wrought a work on the wheels. And the vessel that he
made of clay was marred in the hand of the potter: so he
made it again another vessel, as seemed good
to the potter to make it."

The Lord has a way with words. He always manages to make Himself unmistakably clear. His use of images and stories far surpasses any blockbuster movie, and we are certainly benefited more by them.

God spoke to Jeremiah one day about His willingness to do whatever it takes to save His people. He told Jeremiah to go to a potter's house to observe, and there he would receive His words. Jeremiah did as he was told. He noticed that the pot of clay that the potter was working on had imperfections. The potter, being the master worker that he was, could not be satisfied with the result, so he made it again. The potter was so patient that it did not matter that he had already spent time on the first pot. He needed to do whatever it took to perfect his work.

So it is with God. Hopefully, all of God's children are having the experience of the imperfect pot. We were created by God, yet because of the imperfections caused by sin, we too are marred. The Lord exercises His loving prerogatives to remake us. He loves us so much that as we cooperate with Him, we are renewed into the form He intended from the beginning.

I am sure you have heard it said that the Lord accepts us just as we are. In many cases, the person saying this realizes, to a certain degree, that they are imperfect. It may be that they have cherished sins, which they have not been victorious over. When they encounter the holy standard of

God's law, whether it be through a person or in personal devotion, they make provision for their errors by suggesting that God's loving acceptance of people, is license for us to continue traveling the path of sin. After all, the Lord is still working with us. While it is true that the Lord accepts us as we are, He never leaves us the way He found us. As we experience the Lord more and more, His purpose becomes clear. Whatever is necessary for Him to do in order to make us into the vessels He intended from the beginning, as the master potter did, He must remake us. Can we, if we are the clay, look at the potter and say, "Why have you made me this way?" Oftentimes, the process we must go through to be reformed and perfected is painful, however, we must trust the Lord through the process. Notice what the Lord said to Jeremiah: "O house of Israel, cannot I do with you as this potter? saith the LORD. Behold, as the clay is in the potter's hand, so are ye in mine hand, O house of Israel." Jeremiah 18:6.

It is indeed a blessing, that while the Lord accepts us as we are, He is not willing to accept the fact that as we are, we cannot live with Him eternally. It is our privilege to be remade, reformed, and reconstructed in order to be fit for the kingdom of heaven. The great thing about all of this is that the Lord is interested only in our good, so whatever process He employs, will be used to benefit us in love.

THE LORD OUR RIGHTEOUSNESS

Jeremiah 23:6
"In his days Judah shall be saved, and Israel shall dwell safely: and this is his name whereby he shall be called, THE LORD OUR RIGHTEOUSNESS."

The longer I live, the more I realize that all of my own righteousnesses are as filthy rags (Isaiah 64:6). All of my efforts to live a righteous life are fine as far as they go, but if they are ever to be registered in heaven, I must be seen through the righteousness of Jesus Christ. He is the best. There is none like Him. As I consider the difficulty of resisting the incredible temptations that I am assailed by, I develop a new respect for Jesus. He lived a perfect life while relying solely upon His Father for strength. With authority, He met the intense battle that Satan brought to Him at every step of His life on earth.

False pastors and hirelings had overrun Israel when Israel was supposed to be nurtured and cared for by faithful leaders committed to the Lord. God showed disdain for those commissioned to care for the flock, but allowed pride and self to get in the way. "His watchmen are blind: they are all ignorant, they are all dumb dogs, they cannot bark; sleeping, lying down, loving to slumber. Yea, they are greedy dogs which can never have enough, and they are shepherds that cannot understand: they all look to their own way, every one for his gain, from his quarter." Isaiah 53:10, 11. This type of faithlessness often discourages people from attending church. They see that some leaders are out of control and not loving, therefore they are discouraged from becoming a part of God's body. They wonder how churches can be of God when the leaders are so corrupt. God sees their distress. When these very things were going on in Israel, He sent the message through Jeremiah that He was the only one that was *truly* righteous. While spiritual leaders are to represent God, they are still human. God is ultimately in control and does have His faithful ones in leadership positions. In any case, only Jesus is righteous. As we look to Him for guidance, He will lead us to the right house of worship where He is worshipped faithfully, and His word demonstrated in truth.

Do not allow the corruption of this world or spiritual leaders to sow such a bad seed in your mind that you forget that *God* is the righteous judge. He is the only one above reproach. He is the only one that will save us. Look to Jesus. He will never let you down. *He* is the Lord our righteousness.

HOPEFUL FUTURE

Jeremiah 29:11
***"For I know the thoughts that I think toward you, saith
the LORD, thoughts of peace, and not of evil,
to give you an expected end."***

The Lord prophesied through His servant Jeremiah regarding the end of the Babylonian captivity. This captivity occurred because God's people decided that they did not want to be ruled by Him. They did not adhere to His laws or judgments. They did not listen to the prophets; therefore, God used heathens to get their attention. Near the end of the captivity, Daniel prayed this prayer. "We have sinned, and have committed iniquity, and have done wickedly, and have rebelled, even by departing from thy precepts and from thy judgments: Neither have we hearkened unto thy servants the prophets, which spake in thy name to our kings, our princes, and our fathers, and to all the people of the land. O Lord, righteousness belongeth unto thee, but unto us confusion of faces, as at this day; to the men of Judah, and to the inhabitants of Jerusalem, and unto all Israel, that are near, and that are far off, through all the countries whither thou hast driven them, because of their trespass that they have trespassed against thee." Daniel 9:5-7. You get a sense of Daniel's agony and desperation over the way the people treated God.

The Lord gave Jeremiah a message of hope that all of Israel would look forward to after seventy long years. They must have longed for deliverance much like their foreparents longed for the exodus. "For thus saith the LORD, That after seventy years be accomplished at Babylon I will visit you, and perform my good word toward you, in causing you to return to this place. For I know the thoughts that I think toward you, saith the

LORD, thoughts of peace, and not of evil, to give you an expected end. Then shall ye call upon me, and ye shall go and pray unto me, and I will hearken unto you. And ye shall seek me, and find me, when ye shall search for me with all your heart. And I will be found of you, saith the LORD: and I will turn away your captivity, and I will gather you from all the nations, and from all the places whither I have driven you, saith the LORD; and I will bring you again into the place whence I caused you to be carried away captive." Jeremiah 29:10-14.

This world is like Babylon and Egypt of old. I often feel as if I am a captive here. When will the turmoil end? What hope do we have? Many countries around the world are in constant privation, war, terror, and are faced with plagues. How can they be hopeful? As we diligently seek the Lord and give ourselves to Him, we become His children. As to the Jews of old, He promises that we will have an expected end. We will have a hopeful future. One day soon all evil will cease and peace will be restored to the universe. Let us turn to God with all of our hearts, and we will be delivered. We will finally experience in the fullest sense our hopeful future. "After this I beheld, and, lo, a great multitude, which no man could number, of all nations, and kindreds, and people, and tongues, stood before the throne, and before the Lamb, clothed with white robes, and palms in their hands; And cried with a loud voice, saying, Salvation to our God which sitteth upon the throne, and unto the Lamb." Revelation 7:9, 10. "And I said unto him, Sir, thou knowest. And he said to me, These are they which came out of great tribulation, and have washed their robes, and made them white in the blood of the Lamb. Therefore are they before the throne of God, and serve him day and night in his temple: and he that sitteth on the throne shall dwell among them. They shall hunger no more, neither thirst any more; neither shall the sun light on them, nor any heat. For the Lamb which is in the midst of the throne shall feed them, and shall lead them unto living fountains of waters: and God shall wipe away all tears from their eyes." Revelation 7:14-17.

A GOOD INVESTMENT

Jeremiah 32:24, 25
"Behold the mounts, they are come unto the city to take it; and the city is given into the hand of the Chaldeans, that fight against it, because of the sword, and of the famine, and of the pestilence: and what thou hast spoken is come to pass; and, behold, thou seest it. And thou hast said unto me, O Lord GOD, Buy thee the field for money, and take witnesses; for the city is given into the hand of the Chaldeans."

I have a friend, who after working more than thirty years, just retired from a major corporation. He is still in his fifties and full of life and energy. He and his wife are exploring new opportunities to do things that were not possible to do while he worked at a conventional job. One of their newest ventures is in real estate. They search for so-called distressed properties that have been boarded up and may not be in great shape. Their purpose, in order to make a profit, is to move into one of three options that they have available in the way of investing in these types of properties. Some would see the properties they invest in and wonder why anyone would want to do so, but this couple has a plan. They know the potential, although the immediate view may seem bleak. They do it for investment purposes.

During a bleak time of imminent captivity and destruction, the Lord spoke to Jeremiah concerning an important investment he should make. He commanded that he invest seventeen shekels to buy property in Anathoth, which would soon be overtaken by Nebuchadnezzar's marauders. The Lord commanded that there be witnesses and that a written record be kept of the transaction. In time, this would stand as a testimony of the good ness of God. People would be able to look back to the date of purchase and understand the faith of Jeremiah, and the goodness of God to make such a bold step during such an impossible time. Jeremiah did as he was instructed, but sometimes it was difficult to see the possibility of God's prophetic fulfillment. The Lord told Jeremiah that His people would soon inherit the places wherein they experienced the most trouble. They would be satisfied with abundance in the place where famine and disease once prevailed against them because of their wickedness and idolatry. Jeremiah was perplexed by the Lord's command, simply because of the impending doom by fire and siege. In response, "Then came the word of the LORD unto Jeremiah, saying, Behold, I am the LORD, the God of all flesh: is there any thing too hard for me?" Jeremiah 32:26. "Thus saith the LORD; Again there shall be heard in this place, which ye say shall be desolate without man and without beast, even in the cities of Judah, and in the streets of Jerusalem, that are desolate, without man, and without inhabitant, and without beast, The voice of joy, and the voice of gladness, the voice of the bridegroom, and the voice of the bride, the voice of them that shall say, Praise the LORD of hosts: for the LORD is good; for his mercy endureth for ever: and of them that shall bring the sacrifice of praise into the house of the LORD. For I will cause to return the captivity of the land, as at the first, saith the LORD." Jeremiah 33:10, 11. Needless to say, after the chastisement of God's people had performed its work, the Lord kept His promise and Jeremiah's investment turned out to be a good one.

"Behold, I will gather them out of all countries, whither I have driven them in mine anger, and in my fury, and in great wrath; and I will bring them again unto this place, and I will cause them to dwell safely: And they shall be my people, and I will be their God:" Jeremiah 32:38, 39. Do you realize that this is an object lesson for us? As we face the bleak reality of being almost overrun by our enemy,

Satan, while on this earth, the Lord has instructed in not so many words that we make an investment as well. This world, as it is now, and as beautiful as some places are, will soon be destroyed. The blessing is that the Lord made a promise to us as He did Jeremiah. "Blessed are the meek: for they shall inherit the earth." Matthew 5:5. If we remain faithful, Jesus will give us the earth. It will not be as it is today. After the second coming of Christ, we will live with God, in heaven, for one thousand years. When the one thousand years are finished, the Lord will purify the earth by fire and make it anew. As the Lord said to Jeremiah, He will also be our God, and we will be His people. "And I saw a new heaven and a new earth: for the first heaven and the first earth were passed away; and there was no more sea. And I John saw the holy city, new Jerusalem, coming down from God out of heaven, prepared as a bride adorned for her husband. And I heard a great voice out of heaven saying, Behold, the tabernacle of God is with men, and he will dwell with them, and they shall be his people, and God himself shall be with them, and be their God." Revelation 21:1-3.

LAMENTATIONS

Lamentations 5:15, 16
"The joy of our heart is ceased;
our dance is turned into mourning.
The crown is fallen from our head: woe unto us,
that we have sinned!"

God's people Israel constantly found themselves in dire situations because of habitual disobedience. When the Lord wanted to exalt them, oftentimes they tied His hands through disobedience. They blocked their own blessings. They had the great benefit of having the Lord on their side to be their God, and took Him for granted. They would be obedient and loving toward Him for a season, and then begin worshipping other gods, and giving their friend, the one true God, the last position in their lives. When He delivered them from various types of oppression, they would worship and appreciate Him, and not long afterwards, begin to murmur, complain, and blatantly disobey again.

It is in light of such up and down relationship problems that the fifth chapter of Lamentations was written. Where joy used to prevail with God's people, it ceased. Their relation to God as His royal children was turned into a nomadic relationship. No longer did they understand that they were children of the heavenly king, so they became slaves to the enemy of souls. It was a reproach to see the children of Israel overrun by evil doers.

It is a sad day when God's people are willing trade their royal identities for spiritual slavery. This makes the Lord sad and all of heaven is solemn. In these situations, the Lord waits with outstretched arms, as did the prodigal son's father, as the son returned home. If you have found yourself lacking the royal mentality, in bondage to sin, hear the word of the Lord to your soul, and live. "For I have no pleasure in the death of him that dieth, saith the Lord GOD: wherefore turn yourselves, and live ye." Ezekiel 18:32. "Therefore say unto the house of Israel, Thus saith the Lord GOD; Repent, and turn yourselves from your idols; and turn away your faces from all your abominations." Ezekiel 14:6.

DELIVER THE MESSAGE

Ezekiel 33:7-9
"So thou, O son of man, I have set thee a watchman unto
the house of Israel; therefore thou shalt hear the word at
my mouth, and warn them from me. When I say unto the
wicked, O wicked man, thou shalt surely die; if thou dost
not speak to warn the wicked from his way, that wicked
man shall die in his iniquity; but his blood will I require
at thine hand. Nevertheless, if thou warn the wicked of his
way to turn from it; if he do not turn from his way, he
shall die in his iniquity; but thou hast delivered thy soul."

What if, while you were in a restaurant having a delicious meal with your spouse, you noticed something odd going on at the next table? You realized that while the patron was away from the table, the waiter poured some disinfectant in their orange juice. When the patron returned, would you tell them what you had seen or would you keep it a secret? Would you think it an intrusion to warn the unwary diner? Would you be concerned that that person may not receive your warning well?

What if the Lord gave you a message to a dying *world*? This message is one of repentance and you know that if the people do not heed it, they will be lost eternally? Would you allow the possibility that people may reject the message that God had given you or that they may be offended, to deter you from delivering it? Many of us do just that. We sometimes see people around us languishing and running down the road to, eternal death, yet we do not warn them. The Bible says in that case, that person's blood will be on our hands. We could have delivered someone from eternal condemnation, but we did not.

It is a wonderful thing to be on the positive side of this equation. If the Lord has given us a message and we deliver it faithfully, we have done all that the Lord required, and if, God forbid, they should continue down the wrong path, we are not responsible. Noah is a good example of a faithful messenger whom many people rejected to their own demise. Let us learn a lesson from his life, that no matter how people may respond, we must give them the opportunity to know and love the truth. Pray that the Lord will teach you how to be a good steward of His word. By all means; deliver the message.

HEART TRANSPLANT

Ezekiel 36:26
*"A new heart also will I give you, and a new spirit will I
put within you: and I will take away the stony heart out of
your flesh, and I will give you an heart of flesh."*

There are instances when heart transplant surgery is necessary. When systolic heart failure is severe enough, qualified medical professionals may suggest a heart transplant. Usually a surgeon harvests a heart from someone declared brain dead, whose family consents to anonymously donate the vital organ to someone in need. Before any particular patient is approved to receive a heart donation, they undergo rigorous screenings and are placed on a waiting list. The process of awaiting the much-needed transplant can be overwhelmingly stressful. During this period of waiting, the patient needs a good support system of loved ones, because the anxiety can become unbearable.

The entire human race has experienced heart failure. Because of sin, we all face certain death if we do not receive a new heart from a worthy donor. "Why should ye be stricken any more? ye will revolt more and more: the whole head is sick, and the whole heart faint." Isaiah 1:5. King David understood this fearful reality. When he allowed lust and murder to control him, and saw how far down his choices pulled him, he sought the Lord. He realized that he needed a change of heart. The old failing one would simply not suffice. "Create in me a clean heart, O God; and renew a right spirit within me. Cast me not away from thy presence; and take not thy holy spirit from me. Restore unto me the joy of thy salvation; and uphold me with thy free spirit." Psalms 51:10-12. It is because of our great need that Jesus died and rose again.

Do you know that God is still in the business of spiritual

heart surgery? Do you realize that the surgeon and the donor are the same person? This only works when it is God we are talking about. You see, as the donor must be declared brain dead in the natural world, Jesus died the second death for all mankind. Though natural donors are usually anonymous, Jesus, the supernatural donor, wants us to know that He has given us the blessing of a new heart. "Let this mind be in you, which was also in Christ Jesus:" Philippians 2:5. By faith in Jesus' ministry and perfect sacrifice, we are able to bypass living in anxiety while on a waiting list because His heart is powerful enough to sustain all that are in need.

One of the major differences between natural and supernatural heart transplant surgery is, that the donor in supernatural surgery does not stay dead. Jesus Christ is alive and well. Because of His resurrection from the dead and righteous life, we are able to share in the power of His life. Pray that the Lord will show you how to receive His heart. You cannot live without it.

HEAVENLY RESOLVE

Daniel 3:16-18
"Shadrach, Meshach, and Abed-nego, answered and said to the king, O Nebuchadnezzar, we are not careful to answer thee in this matter. If it be so, our God whom we serve is able to deliver us from the burning fiery furnace, and he will deliver us out of thine hand, O king. But if not, be it known unto thee, O king, that we will not serve thy gods, nor worship the golden image which thou hast set up."

God had given Nebuchadnezzar a dream concerning the succession of world empires. The order in which they would rise and fall was expressed in terms of an image, built with different materials, signifying the strength and longevity of the respective kingdoms. In the interpretation of the dream given him through the prophet Daniel, God revealed that the head of the image made in gold was a symbol of Nebuchadnezzar's Babylon. Seeking to defy the revelation of the end of his absolute rule, he decided to erect an image made entirely of gold, in the plain of Dura. He thought that if the dream depicted him as the head of gold and that his kingdom would have an ending, he would show that he fully intended to remain as the world's absolute ruler forever.

When the image built to boost Nebuchadnezzar's ego was finished and in place, he commanded that a worship ceremony including all kinds of music be organized. As the people, both heathens and Jews were gathered; they were to wait for the pomp of music as the signal to bow themselves to worship before the image. The music began and the majority of people did as commanded; they worshipped. Three boys stood out. Three Hebrew boys, also in captivity, stood erect when all others bowed to the earth. It is clear from what follows in the story that even the professed people of God worshipped the image. The king was informed that these boys did not worship and as one would imagine, he was angry. He called for them and inquired concerning their defiance. The *three worthies*, in spite of a second opportunity extended to them to worship, respectfully yet deliberately said that their God was able to deliver them from his threatened penalty of death, but even if He did not, they would not bow down. The astonished and angered king commanded that these bold young captives be thrown into a furnace that was heated to a temperature seven times hotter than usual. What happened next demonstrates the awsomeness of God. "Then these men were bound in their coats, their hosen, and their hats, and their other garments, and were cast into the midst of the burning fiery furnace. Therefore because the king's commandment was urgent, and the furnace exceeding hot, the flame of the fire slew those men that took up Shadrach, Meshach, and Abednego. And these three men, Shadrach, Meshach, and Abednego, fell down bound into the midst of the burning fiery furnace. Then Nebuchadnezzar the king was astonied, and rose up in haste, and spake, and said unto his counsellers, Did not we cast three men bound into the midst of the fire? They answered and said unto the king, True, O king. He answered and said, Lo, I see four men loose, walking in the midst of the fire, and they have no hurt; and the form of the fourth is like the Son of God. Then Nebuchadnezzar came near to the mouth of the burning fiery furnace, and spake, and said, Shadrach, Meshach, and Abed-nego, ye servants of the most high God, come forth, and come hither. Then Shadrach, Meshach, and Abed-nego, came forth of the midst of the fire. And the princes, governors, and captains, and the king's counsellers, being gathered together, saw these men, upon whose bodies the fire had no power, nor was an hair of their head singed, neither were their coats changed, nor the smell of fire had passed on them. Then

Nebuchadnezzar spake, and said, Blessed be the God of Shadrach, Meshach, and Abed-nego, who hath sent his angel, and delivered his servants that trusted in him, and have changed the king's word, and yielded their bodies, that they might not serve nor worship any god, except their own God." Daniel 3:21-28. The proud king realized that the Lord of Israel was able to deliver His chosen ones. He realized that the only true God was worthy of worship.

It is high time that we too have the resolve of the three faithful Hebrew boys. When, during the end of time, the call is made to worship the beast symbolized in Revelation 13, we must be rooted in the same God, and be willing to lose even our lives rather that defy Him (Revelation 14:9, 10). Pray for the heavenly resolve of the three young Hebrews.

TURNING UP THE HEAT

Daniel 3:25
"He answered and said, Lo, I see four men loose, walking in the midst of the fire, and they have no hurt; and the form of the fourth is like the Son of God."

At about the third year of Jehoiakim, king of Judah's reign, the king of Babylon was permitted by God to besiege Jerusalem. King Nebuchadnezzar carried away God's people as captives. It was because of their collective disobedience that God allowed their captivity (Daniel 9:6). God chastens us when we need it, in order to purify us as fine gold. Though not all were faithless, the faithful shared in the struggles that would come to Jerusalem. The city of peace was now a besieged city. The city where God's house was erected for all to see was also taken captive in the same manner.

As the story continues, there came a point when there was a showdown between the true God of heaven and the false god of Babylon. Many tests had been brought upon the three worthies and they passed with flying colors. God's health plan was put on display through these young men, and His success was revealed for all to see. Now a test of ultimate faithfulness would be required of them. In a prideful attempt to show God that he was boss, Nebuchadnezzar erected a solid gold statue in the plain of Dura. In the king's mind gold represented the longevity of his worldwide reign. Though God had revealed through a dream that he would be usurped by a power greater than himself, he wanted to prove God wrong.

The statue was magnificent. The gold glistened in the sun as a fine jewel. Nebuchadnezzar instructed all to bow and worship his statue when the music began. Most people, including the professed people of God obeyed his command. The three Hebrew boys maintained their fidelity

341

to God and chose to stand erect despite the consequences. The king was outraged and when subtle persuasion failed to impress the young men, he resorted to force. He thought that penalizing them would not only teach them a lesson, but also strike fear in the hearts of all who witnessed what would soon take place. "Now if ye be ready that at what time ye hear the sound of the cornet, flute, harp, sackbut, psaltery, and dulcimer, and all kinds of musick, ye fall down and worship the image which I have made; well: but if ye worship not, ye shall be cast the same hour into the midst of a burning fiery furnace; and who is that God that shall deliver you out of my hands?" Daniel 3:15. As he promised, the king had the heat intensified in the already deadly furnace, so much so that his own servants died while throwing the three Hebrew worthies into the furnace. After the young men were thrown in, in an amazing miracle, Jesus intervened rendering the fire incombustible. Jesus Himself joined the men in the furnace. The king could hardly believe his eyes. He saw Jesus and the three walking loose in the furnace as though there was no flame at all. Immediately He recognized the Son of God.

Through trust in God's providence, the three Hebrew boys went through a fiery trial and immerged as pure as fine gold. When we are faced with intense struggles, let us learn from these three that God is *always* in the midst. The fires will not consume His servants. When the heat of affliction is intensified by seven times, God is still able to appear and bring glory to His own name. He is willing and able to deliver as He sees fit.

Praise the Lord for His willingness to stand with us through trials.

THE HANDWRITING ON THE WALL

Daniel 5:12
"Forasmuch as an excellent spirit, and knowledge, and understanding, interpreting of dreams, and shewing of hard sentences, and dissolving of doubts, were found in the same Daniel, whom the king named Belteshazzar: now let Daniel be called, and he will shew the interpretation."

Daniel served many years in the courts of the king. It was his privilege to be God's spokesperson to both His people and the heathens who did not respect Him. During the reign of Belshazzar, as usual, many gods were worshipped. Among them were the gods of silver, gold, brass, iron, wood, and stone. Materialism ruled the proud hearts of the Babylonians. It was apparent that they had not learned from the mistakes of the king's father, Nebuchadnezzar, who built a golden icon representing himself and an eternal kingdom, which he aspired to rule over, in spite of God's prophesy to the contrary.

"Belshazzar the king made a great feast to a thousand of his lords, and drank wine before the thousand. Belshazzar, whiles he tasted the wine, commanded to bring the golden and silver vessels which his father Nebuchadnezzar had taken out of the temple which was in Jerusalem; that the king, and his princes, his wives, and his concubines, might drink therein. Then they brought the golden vessels that were taken out of the temple of the house of God which was at Jerusalem; and the king, and his princes, his wives, and his concubines, drank in them. They drank wine, and praised the gods of gold, and of silver, of brass, of iron, of wood, and of stone." Daniel 5:1-4. It was a great act of arrogant sacrilege that the king was involved in. He obviously had no respect for the God of heaven.

343

At the appropriate time, God decided to deliver a message to the proud king. Through much inquiry, he was led to Daniel to interpret the message God delivered in the form of a bodiless hand that wrote, "MENE, MENE, TEKEL, UPHARSIN." Daniel 5:25. The interpretation revealed to the king that his rule was to be divided to the Medes and Persians. It was also revealed that he was weighed in the balance and found lacking.

It is a fearful thing to be judged by God, and everything having been weighed, come up lacking. If in His investigation of your case, you are not complete in Him, there is no hope. This is where the wicked king found himself, in spite of the record of His father's experience with pride. "In that night was Belshazzar the king of the Chaldeans slain." Daniel 5:30.

While most of us will never become kings, and never conquer large portions of the globe, the pride that the wicked kings exhibited is not beyond our reach. It is possible to have the same disdain for God that they shared in common. The blessing is that we can also choose to repent when the Lord brings a message of warning to us. It is our privilege to learn from the eternal mistakes of kings like Belshazzar and recognize that God's mercy is not to be taken for granted. Praise the Lord for His willingness to correct us when we are on the wrong path. Praise Him for His willingness to guide to righteousness. By receiving His love by faith, we can be weighed in the balance and be found fully covered by His righteousness, and the handwriting on the wall can say, "Saved and awaiting God's eternal reward."

CONSPIRACY

Daniel 6:5
***"Then said these men, We shall not find any occasion
against this Daniel, except we find it against him
concerning the law of his God."***

I find great encouragement in the story of Daniel. For many years, he faithfully served different rulers. They promoted him because he was humble before God. The power of God compelled the rulers to have the utmost respect and trust for Daniel, although they may not have understood that it was God's power.

During the reign of Darius, the presidents and princes in his courts did not like Daniel. His model character probably fueled their hatred. Oftentimes when you live righteously, unrepentant people develop disdain for you. Because of their evil deeds, they cannot stand the light of God that shines through, because it exposes them. This was the case with Daniel.

No matter how Daniel's enemies wanted to trip him up, they could not, because he was hidden in God. His character was exemplary. They realized that they would never have a reason to accuse him before the law, so they became creative. They decided to use his obedience to God as a stumbling block. I certainly wish that the only way someone could cause trouble for me would be to catch me living righteously. Though they were evil, they took note that he was a stickler for pleasing God.

There is much more to the story, but the point for today is that the Lord wants to empower all of His children to be faithful as was Daniel. The only accusation that He wants to be brought against us is that we pleased God, as well. Why not choose, today, to allow God unrestricted access to your life, and be faithful like brother Daniel?

THE KEY TO UNLOCK CAPTIVITY

Daniel 9:5, 6
"We have sinned, and have committed iniquity, and have done wickedly, and have rebelled, even by departing from thy precepts and from thy judgments: Neither have we hearkened unto thy servants the prophets, which spake in thy name to our kings, our princes, and our fathers, and to all the people of the land."

I remember a lesson that my church was studying a few years ago. The text above was included in that study. I read it with enlightenment that I did not have before. It is a blessing to receive fresh revelations from the word every time you read it. It occurred to me as I considered Daniel's despair, that he had the key to unlock captivity. He prayed to the Lord because he wanted to understand the Babylonian captivity of his people that God revealed through Jeremiah. It concerned him in part because he thought they would be bound much longer, and he could not handle that prospect.

As I read Daniel's prayer, some of the keys became clear. He openly confessed his and his people's iniquities. There was nothing in him that made him think he was worthy of having his prayer answered or his people delivered. His unworthiness was before his eyes. The first key to unlocking captivity is confession of sin. It is a blessing to have the Lord reveal our sins and to give us the strength to confess and forsake them.

The second key to freedom, I discovered as a subset of his confession, is in the specific sins they committed. Daniel said that the people forsook God's precepts and judgments. Whenever we decide to turn away from the laws God has established for our safety, we are certain to be bound and taken captive by Satan at his will (II Timothy 2:26). Conversely, when we submit to God first, and resist the devil, he must flee (James 4:7).

The final key to freedom that I saw in these two verses is listening to the prophets. God has demonstrated His love for us by not doing anything important without first revealing it to us through the prophets (Amos 3:7). Whenever the Lord saw His people in situations when conventional means did not appeal to them, He sent His messengers, the prophets as in the case of King David receiving a visit from the prophet Nathan (II Samuel 12:7). Even today, people are spiritually enslaved because of refusal to adhere to the prophecies of God's word. When we heed the prophecies, the blessings of God are soon to follow.

In short, the key to freedom in Christ is found in submitting to God and obeying His precepts, judgments, and prophets, while confessing our reliance on Him. I praise the Lord for His keys to unlock captivity.

THE VISION

Daniel 9:25
"Know therefore and understand, that from the going forth of the commandment to restore and to build Jerusalem unto the Messiah the Prince shall be seven weeks, and threescore and two weeks: the street shall be built again, and the wall, even in troublous times."

As the prophet Daniel tried to understand the prophecy of the seventy weeks of years, he humbly confessed his sins and the sins of his people. Like the prophet Isaiah as shown in Isaiah chapter 6, he understood fully that he was equally responsible for the iniquities committed against God, which were the cause of the Babylonian captivity.

At the beginning of his prayer, the Bible says that the angel Gabriel was dispatched from heaven to give the sorrowing prophet skill concerning the vision (Daniel 9:23). How fast this mighty angel of God must have been able to move from one place to another, if during a prayer he was able to leave the heavenly courts, and before the prayer was finished, he reached earth? The story continues. This vision in some ways included both the seventy weeks and twenty-three hundred year prophecies since both had the same starting point in history (Daniel 8:2, 14; 9:22, 23). Gabriel reveals the starting point of the vision as "from the commandment to restore and to build Jerusalem," Daniel 9:25. This command, which included not only the rebuilding of the temple, but the city as well, with the return of power to the Jews to rule according to their own laws, occurred in 457 B.C. by Artexerxes (Ezra 4:7-23; Ezra 7:12-26). From the year 457 B.C. to Messiah (which means anointed) the Prince, was sixty-nine prophetic weeks. In symbolic Bible prophecy, one day equals one literal year (Numbers 14:34; Luke 13:31-33). Sixty-nine prophetic weeks equal 483 literal years (sixty-nine times seven days). Did you know that exactly 483 years later (27 A.D. including the year zero), Jesus Christ, whose name means anointed, received the anointing of the Holy Ghost at His baptism explicitly fulfilling the prophecy? "Now when all the people were baptized, it came to pass, that Jesus also being baptized, and praying, the heaven was opened, And the Holy Ghost descended in a bodily shape like a dove upon him, and a voice came from heaven, which said, Thou art my beloved Son; in thee I am well pleased," Luke 3:21, 22. Less than two months later Jesus stood in the synagogue and read from the book of Isaiah. "The Spirit of the Lord is upon me, because he hath anointed me to preach the gospel to the poor; he hath sent me to heal the brokenhearted, to preach deliverance to the captives, and recovering of sight to the blind, to set at liberty them that are bruised, To preach the acceptable year of the Lord. And he closed the book, and he gave it again to the minister, and sat down. And the eyes of all them that were in the synagogue were fastened on him. And he began to say unto them, This day is this scripture fulfilled in your ears," Luke 4:18-21. Gabriel continues by revealing the sacrificial death of Jesus that would occur three and one half years later (31 A.D.), and the rejection of Him in 34 A.D.

What is the moral of this story? At a time when one of God's people was bewildered and seeking Him diligently, God chose to reveal the ministry and sacrifice of the Messiah. Of all the events that would occur between the time of Daniel and the end of time, God chose to give a snapshot of the gospel. God is still revealing Himself through the gospel today. In our times of deepest need, if we persevere in prayer, He will reveal Himself in the light of Jesus Christ. Jesus is still the answer to all of our inner turmoil. Let us search for Him while He can still be found, and live in a constant attitude of prayer.

REJOICING IN THE LAMB KINGDOM

Daniel 9:27
*"And he shall confirm the covenant with many for one
week: and in the midst of the week he shall cause the
sacrifice and the oblation to cease, and for the over-
spreading of abominations he shall make it desolate, even
until the consummation, and that determined shall be
poured upon the desolate."*

In the midst of the last week of Daniel's seventy weeks
prophecy, Messiah was cut off for His people and this
caused the sacrifice and oblation to cease (Ephesians 2:14-
18). In that very moment, type met antitype. The death of
Jesus Christ forever ended the need for animal sacrifices.

As Jesus hung on the cross and died, I can imagine hearing rejoicing in the lamb kingdom. There would be no
further need to sacrifice animals for the remission of sin.
John called Jesus, *the Lamb* of God which taketh away the
sins of the world (John 1:29). This means that all of the
required sacrifices in the Old Testament sanctuary pointed
forward to the genuine article, Jesus Christ. When He died
on the cross, providing the perfect sacrifice, He ended the
entire sacrificial system and gave us access to God's throne.
"And, behold, the veil of the temple was rent in twain from
the top to the bottom; and the earth did quake, and the rocks
rent"; Matthew 27:51. Never more would a lamb of the first
year, without blemish or tears be accepted as payment for
our sins. Now, with faith in Christ, we can be forgiven and
cleansed. We need only to have right relationship with Him
and we will be saved. We are made holy through Christ.

Praise the Lord for His perfect sacrifice!

INVINCIBLE LOVE

Hosea 3:1
*"Then said the LORD unto me, Go yet, love a woman
beloved of her friend, yet an adulteress, according to the
love of the LORD toward the children of Israel, who look
to other gods, and love flagons of wine."*

The topic of divorce is hotly debated amongst God's people
everywhere. Even in the days of Jesus' earthly ministry, the
leaders of Israel used this issue as a way to test Jesus, to
prove His grasp of the Scriptures. "The Pharisees also came
unto him, tempting him, and saying unto him, Is it lawful for
a man to put away his wife for every cause? And he
answered and said unto them, Have ye not read, that he
which made them at the beginning made them male and
female, And said, For this cause shall a man leave father and
mother, and shall cleave to his wife: and they twain shall be
one flesh? Wherefore they are no more twain, but one flesh.
What therefore God hath joined together, let not man put
asunder. They say unto him, Why did Moses then command
to give a writing of divorcement, and to put her away? He
saith unto them, Moses because of the hardness of your
hearts suffered you to put away your wives: but from the
beginning it was not so. And I say unto you, Whosoever shall
put away his wife, except it be for fornication, and shall
marry another, committeth adultery: and whoso marrieth her
which is put away doth commit adultery." Matthew 19:3-9.
God has given very clear guidelines in the Scriptures regarding divorce. He hates divorce, yet there are built in provisions available for it under certain circumstances (Malachi
2:16). As we read above, in the case of sexual unfaithfulness,
it is lawful to divorce. In the case of an unbelieving spouse
insisting on divorce, the believer has no obligation to force
the issue. God is a God of peace (I Corinthians 7:11-16).

Without fasting and praying, and earnestly seeking reconciliation, some people look at the necessary provisions for divorce as a way to escape marriage. What was God's example to us in the Old Testament?

God spoke to Hosea, His servant saying that He should take unto himself an adulterous woman. This was his response. "So I bought her to me for fifteen pieces of silver, and for an homer of barley, and an half homer of barley: And I said unto her, Thou shalt abide for me many days; thou shalt not play the harlot, and thou shalt not be for another man: so will I also be for thee." Hosea 3:2, 3. This is a gospel message if I have ever seen one. In order to demonstrate His invincible love to Israel and Judah, God fine-tuned an object lesson. While it was lawful for Hosea to put away his wife by reason of adultery, he chose instead to purchase her from the adulteress auction block. Hosea sacrificed great expense in order to turn his wife's heart toward him.

Isn't this what the Lord does with those who profess to love Him, yet put other things like work, family, education, money, and self-indulgence before Him? He could very well turn His back, but He doesn't. Instead of turning away, He purchased us from the cold auction block of condemnation with the precious blood of Jesus.

There are sad situations when people just *will not* be redeemed. Some are very resistant. Sometimes after the Lord has done everything He can through conviction, providence, chastening, and sometimes the upheaval of life, we choose not to be with Him. Since He does not force love, He, like the believing spouse, allows the unbeliever to go. He loves peace, not love that is forced.

It is a good day to turn every aspect of our lives over to the Lord. If we have played the harlot, let us accept His pleadings and turn to Him. Please do not waste the precious price of redemption He invested in you.

THE FORMULA

Joel 2:15-18
"Blow the trumpet in Zion, sanctify a fast, call a solemn
assembly: Gather the people, sanctify the congregation,
assemble the elders, gather the children, and those that
suck the breasts: let the bridegroom go forth of his cham-
ber, and the bride out of her closet. Let the priests, the
ministers of the LORD, weep between the porch and the
altar, and let them say, Spare thy people, O LORD, and
give not thine heritage to reproach, that the heathen
should rule over them: wherefore should they say among
the people, Where is their God? Then will the LORD be
jealous for his land, and pity his people."

Israel's interaction with God has always been particularly
fascinating to me. It speaks to the mercy of God and His
extreme patience. It seems as though they lived on a pendu-
lum. Back and forth, they swung between repentance and
iniquity. Left and right, they swung between confession and
transgression. It shows that the Lord is determined to save
people. Many times they deserved to be utterly wiped out,
but the Lord extended His mercy. It is true that sometimes in
mercy there is chastisement.

Such was the case in the days of Joel, the prophet. He
was given a solemn message of warning for God's people.
After having gone into detail, He gave them the formula to
turn the tide. He gave them the formula for having favor
with God through humility. He said that the people should
gather the children, elders, and congregation together for a
solemn assembly. They were to diligently seek the Lord for
mercy, while recommitting themselves to the Him. The
priests were to intercede for the people between the porch
and the altar, entreating the Lord not to bring reproach upon
His children by allowing the heathen to rule over them. The

Lord told the children of Israel that He would restore the crops and all that had been taken away due to their iniquity. He promised the early and latter rains would come to refresh the land.

The Lord is still answering the sincere prayers of diligent seekers today. He delights to know that sinners have chosen to forsake their wickedness in order to follow Him. As we seek His presence through revival, reformation, prayer, and Bible study, He will refresh us with the early and latter rains of His Spirit. He will saturate us with His power that the world may see our good experience with Him and glorify Him. Let us come together whenever necessary to seek the Lord's face, that we may please Him and bring honor to His matchless name.

THE LORD SPEAKS

Amos 3:7
"Surely the Lord GOD will do nothing, but he revealeth his secret unto his servants the prophets."

The Lord spoke in almost deafening tones to the children of Israel, whom He delivered from Egypt. As usual, they committed iniquity to the point that it aroused the Lord to address them with unmistakable language. He used example after example of things that should have gotten their attention. "Will a lion roar in the forest, when he hath no prey? will a young lion cry out of his den, if he have taken nothing? Can a bird fall in a snare upon the earth, where no gin is for him? shall one take up a snare from the earth, and have taken nothing at all? Shall a trumpet be blown in the city, and the people not be afraid? shall there be evil in a city, and the LORD hath not done it?" Amos 3:4-6. The message of warning should have been clearly understood. When the Lord spoke, He wanted their undivided attention. If He spoke through the prophets, His people needed to get an important message.

The Lord said to His people, in essence, that He does not do anything important without informing His people through the gift of prophecy. Such is the case even today. Countless numbers of people are groping around in darkness, searching for a sign, or word from the Lord. He has given us the best gift for guidance second only to the Holy Ghost in the Bible. When we diligently search its pages, we are able to walk through the messages of prophets. We are able to see by the power of His Spirit, truths that transform. In the last days, it is especially important to know that He speaks through prophecy. The books of Daniel and Revelation are full of the Lord speaking important things concerning the times in which *we* live. It would be well if we studied them side by side, searching through the truths depicted there. The symbols and allegories are unlocked by comparing them with one another. The truth now present comes to more and more light as we labor over the prophecies. I thank God for giving us a key to unlocking what is important to Him. Prophecy is that key. "Surely the Lord GOD will do nothing, but he revealeth his secret unto his servants the prophets." Amos 3:7.

PRIDE IS A TERRIBLE THING

Obadiah 1:3, 4
"The pride of thine heart hath deceived thee, thou that dwellest in the clefts of the rock, whose habitation is high; that saith in his heart, Who shall bring me down to the ground? Though thou exalt thyself as the eagle, and though thou set thy nest among the stars, thence will I bring thee down, saith the LORD."

Pride must be one of the sins God despises the most. It is the root of all sin. It makes salvation impossible to for those who cherish it. The former son of the morning, Luficer himself became proud because of his beauty. He also, thought that his supreme intellect made him exempt from the law of God. In fact, he thought that he could be above the Supreme Lawgiver. He said in his heart that he would be like the Most High.

This attitude of pride was cherished by Edom. The Lord showed such disdain for it that He prophesied that all of the heathen nations would be greater than him. There would be pillage far greater than anything they had seen before. Usually, those who plundered a town would leave something behind; something unharmed, but the Lord said it would not be so with Edom. "Shall I not in that day, saith the LORD, even destroy the wise men out of Edom, and understanding out of the mount of Esau? And thy mighty men, O Teman, shall be dismayed, to the end that every one of the mount of Esau may be cut off by slaughter. For thy violence against thy brother Jacob shame shall cover thee, and thou shalt be cut off for ever." Obadiah 1:8-10.

More than the details that brought Edom to this point of pride and to the point of inciting God's anger, I think about the similarities in the language concerning the land of Edom and Satan on judgment day. Both betrayed their families –

Satan used to be a part of the family of God. They both exalted themselves, one like the eagles, and the other like the stars of God. They both were deceived because of their perceived superiority. They both face utter destruction. The devil will soon bear the weight of punishment he deserves. One day the Lord will repay him for his evil deeds against heaven and the son's and daughters of men. Speaking about Satan the Bible says, "All they that know thee among the people shall be astonished at thee: thou shalt be a terror, and never shalt thou be any more." Ezekiel 28:19.

I look forward to the day when sin and sickness will no longer exist. While I am waiting, I encourage you to make you calling and election sure. Pray that the Lord's sacrifice for you will not be in vain. Soon he that said He was coming will come to take His people home. I want to be ready. How about you?

IT IS HARD TO KICK AGAINST THE PRICKS

Jonah 1:4
"But the LORD sent out a great wind into the sea,
and there was a mighty tempest in the sea,
so that the ship was like to be broken."

When I think about the story of Saul of Tarsus' conversion, Jonah immediately comes to mind. You see, Saul of Tarsus was educated in the things of God to the point of becoming a stout Pharisee. They memorized the first five books of the Bible in their entirety, and were well versed in many other areas of religious beliefs, yet Saul persecuted the church of God. On one of His trips to persecute the church, Jesus confronted him. "And he said, Who art thou, Lord? And the Lord said, I am Jesus whom thou persecutest: it is hard for thee to kick against the pricks." Acts 9:5. It is very difficult to be confronted by God and ignore Him, choosing to do the opposite of what He commanded. Certainly, the Lord had convicted Saul of his errors before this confrontation, but he chose to fight against the convictions, and the Lord pursued him further.

As in the story of Saul, God needed to confront one of His prophets. He commanded that Jonah go to the city of Ninevah to warn them of the inevitable judgements of God, which would befall them if they did not repent. Instead of doing exactly what God said, the prophet decided to do the opposite. He chose to get on a ship going the opposite direction so-to-speak, and travel to Tarshish instead. He went to extreme lengths to avoid the call of God in order to protect His reputation. He probably did not want the Ninevites to think he was a false prophet if God decided to spare them in the end them.

The Lord demonstrated His tenacity in pursuing Jonah. Just as Jesus struck Saul with brightness causing him to lose his eyesight, God chose to agitate nature to get Jonah's attention. "But the LORD sent out a great wind into the sea, and there was a mighty tempest in the sea, so that the ship was like to be broken. Now the LORD had prepared a great fish to swallow up Jonah. And Jonah was in the belly of the fish three days and three nights." Jonah 1:3, 17.

The story of Jonah did not end there, but the point we need to get today is that God is willing to do whatever it takes to get our attention. He will confront us in whatever way He needs to, in order to get us to listen. It is hard to ignore the Lord. Let us choose not to turn away from the commands of God. We can become so strong in resisting Him that one day we may no longer hear His voice.

UNPLEASANT DREAMS

Micah 2:1
"Woe to them that devise iniquity, and work evil upon their beds! when the morning is light, they practice it, because it is in the power of their hand."

Sometimes when I listen to the news on my way to work, I wonder what this world is coming to. I know the prophecies of the last days are clear. We have been told that people's hearts will wax cold. We have seen in scripture that during the time of Noah, people thought only evil continually. Jesus said that these days would be just like the days preceding the flood. Even with all of this forewarning, some of the things going on in our world are astonishing.

The media now glamorizes sins that were shameful fifty years ago. Entire sitcoms and movies have been written with these glamorized sins as the theme. Blockbuster hits are growing by leaps and bounds with graphic material as the enticing element. I wonder what lude behavior has not yet been popularized in our society. It almost seems that it cannot get any worse.

There are many who dream up ways to flaunt evil. Many are enticed by capitalism to devise twisted plots and write them in books, and direct movies with scenes that are beyond offensive. Instead of meditating on the word of God, they meditate on different ways to provoke the public. Is there any hope?

The Lord has always taken into account the level of wickedness He would allow before He did something drastic in order to correct the issues, as in the days of Sodom and Gomorrah. The Lord is no less in touch with our woes today than in those days. One day soon, He will have allowed sin to run its final course, and put an end to it. He will rise from His throne as the conquering King who will keep the door of His tender mercy ajar no longer. Sin and suffering will cease. The pure pulses of righteousness will move by waves over the entire universe, and order will be restored. He that said He would return will at last set His faithful ones free. Are you ready? Are you ready for Jesus to come? I certainly am. Pray that we will all be found faithful.

"And God shall wipe away all tears from their eyes; and there shall be no more death, neither sorrow, nor crying, neither shall there be any more pain: for the former things are passed away." Revelation 21:4.

CAST DOWN

Micah 5:9
"Thine hand shall be lifted up upon thine adversaries,
and all thine enemies shall be cut off."

Israel was constantly involved in a passionate push and pull match with God. He would bless them with all of the advantages a people could ever hope for. He gave them His direct rulership, prophets, judges, the sanctuary service, and protection so the entire heathen world knew that they served an invincible God. Oftentimes, they became dissatisfied, and chose to erect idols and places of false-worship. In those times, the enemies of God blasphemed because of Israel's unfaithfulness. As well, their enemies sorely pursued Israel. War seemed always to be looming.

Micah prophesied that the Eternal Ruler of Israel would come from Bethlehem to deliver His people (Micah 5:2, 3). Their enemies would soon see that their God was like no other. During the time of Jesus, many people read prophecies like this one, and determined in their own minds that Messiah would come and break the yoke of Roman power for Israel to rise to her former glory. When Jesus appeared from Bethlehem as a humble servant, and preached about another world kingdom, many people did not accept Him because He did not fit their preconceived ideas. Could the prophecies pointing to the victory of Israel be fulfilled in a humble man named Jesus? "And the remnant of Jacob shall be among the Gentiles in the midst of many people as a lion among the beasts of the forest, as a young lion among the flocks of sheep: who, if he go through, both treadeth down, and teareth in pieces, and none can deliver." Micah 5:8. I know that there was a historical application of this prophecy to be realized long before Jesus took on human flesh, but God was also trying to tell those who would become spiritual Israel that He would deliver them from the bondage of the devil (Galatians 3). "And I heard a loud voice saying in heaven, Now is come salvation, and strength, and the kingdom of our God, and the power of his Christ: for the accuser of our brethren is cast down, which accused them before our God day and night." Revelation 12:10.

In Christ, there is victory. In the power of His resurrection, we find the devil being vanquished forever. The mighty King of Israel has come to us and He has the keys of hell and death (Revelation 1:18). One day soon, we will finally experience the full reality of His victory over our adversary, the devil. "He which testifieth these things saith, Surely I come quickly. Amen. Even so, come, Lord Jesus." Revelation 22:20.

NEVERMORE TO RISE

Nahum 1:15
"Behold upon the mountains the feet of him that bringeth good tidings, that publisheth peace! O Judah, keep thy solemn feasts, perform thy vows: for the wicked shall no more pass through thee; he is utterly cut off."

Many of the exhortations that the Lord gave to His children Israel, are for our learning today. When He said that He did not love the death of unrepentant people, therefore repent and live, it was for our learning. When He said that He would write His laws on our hearts and in our minds, that we may know Him, it was for our learning. When He said that one day, He would create a new heaven and a new earth, it was for our learning.

He promised His people Judah that eventually the affliction brought about by iniquity; the distress, tribulation and pain would never rise again. It would be utterly cut off. His promises are made on condition. He admonished them to perform their solemn feasts and vows in faith, and they would experience the peace of which He spoke.

This is the same promise made to us upon whom the ends of the world are come. He says through Nahum, "The mountains quake at him, and the hills melt, and the earth is burned at his presence, yea, the world, and all that dwell therein. Who can stand before his indignation? and who can abide in the fierceness of his anger? his fury is poured out like fire, and the rocks are thrown down by him. The LORD is good, a strong hold in the day of trouble; and he knoweth them that trust in him. But with an overrunning flood he will make an utter end of the place thereof, and darkness shall pursue his enemies. What do ye imagine against the LORD? he will make an utter end: affliction shall not rise up the second time." Nahum 1:5-9. The Lord is soon to make an utter and complete end to all sin. He will destroy it, both root and branch. It will be at the Lord's proclamation, near the end of time that we all will have made our final decisions either to love or leave the Lord. "And he saith unto me, Seal not the sayings of the prophecy of this book: for the time is at hand. He that is unjust, let him be unjust still: and he which is filthy, let him be filthy still: and he that is righteous, let him be righteous still: and he that is holy, let him be holy still. And, behold, I come quickly; and my reward is with me, to give every man according as his work shall be." Revelation 22:10-12. With this safeguard in place and the fact that all the righteous will be fully persuaded that sin never pays, affliction shall not rise a second time. "And I saw the dead, small and great, stand before God; and the books were opened: and another book was opened, which is the book of life: and the dead were judged out of those things which were written in the books, according to their works. And the sea gave up the dead which were in it; and death and hell delivered up the dead which were in them: and they were judged every man according to their works. And death and hell were cast into the lake of fire. This is the second death." Revelation 20:12-14.

KEEP SILENT BEFORE HIM

Habakkuk 2:19, 20
*"Woe unto him that saith to the wood, Awake; to the dumb
stone, Arise, it shall teach! Behold, it is laid over with
gold and silver, and there is no breath at all in the midst
of it. But the LORD is in his holy temple:
let all the earth keep silence before him."*

It is important to remember in the times of deepest trials,
that the Lord is in control. This is a lesson that Habakkuk
learned well. He wanted to know how long the Lord would
put up with the wiles of wicked people. He wondered how
long the Lord would allow them to appear to prosper while
God's people languished. "And the LORD answered me,
and said, Write the vision, and make it plain upon tables,
that he may run that readeth it. For the vision is yet for an
appointed time, but at the end it shall speak, and not lie:
though it tarry, wait for it; because it will surely come, it
will not tarry. Behold, his soul which is lifted up is not
upright in him: but the just shall live by his faith."
Habakkuk 2:2-4. The Lord proceeded to tell his son of the
woes of the wicked. He made it clear that their evil would
not go unpunished. They could consult their idols and
command that they speak all they wanted to, but to no
avail. Stones and wood cannot instruct anyone. There is no
life in them.

The Lord distinguished Himself to Habakkuk and
anyone else, in the future, that would know the vision. The
Lord, not idols, is in control. The Lord, not impotent statues
of beasts and other creatures, is worthy of worship. The
Lord, not the enemy, will triumph in the end. Anytime you
are tempted to think that the Lord will allow wickedness to
continue unchecked, remember the counsel He gave to
Habakkuk. Anytime you think to resort to some inferior

medium to receive light in place of God, remember the two edged counsel given. "But the LORD is in his holy temple: let all the earth keep silence before him." Habakkuk 2:20.

DO IT AGAIN LORD

Habakkuk 3:1, 2
"A prayer of Habakkuk the prophet upon Shigionoth.
O LORD, I have heard thy speech, and was afraid:
O LORD, revive thy work in the midst of the years,
in the midst of the years make known;
in wrath remember mercy."

Have you ever been so overwhelmed by the works of Satan that you could hardly take it anymore? Have you been tempted to think that the Lord has allowed the enemy to triumph over you? Does the burden of Satan's constant attacks make you feel like giving up? Learn a lesson from the seldom-read prophet, Habakkuk.

Habakkuk was in a state of despondency because the enemies of God seemed to triumph. It seemed like they had unfettered ability to oppress God's people and His cause. After inquiring of the Lord, and receiving counsel as did Job in the midst of *his* distress, he began to evaluate God's resume. He said that He had heard of the mighty works God had performed for His people of old, and longed to see the same mighty works in his day. He wanted the Lord to be vigilant over the wicked, yet merciful to His own people.

As Habakkuk recounted the incredible acts of God, he spoke of the power God had over the land, air, and rivers of water. He spoke of the command God demonstrated over the sun, moon, and stars. He recalled the fact that the Lord has dominion over even the mountains, which have stood for centuries. They all tremble at the voice of God. Likewise, His enemies trembled when He has appeared to vindicate His people. "Thou wentest forth for the salvation of thy people, even for salvation with thine anointed; thou woundedst the head out of the house of the wicked, by discovering the foundation unto the neck. Selah. Thou didst strike through with his staves the head of his villages: they came out as a whirlwind to scatter me: their rejoicing was as to devour the poor secretly." Habakkuk 3:13, 14.

As the Lord has vanquished His human enemies, He has utterly defeated the enemy of us all. The Bible says that the promised seed, Jesus Christ, would crush the head of the serpent, and certainly that *is* the case. At Calvary, the Lord struck the enemy with a deadly blow. Over the devil's weapon of death, the Lord emerged victoriously. The devil thought he could keep our Savior in the grave, but early one Sunday morning, Jesus arose as the absolute victor over the grave, hell, and death.

Whenever you feel taken advantage of by the devil, recount the mighty works that the Lord has performed in the past. Remember His works of old and be encouraged. Ask Him to strengthen your faith making you His faithful follower. One day, sin and sinners will be no more. God's people will finally experience ultimate rest, and we shall reign forever with the Lord. Until then, praise His holy name. "When I heard, my belly trembled; my lips quivered at the voice: rottenness entered into my bones, and I trembled in myself, that I might rest in the day of trouble: when he cometh up unto the people, he will invade them with his troops. Although the fig tree shall not blossom, neither shall fruit be in the vines; the labour of the olive shall fail, and the fields shall yield no meat; the flock shall be cut off from the fold, and there shall be no herd in the stalls: Yet I will rejoice in the LORD, I will joy in the God of my salvation. The LORD God is my strength, and he will make my feet like hinds' feet, and he will make me to walk upon mine high places. To the chief singer on my stringed instruments." Habakkuk 3:16-19.

TWO DIFFERENT OUTCOMES

Zephaniah 1:12-15
"And it shall come to pass at that time, that I will search Jerusalem with candles, and punish the men that are settled on their lees: that say in their heart, The LORD will not do good, neither will he do evil. Therefore their goods shall become a booty, and their houses a desolation: they shall also build houses, but not inhabit them; and they shall plant vineyards, but not drink the wine thereof. The great day of the LORD is near, it is near, and hasteth greatly, even the voice of the day of the LORD: the mighty man shall cry there bitterly. That day is a day of wrath, a day of trouble and distress, a day of wasteness and desolation, a day of darkness and gloominess, a day of clouds and thick darkness,"

Often we see events depicted in the Scriptures with different outcomes for people, depending on their attitude toward the Lord. For instance, in the parable of Matthew 22, the king invited guests to the wedding feast of his son. There were those who refused to attend. There were those who chose to attend and have a wonderful time in honoring the son. Eventually, the king is depicted as visiting with the invited guests. Much to his dismay, he discovered a man that chose not to have on the garment that was appropriate for the event. The king asked him how he got in not having on the appropriate attire. The man was speechless, and the king commanded that he be tied up, taken out, and punished.

Two groups are represented as being at the feast. The ones that had on the garment representing the righteousness of Christ, and those who chose to present their own insufficient righteousness. The king saw both, but between the two, there were different outcomes.

Such is the case in the first chapter of Zephaniah. The

Lord is depicted as being on the verge of unleashing His wrath upon all idolaters. He is especially concerned with those who claimed to be His people, yet chose to worship Baal, Molech, and Dagon instead. The Lord said, "Hold thy peace at the presence of the Lord GOD: for the day of the LORD is at hand: for the LORD hath prepared a sacrifice, he hath bid his guests. And it shall come to pass in the day of the LORD's sacrifice, that I will punish the princes, and the king's children, and all such as are clothed with strange apparel." Zephaniah 1:7. Although Matthew and Zephaniah are not speaking of the same event, the imagery is clear. Those who choose to trust in anything other than the Lord, will always lose. God is a jealous God.

The contrast is made between those who love the Lord and others who do not. "And it shall come to pass at that time, that I will search Jerusalem with candles, and punish the men that are settled on their lees: that say in their heart, The LORD will not do good, neither will he do evil. Therefore their goods shall become a booty, and their houses a desolation: they shall also build houses, but not inhabit them; and they shall plant vineyards, but not drink the wine thereof." Zephaniah 1:12, 13. "And I will rejoice in Jerusalem, and joy in my people: and the voice of weeping shall be no more heard in her, nor the voice of crying. And they shall build houses, and inhabit them; and they shall plant vineyards, and eat the fruit of them. They shall not build, and another inhabit; they shall not plant, and another eat: for as the days of a tree are the days of my people, and mine elect shall long enjoy the work of their hands." Isaiah 65:21, 22. When the Lord unleashes His wrath against wickedness, there are two groups present. To one group it is promised that they will build on earth in vain, and in the end, be utterly destroyed. The other group will build on the new earth and benefit fully from the fruit of their labor. The distinguishing mark between the two is their relationship with God. If we choose to honor the Lord for all He has done for us and by His grace remain faithful to Him, we soon will enter into eternity without sin unto salvation. If we choose to despise the blessed gift of salvation and put anything above God, we will be bitterly disappointed and reap the bitter reward of wickedness, which is eternal ruin. Which group are you choosing to be a part of? "And if it seem evil unto you to serve the LORD, choose you this day whom ye will serve; whether the gods which your fathers served that were on the other side of the flood, or the gods of the Amorites, in whose land ye dwell: but as for me and my house, we will serve the LORD." Joshua 24:15.

CONSIDER YOUR WAYS

Haggai 1:3-5
"Then came the word of the LORD by Haggai the prophet, saying, Is it time for you, O ye, to dwell in your cieled houses, and this house lie waste? Now therefore thus saith the LORD of hosts; Consider your ways."

During King Cyrus' reign, the Lord commanded that Israel rebuild His house. They started the work as He had commanded, but as usual, they were met with adversity. Their adversaries went to Zerubbabel and the chief of the fathers and suggested that they lend a helping hand. They said that they also had worshipped the God of Israel, since the days of Esar-haddon. "But Zerubbabel, and Jeshua, and the rest of the chief of the fathers of Israel, said unto them, Ye have nothing to do with us to build an house unto our God; but we ourselves together will build unto the LORD God of Israel, as king Cyrus the king of Persia hath commanded us. Then the people of the land weakened the hands of the people of Judah, and troubled them in building, And hired counsellers against them, to frustrate their purpose, all the days of Cyrus king of Persia, even until the reign of Darius king of Persia." Ezra 4:3-5. Because of Israel's lack of faith during this time of opposition, they decided to stop building the house of God for a while. Perhaps, they thought that since the Lord was with them, their work should have been much easier, although no such promise has ever been made to God's people.

A few years later, in the second year of King Darius' reign, the Lord spoke concerning the matter. It was clear from His tone that the people had disobeyed. As He had referred to them so many times during the days of Moses, so it was in this case. The Lord called them *this* people, rather than *His* people, signifying their blatant disobedience. He said that this people said, the time had not truly come to build His house where they could worship, but has the time come for you to build you own beautiful homes? While my house is left undone, is it time for you to build monuments of you own pride? Consider your ways (Haggai 1:2-4). These words of rebuke are timely for us even in these days. There are so many of us whom the Lord has told to do special things for the sake of the gospel, yet when opposition or discomfort comes, we stop. When the rubber really meets the road and our faith is tried, sometimes we falter. It is interesting that we can often find the energy, in the midst of opposition, to do other things more desirable to us. I know that this does not make the Lord happy.

On a more basic level than some great work that the Lord may have commanded, He wants us to spend time with Him each day. During the era of the Old Testament sanctuary services, the Lord commanded that there be brought morning and evening sacrifices, besides the other offerings. This is where we get the idea of morning and evening worship. Have you ever set time aside for morning worship, but something interfered? Did you allow the matter to take the place of your devotion? When the matter was resolved, did you return to your time with the Lord? That has happened to me before, and I realized that I chose to deal with the issue and neglected devotion. Once I was finished, I did not even consider neglecting to brushing my teeth or taking a shower. It was clear to me, in those instances, that I made other things more important than my time with the Lord. While I would not dare put off the things that were important to me, I almost had no problem postponing worship. Even in these types of issues, the Lord says, "Consider your ways."

Pray that we will learn to make the Lord's priorities ours. I want to do what He says, how about you? He has made us special in His life. It would be wonderful if we consistently did the same.

A SOLEMN EXPERIENCE

Zechariah 3:3
"Now Joshua was clothed with filthy garments,
and stood before the angel."

It is a solemn experience to appear before the Lord. When we consider the extreme contrast in holiness, it is intimidating. He is absolutely holy to the point of being called a consuming fire. We are poor, wretched, miserable, blind, and naked. How is it that He is willing to dwell with us? Why don't we die instantly? These questions and more are answered in the story of Joshua and his accuser.

The high priest Joshua appeared before the angel of the Lord with the devil standing by to accuse him. Immediately, God's indignation was kindled against the accuser. "And the LORD said unto Satan, The LORD rebuke thee, O Satan; even the LORD that hath chosen Jerusalem rebuke thee: is not this a brand plucked out of the fire?" Zechariah 3:2. Joshua was one redeemed by the Lord, therefore, the accuser had no case. All that was necessary for a sinner to be made righteous was laid to his account. "Now Joshua was clothed with filthy garments, and stood before the angel. And he answered and spake unto those that stood before him, saying, Take away the filthy garments from him. And unto him he said, Behold, I have caused thine iniquity to pass from thee, and I will clothe thee with change of raiment." Zechariah 3:3, 4. The Lord saw Joshua's need of cleansing, which was represented by filthy garments, and chose to supply his need, rather than rebuking him. He demonstrated in a tangible way, His unwillingness to let a sinner die in his sin without giving him the privilege of being in a saving relationship with Himself. The filthy garments of iniquity that separated between them were replaced by clean ones. These garments represented the righteous life of Christ, which was to come in the future. As a guarantee, by faith, God gave Joshua the righteous covering of salvation.

I thank God that He does not allow the devil to innumerate my sins and make a solid case for my destruction. When we have faith in the perfect life, sacrifice, and heavenly ministry of Jesus Christ, and are willing to live according to the light of God's word, He sees it as an opportunity to bestow the blessing of righteousness. Having received the righteousness that is of God by faith, we have peace with God. We verily have received the gift of eternal life and nobody can bring a railing accusation against us. We have indeed passed from death to life.

UNCHANGEABLE

Malachi 3:6
"For I am the LORD, I change not; therefore ye sons of Jacob are not consumed."

During reign of Darius, the Medo-Persian king, Daniel, the faithful prophet, served in the royal courts as a special advisor. For many years, evil men sought a way to destroy Daniel, because his stark dedication to God was offensive to their irreverent lifestyles.

There was a point when the king's presidents and princes devised a diabolical plan to accomplish their objective of destroying Daniel. They knew that his custom was to pray only to the God of heaven, so they convinced the king to sign a decree stating that anyone who did not exclusively worship the king, should be cast into the den of lions. They said, "Now, O king, establish the decree, and sign the writing, that it be not changed, according to the law of the Medes and Persians, which altereth not. Wherefore King Darius signed the writing and the decree." Daniel 6:8, 9. They knew that even the king could not change the law.

The enemies of Daniel's God came to the king when they witnessed Daniel's pedictable obeisance to God and charged him with the crime of not worshipping the king. "Then the king, when he heard these words, was sore displeased with himself, and set his heart on Daniel to deliver him: and he laboured till the going down of the sun to deliver him. Then these men assembled unto the king, and said unto the king, Know, O king, that the law of the Medes and Persians is, that no decree nor statute which the king establisheth may be changed. Then the king commanded, and they brought Daniel, and cast him into the den of lions. Now the king spake and said unto Daniel, Thy God whom thou servest continually, he will deliver thee."

Daniel 6:14-16. In the end, God delivered Daniel just as the king had hoped.

The plots of evil people to persecute God's people continued even until Jesus' day. One day at a party that King Herod hosted, his niece came in to dance for him and his guests. Since he was drunk and well pleased, he told her to ask for anything she wanted and he would grant her wish. She consulted her mother Herodias, who was angry with John the Baptist for reproving her unlawful marriage to the king and she asked for the head of John the Baptist. "And the king was exceeding sorry; yet for his oath's sake, and for their sakes which sat with him, he would not reject her. And immediately the king sent an executioner, and commanded his head to be brought: and he went and beheaded him in the prison." Mark 6:26, 27.

We have read two examples of kings being obligated to follow evil edicts because the laws were irreversible. Even the kings could not abrogate their own laws. In these cases, the laws were evil and devised to hurt the cause of God. God's law is different. "Wherefore the law is holy, and the commandment holy, and just, and good. For we know that the law is spiritual: but I am carnal, sold under sin." Romans 7:12, 14. Just as a king could not change their evil laws, the King of kings cannot change His holy law which He set in place for our protection (Matthew 5:17, 18). Just as the offense of human kings' laws brought the consequence of death, so the offence of God's holy law brings eternal death.

The fact that God's law is unchangeable brings stability to the universe. Otherwise no safeguards would exist to ensure a blissful eternity. Sin, which is the violation of God's law, is not tolerated by a holy God (I John 3:4; Romans 6:23). The blessing in all of this is that while God does not change His law in order to free those whom He loves from the penalty of transgression, He does provide the perfect plan to satisfy justice, yet deliver offenders from eternal death. "For God so loved the world, that he gave his only begotten Son, that whosoever believeth in him should not perish, but have everlasting life. For God sent not his Son into the world to condemn the world; but that the world through him might be saved." John 3:16, 17.

If God's law were changeable, Jesus would not have needed to die for our sins. No, God cannot change His law, but He can take the punishment that we deserve in order to give us the righteous reward that we do not deserve; and He did. "For what the law could not do, in that it was weak through the flesh, God sending his own Son in the likeness of sinful flesh, and for sin, condemned sin in the flesh: That the righteousness of the law might be fulfilled in us, who walk not after the flesh, but after the Spirit." Romans 8:3, 4

BONUS READING MATERIAL

COMPLETE AND FREE PART 1
OFF THE DRIBBLE

In 1996, Allen Iverson was the first pick in the NBA draft and began playing with the Philadelphia 76ers even though he was just a college sophomore. In one of the games of his rookie season, Allen Iverson got the ball and heard Phil Jackson, the Chicago Bulls coach say, "Michael!" The commentator said, "Iverson has Michael, the crowd is in to it!" Allen Iverson said in an interview, while watching the highlights of that game, "I gave him a little cross to see would he bite on it. I let him set his feet and I stepped it back again..." The commentator said, "Allen shakes...gets two... Mike said NO! Allen said YES! The bucket...the crowd loves it!" That year Allen Iverson finished sixth in the league in scoring, broke a thirty-seven year old record set by Wilt Chamberlain, and received the NBA, Schick Rookie of the Year Award. Allen Iverson is also known as "The Answer."

In basketball there is a term used, that when executed properly, violently hurls both the player with the ball and the defender off balance, while the one with the ball blows passed the defender, recovering his or her own balance, and executing a shot to score for their team. This term is *first step*, and is known also as beating someone *off the dribble*. Allen Iverson has an incredible ability to execute this move effectively in games at will. Although the so-called quick first step is a killer move, it does not guarantee the score. Only the most agile and proficient player combines a quick first step, and scores consistently.

Imagine if a mediocre player faced off with Michael Jordan who is, arguably, the best overall player the NBA has seen thus far. Do you think they could beat him off the dribble? I know, for a fact, that I could have a huge bowl of Wheaties, a bottle of Gatorade, and watch every AI highlight video ever produced, and I would never be able to beat MJ off the dribble. Even if by some strange miracle I got by him, he would probably come from behind just when I was about to score and bat my shot into the stands.

OUR SALVATION

The Bible says, "For it is by grace you have been saved, through faith—and this not from yourselves, it is the gift of God—not by works, so that no one can boast." Ephesians 2:8, 9. Is salvation free? I mean, doesn't God require something from me? If He requires obedience, how then can it be free?

Do you remember reading about when Adam and Eve sinned in the Garden of Eden? You can find this story in Genesis chapter 3. From what you have read, who made the first step in their salvation? Did Adam say, "Oh my...I have sinned. I shall seek the Lord and He shall forgive me?" No, that is not the way it happened. The Bible says, after they had sinned, God was walking in the cool part of the day, and called out saying, "Adam...where are you?" Genesis 3: 8, 9. God knew where he was, but Adam could only say that he was naked, so he hid himself. *Adam* needed to know where he was. Adam was hiding because of his poor decision to sin. God is the One who made the first and most critical step so Adam and Eve could be saved. The Bible says that God took the aprons off that they made for themselves (that was their attempt to make a first step) and put on them coats of skins. These coats of skins represent the righteousness of Christ (Isaiah 61:10).

Have you ever heard the cliche', "You take one step and God will take two?" How about, "You do your best and God will do the rest?" I suppose these clichés have a little truth in them, just not enough. At the center is sinful me having something valuable to offer God in my salvation. You see, in order for salvation to be free, God must supply everything. I can hear it now, "But my pastor and parents say that

I have to do my part." To close us out, we will look briefly at this singular question, "How can God require so much, yet say that salvation is free?"

What are some of the things God requires in order for me to be saved? He requires faith, repentance, love, and for me to exert my will to do right since God doesn't force anybody, and perfect obedience one hundred percent of the time. These are the most essential elements of our responsibility. I think they are sufficient to make the point. Do you realize that even the faith we need is a gift from God? Not only is it a gift, but God gives a measure to everyone on which to act (Ephesians 2:8, 9; Hebrews 12:2 Romans 12:3). I remember reading in Acts 2:36-39 what Peter said in answer to the question, "Brothers, what shall we do?" "Repent every one of you!" In Romans 2:4 and Acts 5:30-32 the Bible says the *God* gives us repentance, which is the ability to be truly sorry for sin, and turning away from it. Jesus said, "If you love me, you will obey what I command." John 14:15. Love is also a gift that God gives. Doesn't the Bible say that we love Him because He first loved us (I John 4:19)? If I were to paraphrase this text I would say that the reason we can love God is *because* He first loved us, and with His love comes the ability to love Him back. Everyone needs to work out their own salvation and exert their decision-making abilities to do choose to do right. Did you know that it is God that works in us both to will and to do of His good pleasure? (Philippians 2:12, 13)? Therefore, God gives us the choice to do right or wrong and empowers us to choose right. Though we are not saved because we are obedient to God, we cannot be saved if we are not obedient. The Bible says that Jesus condemned sin while living as a human being so the righteous requirements of the law could be perfectly fulfilled in us when we live in the Spirit (Romans 8:3,4). In order for God to require so much of us, and at the same time make salvation a gift, He must first supply us what He requires and then expect us to act on it. It is like using a person's money to buy something from that person. Jesus paid it all and now says buy from Him without money, and without price (Isaiah 55).

COMPLETE AND FREE PART 2
STILL IN MY SINS?

I cannot even imagine where I would be if, one day in 1995, the Lord had not been kind enough to send someone to invite me to church. The person knew that I had prior church affiliation, but he certainly did not know that I did not pray; attend church, read the Bible or anything else like that. I was impressed to go when he said that one of my former college mates was scheduled to preach.

I will never forget it. It was weird going to church again. I had no real expectations regarding this trip to church, but I was there—front and center. While preaching the sermon, the young pastor said something like this: "Fellas, when you choose Jesus, you will go to the basketball court, and the guys will hear you talk about your decision to be with Jesus and they will talk about all of the stuff they saw you do in the past. You can say to them that it doesn't matter what you saw me do last month, last week, yesterday; I have chosen to follow Jesus today!" Man, that is all I needed to hear. I tried on two separate occasions to modify my behavior in the name of changing my life. Well, as you might imagine I failed miserably and everybody knew it. So, let me get this straight, I can give my life to Jesus, my sins will be forgiven, and it does not matter what people have seen me do in the past? I'll take it! Freedom! You mean, I can go back to work on Tuesday, a changed person, and the sins I used to be popular for can be behind me? Where do I sign up? The appeal at the end of the sermon could not come quickly enough.

Jesus is the One who makes the first and most critical step in our salvation. If it were left up to us, we would be lost forever. Being saved from sin by God is a one hundred percent free gift and not based on our good works

(Ephesians 2:8, 9). Part of God's first step was Jesus coming in human flesh, living a perfect life, and then dying in our place so we could one day live forever in a sinless universe. This is the question. Were these aspects of God's first step in our salvation enough? What I mean is, was the cross it? I know many people think that was the end of it because Jesus said, "It is finished!"

WHAT WAS FINISHED AT THE CROSS?

When Jesus was on the cross taking my eternal punishment and proclaimed, "It is finished!" here are some of the most critical things that He meant:

1. Jesus would never again suffer on the cross for our sins; He died once for us (Romans 6:9,10).
2. The need for human priests ended (Hebrews 7:18-28).
3. Animal sacrifices were no longer valid or necessary; the ceremonial laws were nailed to the cross (Matthew 27:51; Daniel 9:27; Colossians 2:14).
4. The "antidote" for sin was fully mixed and ready to be administered.

WHAT IF JESUS WAS STILL DEAD?

Check this out. "And if Christ has not been raised, your faith is futile; you are still in your sins. Then those also who have fallen asleep in Christ are lost. If only for this life we have hope in Christ, we are to be pitied more than all men." I Corinthians 15:17-19. What Jesus did for me on the cross was critical, and necessary. Jesus did not come to earth to stay dead. Paul said that we would still be in our sins if Jesus was still dead, and our faith would be in vain. Aren't you glad that the story did not stop there? You see, a dead Jesus cannot help us very much. If Jesus was still dead, whose name would we pray in, who would be our Advocate in heaven, how would we get to heaven, what assurance would we have that we could live like God wants us to live?

HOW DOES JESUS BEING ALIVE HELP ME?

Take out your Bible and read aloud Romans 6:5-11. Texts like this are not very helpful if I cannot use them everyday. When we receive Jesus into our lives and accept everything He has done for us as the only means of salvation, we are included in the text above. Jesus being raised from the dead is my assurance that I can be forgiven for all of the sins I have ever committed (Romans 3:22-26). Do you remember the woman caught in the very act of adultery in John chapter 8? The Bible says that when Jesus forgave her, He empowered her to be free from sin. When Jesus forgives us, He also gives us the power to resist sin (I Corinthians 10:13; James 4:7-10). It is similar to when Jesus forgave and healed a paralyzed man in Mark chapter 2. Jesus forgave Him, and with a command full of love and power said, "Get up, take your mat and go home." He too could "go and sin no more."

When I am at work or school, and someone wants me to do something ungodly, I can talk to God about it and He will empower me to do the right thing. I don't have to watch explicit movies, listen to Hip-Hop, R&B or Rock music anymore, because Jesus has delivered me. Anything that is against what God says in the Bible is sin. I can now walk away from smoking weed, and ecstasy. I no longer need to be involved in sex with anyone before I get married because I am free from sin. Drinking beer, and other alcoholic beverages does not make me cool in my mind anymore, because being cool in God's eyes is having eternal life.

When I accept Jesus and His victory over sin, I have a new outlook on life. I have new friends who help me grow in Jesus, instead of away from Him (Mark 10:26-31). We can now understand that we don't have to sin, but if we do, because we are still weak, Jesus will help (I John 2:1). Jesus

being alive is one of the greatest reasons I can live a godly life here on earth, and then one day live with God eternally.
Remember, God loves you.

COMPLETE AND FREE PART 3
THE ACQUITTAL

Order in the Court! All rise; the honorable Judge Noname presiding. We are in a courtroom scene on the set of NBC's Law and Order. Each participant is in place, including the tough Executive Assistant Attorney, Jack McCoy along with his partners from the District Attorney's office. Also in the courtroom are Detectives Green and Briscoe, with Lt. Anita Van Buren. You know that if all of these folks are there at the same time, this case must be serious. Obviously, the judge is there, but this judge seems to be biased. You are the one accused and because you have no money, you are stuck with a public defender, instead of a paid attorney who would have your best interest at heart. The case seems hopeless because you are on trial for a crime, which, if convicted you could face the death penalty. We don't even need to discuss the jury, who after McKoy's opening arguments, seem already swayed against you. Their facial expressions leave little room for optimism. What is going on? If that is not enough, the victim's family, media, and even your own conscience side with the District Attorney to prosecute you, which, incidentally, feels like they are *persecuting* you. After all, you know, and they know that you are guilty as charged. What are the odds of you being acquitted? All eyes are on you and the outcome seems certain.

Jesus gives us forgiveness, and the power to be victorious over sin in real life situations. We are going to shift our focus to the heavenly judgment hall where eternal destinies are determined.

BRINGING YOU UP TO SPEED

The courtroom introduction above leaves you on the edge of your seat, doesn't it? What's going to happen to the defendant [accused]? We will now shift our attention to the way court was held in the ancient Jewish economy. Present in the courtroom scene would be the accused, the accuser, the judge, and the advocate. These four were the only major players. This is the way the heavenly pre-second coming judgment is structured. In this case, the accused has actually committed the crime worthy of eternal death. What was the crime? The Bible says, "For all have sinned and fallen short of the glory of God." Romans 3:23. Further, the Bible says, "For the wages of sin is death, but the gift of God is eternal life in Christ Jesus our Lord." Romans 6:23. The crime is sin, punishable by eternal death. Since when we receive the gift of salvation, we become God's children, we know that something wonderful must be about to happen in this case, though on the one hand it seems hopeless.

ON YOUR SIDE

Let's identify the courtroom players more closely, shall we? We have already said that we as sinners are the accused, and we are guilty. The accuser is Satan. "And there was war in heaven. Michael and his angels fought against the dragon, and the dragon and his angels fought back. However, he was not strong enough, and they lost their place in heaven. The great dragon was hurled down—that ancient serpent called the devil, or Satan, who leads the whole world astray. He was hurled to the earth, and his angels with him. Then I heard a loud voice in heaven say: "Now have come the salvation and the power and the kingdom of our God, and the authority of his Christ. For the accuser of our brothers, who accuses them before our God day and night, has been hurled down." Revelation 12:7-10. Who is the advocate or defense attorney? "My dear children, I write this to you so that you will not sin. But if anybody does sin, we have one who speaks to the Father in our defense—Jesus Christ, the Righteous One. He is the atoning sacrifice for our sins, and not only for ours but also for the sins of the whole world." I John 2:1,2. Jesus Christ, the Righteous One is our defense attorney. An interesting question to ask following this description of our advocate is, "Who is the judge?" The text we just read said that Jesus is our Advocate with the Father, which suggests that the Father is our judge, and, in a way, He is. However, an incredible shift of responsibility occurs here. "For just as the Father raises the dead and gives them life, even so the Son gives life to whom he is pleased to give it. Moreover, the Father judges no one, but has entrusted all judgment to the Son, that all may honor the Son just as they honor the Father. He who does not honor the Son does not honor the Father, who sent him." John 5:21-23. Jesus is also our judge.

How does it feel to know that the accuser is "hurled down", meaning defeated, the defense attorney is your friend, and the judge is your friend? Does the case still seem hopeless knowing that you are guilty as charged? Check this out. I neglected to mention that when it comes to the judgment, if there is any hope of acquittal, somebody has to be punished in order for justice to be satisfied. Well, we have already read in I John 2:1, 2 that Jesus is the atoning sacrifice for our sins. This means that Jesus volunteered to take our punishment on the cross, which was equal to eternal death. Knowing that Jesus is our Advocate, Judge, and the One who paid the eternal death penalty for us, how does the trial make you feel now? Are you hopeless with all odds against you, or hopeful because you are friends with the only One who can acquit you?

In your spare time read Zechariah 3:1-5. These verses paint a living-color portrait of all that we have said. They portray an image of the accused receiving clean garments, representing the free righteousness of Christ in place of the filthy garments, representing self-righteousness. Since Jesus never sinned, and we are seen wearing Jesus like a garment, heaven's verdict is that we are *innocent*. In heaven's eyes, we never sinned.

One critical question must be answered in closing, with all of this talk about free salvation and righteousness, does that mean that it doesn't matter what we do, and expect to still be saved? I will answer this with a question. If you were wearing a brand new full length Sean John leather coat or Donna Karan Chinchilla fur, would you pick the rainiest day to go outside and find the sloppiest puddle to wallow in? I don't think so. When a person receives the gift of Christ's righteousness, they are empowered to stay far away from the mud puddles of sin just as Jesus did.

My friends, I have chosen personally to receive the free gift of salvation. I think it would be a good idea if you did the same, besides, it wouldn't make sense not to. Remember, God loves you.

TWO GREAT VOLUMES
WITH A UNIFIED MESSAGE

The gospel of Jesus Christ is the most influential story
ever told. It is an eternal, panoramic movie projected
on a universe-sized monitor for all generations to see.
Alive at 5—Victory in Retrospect, Volumes 1 & 2
will leave you spellbound as this story is
passionately brought into focus.

Share the *Alive at 5—Victory in Retrospect* set with friends,
family and associates. It is truly a gift for all occasions
and a great witnessing tool. Get yours today.
*Available in paperback and hardcover.

www.AliveatFive.com

Printed in the United States
23230LVS00003B/334-342

9 781594 678387